W9-BUO-259

# TWENTIETH CENTURY VIEWS

The aim of this series is to present the best in contemporary critical opinion on major authors, providing a twentieth century perspective on their changing status in an era of profound revaluation.

Maynard Mack, *Series Editor*
Yale University

# SHERWOOD ANDERSON

# SHERWOOD ANDERSON

## A COLLECTION OF CRITICAL ESSAYS

Edited by

*Walter B. Rideout*

Prentice-Hall, Inc.  *Englewood Cliffs, N.J.*

A SPECTRUM BOOK

*Library of Congress Cataloging in Publication Data*

RIDEOUT, WALTER BATES, COMP.
  Sherwood Anderson; a collection of critical essays.

  (Twentieth century views) (A Spectrum Book)
  CONTENTS:   Waldo, F.   Emerging greatness.—Phillips,
W. L.   How Sherwood Anderson wrote Winesburg, Ohio.—
Fussell, E.   Winesburg, Ohio: art and isolation.   [etc.]
  1. Anderson, Sherwood, 1876–1941.
PS3501.N4Z77      813'.5'2      74–3397
ISBN 0–13–036558–0
ISBN 0–13–036533–5 (pbk.)

© 1974 by Prentice-Hall, Inc., Englewood Cliffs, New Jersey. A SPECTRUM BOOK.
All rights reserved. No part of this book may be reproduced in any form or by any
means without permission in writing from the publisher. Printed in the United States
of America.

10   9   8   7   6   5   4   3   2   1

PRENTICE-HALL INTERNATIONAL, INC. (*London*)
PRENTICE-HALL OF AUSTRALIA PTY., LTD. (*Sydney*)
PRENTICE-HALL OF CANADA LTD. (*Toronto*)
PRENTICE-HALL OF INDIA PRIVATE LIMITED (*New Delhi*)
PRENTICE-HALL OF JAPAN, INC. (*Tokyo*)

Acknowledgment is gratefully made to the following for granting permission to reprint selections from the works of Sherwood Anderson:

To Harold Ober Associates Incorporated for quotations from

*A Story Teller's Story* (copyright 1924 by B. W. Huebsch, Inc. Renewed 1952 by Eleanor Copenhaver Anderson).

*Poor White* (copyright 1920 by Eleanor Anderson. Copyright renewed).

To Little, Brown and Company, and Harold Ober Associates, for quotations from

*Letters of Sherwood Anderson,* edited by Howard Mumford Jones in Association with Walter B. Rideout (copyright 1953 by Eleanor Anderson).

# Contents

*To Eleanor Anderson*

# SHERWOOD ANDERSON

# Introduction

## by Walter B. Rideout

Readers of Sherwood Anderson have always disagreed, and probably always will, concerning the nature of his art and his worth as a writer. In the posthumously published *Memoirs* Anderson himself declared that "For all my egotism I know I am but a minor figure," and it must have taken the same kind of courage to make such a remark late in life as it did for him to break away from a career as businessman in 1913 and to direct his chief energies toward a career as writer, this at thirty-six, an age when most American men are expected to have settled, happily or resignedly, on their life goals.

Adverse critics and readers go beyond Anderson's modest self-assessment; they find his novels disorganized, his essays mannered and intellectually limited, his short stories thin in substance and awkward in technique. More sympathetic readers, however, find a few of the novels and parts of all of them impressive, though they recognize that Anderson was not at his best at the long haul. They observe that in the essays, whatever the level of intellectual analysis, Anderson had at least intuited correctly what some of the basic issues in American life were, and are—the ambivalence of our attitudes toward the machine, the phenomenon of alienation in technological society, the subtle corruptions of success defined in material terms, or any other terms, the threat of standardization to individualism, and the desperate need of individuals for a sense of community. These sympathetic critics and readers likewise admire a considerable number of the short stories for their shrewd, sometimes stunningly acute insights into human psyches, for the technical skill with which Anderson can conceal his technical skill, for the way in which the best of the tales give the reader a sudden, intense sensation of being connected with what one can only vaguely name as fundamental rhythms of existence. And so the disagreement goes on.

There are, it seems to me, several reasons why Anderson's work has always been hard to describe and assess. More, perhaps, than with most authors, liking or disliking it may come down abruptly to a matter of the reader's personal temperament. One does or definitely does not feel comfortable with Anderson's storyteller method, with its apparently (but only apparently) aimless circling of its subject and its intrusive narrator, who may suddenly protest that he is hopelessly puzzled by life or, contrariwise, may make large, confident assertions about the especial loneliness of Americans or the need to liberate the self that it may grow into something which the narrator does not very clearly define. Since the voice of the narrator often seems to, in fact sometimes does, merge with that of the author, the reader of an Anderson fiction tends to respond directly to the author himself. One of the most personal of American writers in any case, Anderson thus immediately evokes in his readers, not critical judgment, but varying degrees of affection or antipathy.

Another reason for the difficulty in assessing Anderson's work is that, as Robert Morss Lovett writes, it is "amazingly uneven in execution" from book to book or even within books.[1] Several reviewers of Anderson's first novel, *Windy McPherson's Son,* which he published in 1916 at the age of forty, noted that the hero's rise to wealth in the first part was more convincing than his wanderings around America in search of truth in the last; and most reviewers of the final novel, *Kit Brandon,* published twenty years later, similarly found short-storylike sections of it better than the whole. The stories collected in *The Triumph of the Egg, Horses and Men,* and *Death in the Woods* vary considerably in quality—I happen to find every odd-numbered story in *Horses and Men* much superior to every even-numbered one—and not all the tales in *Winesburg, Ohio* are as extraordinarily good as, say, "Hands" or "The Untold Lie." Other writers besides Anderson—Hemingway and Faulkner, for example—really do not maintain a dead level of excellence either, but their stories and novels are not subject to quite such sharp fluctuations of quality as Anderson's. I suspect that those who dislike Anderson tend to judge him by the weak tales, those who like him by the strong.

Yet a third reason why Anderson's work has been hard to assess is that during his literary career his writings were at times overvalued, at times undervalued on grounds having as much to do with current general attitudes as with the work itself. The effects of such tendentious or distorted readings, by which one saw what one wanted to see in an Anderson book rather than what was actually there, are still with us, furthermore, and distort our own readings of Anderson in ways we may not recognize. Because this point is an important one, it is worth illustrating at some length in relation to *Winesburg, Ohio.*

Whether they like the book or not, most general readers and critics have considered *Winesburg* to be Anderson's best—rightly, I think,

1 See Lovett's "The Promise of Sherwood Anderson," reprinted in this volume.

though the repetition of this judgment has tended to make us under-rate his quite different achievements in the volume of experimental tales, *Horses and Men,* or that symbolic "autobiography," *A Story Teller's Story.* The reviews of *Winesburg* back in 1919 were in fact much more favorable than is now usually assumed, for in his own tendentious fashion Anderson preferred to think of this book as hav-ing been "widely condemned, called nasty and dirty by most of its critics," and so wrote in his *Memoirs* and so led us to believe. To be sure, an anonymous and proper reviewer in the *Springfield Republican* found the tales, with some exceptions, to be "descriptions[,] somewhat boldly naked, of the commonplace, without a spark of life or creative feeling"; another anonymous, even more proper reviewer asserted in the *New York Sun* that "Mr. Anderson has reduced his material from human clay to plain dirt" and moreover had done so in "very bad English"; and H. W. Boynton in that staid periodical *The Bookman* tempered his considerable praise for Winesburg with the reservation that Anderson had "too freely imbibed the doctrine of the psycho-analysts" and that "with this writer sex is wellnigh the mainspring of human action." On the other hand, H. L. Mencken in his *Smart Set* review hailed Anderson as belonging to "a small group that has some-how emancipated itself from the prevailing imitativeness and banality of the national letters"; Burton Rascoe and Llewellyn Jones praised *Winesburg* in Chicago newspapers, Rascoe taking direct issue with "the inert and vegetative organism on an eastern paper"—that is, the *New York Sun*'s prim reviewer; and even two New Englanders wrote favor-ably of the book, William Stanley Braithwaite in, of all places, the *Boston Transcript,* and that ebullient Yale professor William Lyon Phelps in *The New York Times Book Review.*

By the standards of its time, of course, *Winesburg, Ohio* was a dar-ing book in its subject matter and technique as well as in its willingness to consider sex as a real force in people's lives, but the fact that a few (not "most") critics could condemn Anderson as sex-obsessed im-pelled his advocates later on in the Twenties to defend the book as sexually honest. Making the question of sexual morality a central issue in judging the book obscured for many readers then, and for some readers now, the significant point that for the author sexual expression primarily symbolizes the desire for intuitive communication between individuals which, as the narrator of *Winesburg* puts it, "makes the mature life of men and women in the modern world possible."

In another way many readers of the Twenties, and many since, saw *Winesburg, Ohio* distortedly. Like Edgar Lee Masters's *Spoon River Anthology,* Zona Gale's *Miss Lulu Bett,* Sinclair Lewis's *Main Street,* and other books of the time which found American small-town life to be less than idyllic, Anderson's volume of tales was taken to be another example of what was quickly categorized as The Revolt from the Village, a useful enough term that will probably remain imbedded eternally in our literary history. Viewing the town of Winesburg as something to revolt from, one concludes that the smartest thing George Willard ever did was to leave a place so full of messed-up human failures and go off to the city, that place where, as the narrator says in "Paper Pills" with an irony so quiet one hardly hears it, the perfect apples picked from the Winesburg orchards "will be eaten in apartments that are filled with books, magazines, furniture, and people." Those who read *Winesburg, Ohio* as an example of The Revolt from the Village quite miss Anderson's notion that his "grotesques" possess "the sweetness of the twisted apples" that are left unpicked in the orchards of Winesburg.

Linked to such a reading of *Winesburg, Ohio* as an example of a category rather than uniquely itself is the assumption that its author was in fictional technique a realist, and an inferior practitioner at that. The acutest of his critics in the Twenties, such as Lovett and T. K. Whipple, perceived that this was not the case with Anderson, who once protested to Mencken that he cared just as much for realism as he did for "worn out underwear." To assume that Anderson was, or ought to be, a realist in the usual sense of one who attempts to show visualizable characters moving through densely specific environments was, and is, to miss both Anderson's concern for the "essences" that lie "beneath the surface of lives" and his strong attraction toward fantasy, which resulted from his belief that what his characters and people in general imagine about themselves constitutes part of their "reality."

So Anderson's highly personal manner of writing, the unevenness of his work, the susceptibility of it to distorted reading, all have made it difficult to assess fairly his worth as a writer, and his literary reputation has accordingly fluctuated. It has to be admitted that Anderson, for years a successful advertising man, was always quite willing to assist in the creation of certain images of himself that have affected the way he was read and evaluated. In the poems he wrote early in 1917 and published in the following year as *Mid-American Chants* he presents himself as the bard of the people of Mid-America, that wide land resting between the two great mountain ranges and drained by the Mississippi. In the early Twenties he wanted his readers to regard him as a kind of neopagan liberator come to purge the American psyche of the twin evils spawned, he believed with Van Wyck Brooks, from "Puritanism" —the devotion to materialistic gain and the repression, hence perversion, of the inner self. The best-known of these personas, one that markedly affected the way he and his work were perceived in the

Twenties, was that which he created in *A Story Teller's Story* (1924) to explain his career change from businessman to artist. According to that account he one day chose to appear slightly insane and deliberately walked out of his paint factory in Elyria, Ohio, in a single moment leaping from the kingdom of necessity to the kingdom of freedom. Anderson's revolt against the business life was real enough, though the facts of his not-so-deliberate nervous breakdown at the time came to his readers only later with William Sutton's 1943 doctoral dissertation, "Sherwood Anderson's Formative Years," and the publication in the September 4, 1948, issue of the *Saturday Review of Literature* of Karl Anderson's article, "My Brother, Sherwood Anderson." But by his presentation of his revolt in *A Story Teller's Story* as a fully willed act, Anderson almost guaranteed that he and his writings would be viewed in terms of one of the powerful myths of the Twenties, indeed one of the most powerful myths of the Romantic Movement, that of the liberated artist as culture hero. In the mid-Twenties this association with myth made Anderson loom larger than he was.

In the Thirties, however, his reputation as a writer fell off drastically. With some exceptions his fiction is certainly less good than in the Twenties, and the best of his later tales are told with a bareness and simplicity so deceptive that they have not even yet been sufficiently examined. Again, he turned more often at this time from fiction to journalism, to nonfictional descriptions of American lives during the Great Depression; and his undogmatic tone in this journalism, his willingness not to know the answers but to admit that he was as puzzled by the general calamity as were the decent ordinary people he talked with, offended the dogmatists of that very dogmatic decade. The attacks of many of the literary critics against Anderson and his work took on a hostility not warranted even by the decline of his powers. Reacting against the overevaluation of him in the Twenties, his critics now rejected him almost with contempt as one hopelessly out of touch with the times.

Since Anderson's death in 1941 there has slowly developed an attempt to get past immediate temperamental responses to the writer and his work, to overcome the tendency to read him in terms of categories, to avoid indiscriminate praise or censure, and instead to define the peculiar qualities of the work that do in fact make Anderson so hard to sum up. Some of the individual attempts at revaluation have been more successful than others, but the major early ones deserve notice here. An "Homage to Sherwood Anderson" issue of *Story* magazine (September–October, 1941) was for the most part an expression by the contributors of personal loss at his death. The true revaluation process began in the late Forties with several events: the appearance of Max-

well Geismar's long, and far from uncritical, chapter on Anderson in
*The Last of the Provincials*;[2] the publication of two admirable an-
thologies, Paul Rosenfeld's *The Sherwood Anderson Reader* and
Horace Gregory's *The Portable Sherwood Anderson*; the availability
in typewritten form of William L. Phillips's exemplary dissertation on
*Winesburg, Ohio* and his publication in *American Literature* of a
significant scholarly article based on that dissertation;[3] and (perhaps
most of all) the generous gift to the Newberry Library in Chicago by
Eleanor Copenhaver Anderson of her late husband's papers, a collection
essential for subsequent studies of Anderson, including the first full-
length critical biographies by Irving Howe and James Schevill in 1951.
In 1950 Lionel Trilling published his final version of the most devastating attack ever made on Anderson, but from the late Forties on-
ward most of the criticism of Anderson has sought some middle ground
between, generally speaking, the adulation of him in the Twenties and
the rejection of him in the Thirties.

The present collection of essays brings together a range of critical
opinion on Anderson, but in selecting from among the best pieces
written about him, I have deliberately emphasized "middle ground"
ones in order to give the reader the greatest possible assistance toward
accurate assessment of his work. The arrangement of the essays in the
collection is not, with some exceptions, according to the date of
publication of the essays themselves, but rather according to the
chronology of events in Anderson's literary career. Thus, while the
first piece, dating from 1916, is the most significant review of his first
book, the immediately following essays on *Winesburg, Ohio* were all
published after 1950. Three other contemporaneous reviews are included in sequence and also a remarkable analysis by T. K. Whipple
based on what Anderson had then published up through *A New Testament* (1927). The remaining pieces all appeared subsequent to Anderson's death, the latest in 1969, and represent the recent reassessment of
his work. Generally the essays are arranged so that they move from
discussions of Anderson's individual books in order of their publication to considerations of his achievement as a whole.

Some discussion of the essays and their backgrounds will be helpful.

2 See "Sherwood Anderson: Last of the Townsmen," Chapter Four, pp. 223–84
in Maxwell Geismar, *The Last of the Provincials: The American Novel, 1915–1925*
(Boston: Houghton Mifflin Company, 1947). Unfortunately, space limitations prevent inclusion of this piece. Some may question Geismar's method, a combination
of literary history and literary psychoanalysis; yet the chapter is important as
the first extended attempt, and an often penetrating one, to see Anderson's whole
literary career in perspective, the writings of the Thirties as well as those of the
previous two decades, the articles, journalism, poetry, fanciful and less fanciful
memoirs as well as the fiction.

3 "How Sherwood Anderson Wrote *Winesburg, Ohio*," reprinted in this volume.

Waldo Frank's review of *Windy McPherson's Son* appeared in the first number of the short-lived *Seven Arts*, a monthly magazine founded in New York in 1916 by two young literary men, Frank himself and James Oppenheim (later joined by Van Wyck Brooks) to demonstrate that "we are living in the first days of a renascent period, a time which means for America the coming of that national self-consciousness which is the beginning of greatness." Grand as this idea and his expression of it in the review may be, Frank saw the significance of Anderson as an American artist working in native materials. Present-day critics are more likely to emphasize the depiction of Sam McPherson's youth in a small Iowa town like Winesburg rather than that of his rise to success and rejection of it, and Frank himself recognizes that the "quest" section of the novel is "Puerile, fumbling stuff"; but the intense young "cultural nationalist" in New York understood that this middle-aged Midwesterner was likewise engaged in an important enough search for the appropriate symbols with which to express his ideas—intuitions, rather—as to America's current stage of emotional development. Anderson's whole literary career may in fact be charted according to his successes, and failures, in finding such symbols.

*Winesburg, Ohio,* as I have indicated, received more favorable than unfavorable reviews on its publication, nor were the former mere enthusiastic puffs without any comprehension of Anderson's art, which, as Burton Rascoe thoughtfully noted in the *Chicago Tribune*, "suggests rather than depicts . . . is selective, indefinite, and provocative instead of inclusive, precise, and explanatory." Still, the longest and best discussions of *Winesburg* have almost all appeared since Anderson's death. Many persons who know the fairly extensive body of criticism that has accumulated around the book may have a favorite essay or two they believe I should also have included, but none, I think, will object to my including the pieces by William L. Phillips, Edwin Fussell, and Malcolm Cowley. Each of these tells much about Anderson's writing methods and about the combination of complex and simple elements that has made this particular book mean, validly, many things to many readers—which is, of course, one definition of a classic. Having examined these three superlative commentaries on *Winesburg*, the interested reader should go on to other valuable ones listed in the *Selected Bibliography*, such as Waldo Frank's "*Winesburg, Ohio* After Twenty Years" (reprinted in the Appel volume), Irving Howe's chapter on "The Book of the Grotesque" in his *Sherwood Anderson*, Epifanio San Juan, Jr.'s "Vision and Reality: A Reconsideration of Sherwood Anderson's *Winesburg, Ohio*," and Jarvis Thurston's "Anderson and 'Winesburg': Mysticism and Craft."

*Winesburg, Ohio,* which may derive its form in part from George Moore's collection of Irish tales, *The Untilled Field* (1903), is a "short

story cycle" or "composite novel" from which in turn may partly derive such works as Hemingway's *In Our Time,* Steinbeck's *The Pastures
of Heaven,* and Faulkner's *The Unvanquished* and *Go Down, Moses.*
When Anderson's best true novel, *Poor White,* appeared in 1920, this
study of a small town being industrialized received generally favorable
reviews by Hart Crane, Robert Morss Lovett, H. L. Mencken, and
Constance Rourke, along with other less complimentary ones. Crane
especially praised the "descriptions of modern city life with its mechanical distortions of humanity," and Lovett observed that the inventor-hero of the book was "a symbol of the country itself in its industrial progress and spiritual impotence." A standard criticism of *Poor
White* has been that the book suffers from a split between the scenes
showing the disruptive effects of industrialization and those showing the
hero and heroine's difficult struggle to achieve a love relationship. In
the section of her chapter on *Poor White* in *The American City Novel*
Blanche Gelfant demonstrates, however, that the sociological and the
psychological themes are not disjoined but complementary; for, she
argues, the "bizarre relationship between Hugh and Clara externalizes
man's inner state of dissociation in the machine age." Although *Poor
White* may be read more frequently as a sociological document than as
the highly original fiction it is, Gelfant's analysis shows how Anderson's
writings will often supply the right answers if the right questions are
asked of them.

Three reviews from the Twenties show that, overall, Anderson was
probably as fortunate in his reviewers, despite their disagreements, as
most writers are. Robert Morss Lovett, who often commented on
Anderson's books, was a famous teacher at the University of Chicago
and a person unusually open to new writing. His summary of Anderson's qualities, as shown by the six books the latter had published up
to that point, one each year from 1916 to 1921, seems to me balanced
and fair as well as penetrating. By the time of the publication of *The
Triumph of the Egg* Lovett could dispassionately sum up the flaws and
peculiar strengths in the three novels, surmise that the author was at
his best in the short story, and identify the unifying element of his
writings as his desire to understand existence from the standpoint of
those who live it, not from the standpoint of an imposed philosophy.

A similar view of what Anderson was trying to do, to "express" life
rather than "reflect . . . or describe . . . or embroider . . . or photograph" it is advanced by Gertrude Stein in her brief review of *A Story
Teller's Story.* One does not need to accept her short list of American
writers "who have essential intelligence" or even accept her definition
of what essential intelligence is in order to see that this expatriate experimenter with words understood those of an experimenter who had
stayed in his (their) own country. Stein and Anderson were of sharply

different backgrounds but of the same generation, and one thing that bound them in a warm but not close friendship was their awareness of having become middle-aged before they had achieved any literary fame.[4] Ernest Hemingway, the other reviewer of *A Story Teller's Story,* however, was of the next age group of writers who came to early maturity during and shortly after World War I and whose brilliant achievements in the Twenties were partially made possible by the risks taken by Stein's and Anderson's generation. The friendship between Anderson and Hemingway, whom William L. Phillips coupled with Faulkner as the first of "Sherwood Anderson's Two Prize Pupils," is best known for the way it ended with Hemingway's parody in *The Torrents of Spring* of his former "teacher's" style in *Dark Laughter*. It is a pleasure, therefore, to include in this collection Hemingway's review, recently reprinted by Matthew Bruccoli from *Ex Libris,* the journal of the American Library in Paris; for it shows Hemingway, prior to the parody, paying deserved respects to a writer who had encouraged him and influenced his early work.

Like Hemingway and Stein most other reviewers had praised *A Story Teller's Story* when it appeared in the mid-Twenties. As Anderson's reputation declined in the Thirties and early Forties, however, this fanciful autobiography was dismissed as self-indulgent in manner and unreliable in its facts—Anderson had of course made that latter point himself quite openly on the title page—and *A Story Teller's Story* became one of Anderson's least known books. Rex Burbank's analysis of the themes and structure implicit in this casual-seeming life "journey" is one of the best parts of his *Sherwood Anderson* (1964) and has redirected recent readers toward seeing that this book is in fact carefully organized and highly suggestive about the fate of artists in America. Burbank's chapter severely downgrades *Dark Laughter,* Anderson's one popular success, and that odd half-fantasy *Many Marriages,* but it puts into clear perspective the author's very limited debts to D. H. Lawrence and to Freud, his greater debt to the Henry Adams of *The Education*. It will help the reader of this piece to know that Trigant Burrow (1875–1950), to whom Burbank refers, was one of the first Freudian psychoanalysts in the United States, that Burrow and Anderson met and talked often in the summer of 1916, and that according to a later statement by Burrow, who admired the writer's intuitive insights, Anderson had strongly opposed "delving" into "human life" with such "surgical probes" as Freudian analysis.

That Anderson's own probing into human life was not by "analytic dissection" but by "an intuitive and imaginative process" is one of the

---

[4] For the documents resulting from this friendship see Ray Lewis White, ed., *Sherwood Anderson/Gertrude Stein: Correspondence and Personal Essays* (Chapel Hill, N.C.: The University of North Carolina Press, 1972).

points made by T. K. Whipple. This chapter from Whipple's *Spokes-men* (1928), a volume of essays on contemporary writers, is one of the most perceptive discussions of Anderson's art published during his lifetime. It is included here partly to bring back into wider knowledge the insights of a still too little known book (though Mark Schorer edited a paperback reissue in 1963), partly to show that in the Twenties Anderson and other figures in then contemporary literature had already begun to receive a sympathetic hearing among some university scholar-critics. (One of the significant developments in university English departments over the last half century, it may be noted parenthetically, is the sharply increasing attention shown contemporary writing by those whom H. L. Mencken used to refer to disparagingly as "professors of English.")

Among the university critics who have more recently attempted to come to terms with Anderson's work are Irving Howe and Jon Lawry. Although both are emphatic about Anderson's limitations and tend to divide his writings into the few successes and the many failures, with almost no intermediate accomplishments, both are alert to characteristics of his work at its best. In his *Sherwood Anderson,* Howe disappointingly dismisses *A Story Teller's Story* in a paragraph as being false in every respect; but his chapter on *Winesburg, Ohio* is eloquent, and that on the short stories, here reprinted, is the best brief examination of Anderson's storytelling technique I know. Likewise Jon Lawry's discussion of "Death in the Woods," one of the few Anderson stories critics are united in praising, seems to me the best of many discussions of that tale.

The last four pieces in this collection are summings-up of the nature of Anderson's art and his place in twentieth-century American literature. Unsurprisingly these overall assessments vary considerably. For Lionel Trilling, Anderson was a questioner, but one who lacked power of mind to go beyond an adolescent stage of inquiry. Anderson's anti-rationalism and dependence on his own feelings, Trilling asserts, paradoxically produced, not a rich, but an abstract fictional world in which there is little sensory or social experience. Anderson's language also assists in making the world of actuality appear remote, and the salvation of which this quasi-religious language speaks is vague and limited. Although I do not myself find Trilling's negative judgment of Anderson particularly persuasive, I have included it because Trilling, one of our very best cultural critics, summarizes so well the dissatisfactions that some, perhaps a number, of readers feel with Anderson's work.

Far more sympathetic in their evaluations are two other scholar-critics, Howard Mumford Jones and Benjamin Spencer. Jones's introduction to a selection of Anderson's letters points out that these writings too are part of his total work, in fact are sometimes indistinguishable from his published fiction and nonfiction. Drawing on the evidence of the correspondence, Jones independently corroborates some of Trilling's premises about Anderson—his reliance on feeling, his expression of a mode of mysticism, his desire for a secular salvation —but comes to quite opposite conclusions. Jones finds Anderson's distrust of the intellect and the intellectuals to be at least partly defensible, his emotionalism to be productive of a joyful expression of ordinary life rather than a negation of it, his search for salvation to be a humanistic desire to abandon preoccupation with self and to apprehend the unity underlying separate lives. Clearly Trilling and Jones point the reader of Anderson along very divergent paths.

In an essay that I consider a key one for understanding Anderson, Benjamin Spencer also takes issue implicitly with Trilling's conclusions. Agreeing that Anderson is little involved with the Western European intellectualist tradition, Spencer finds that his strengths— and his deficiencies as well—come from his commitment instead to "a major native tradition initiated by the Transcendentalists." By an intuitive apprehension of the "essence" of specifically American lives, Spencer argues, Anderson consciously sought in his writing to proceed from the local to the universal, from the individual to the archetype. Such a view of Anderson is to an extent supported by the final essay in the collection, the appreciation of him by William Faulkner, Anderson's other "prize pupil," who for a few months in 1925 in New Orleans had come to know Anderson well, who had been warmly encouraged by him in his own writing, who then went on to far surpass his "teacher," and who, despite a personal rift between them, continued to acknowledge his debt as younger writer to older one. For, Faulkner asserts (in words reminiscent of his own attempt to do so), what Anderson wished to express through the purity of his style was the "meaning"—that is, the myth—of America, even though that meaning, by the very nature of myths, could not be rationally understood but only "believed."

The reader of this collection, then, will find in it a wide choice of views of Anderson, that "amazingly uneven," hard-to-define writer, who, to paraphrase Howard Mumford Jones, stands like his letters at the fountainhead of modernism. Once having considered other people's views, the reader is advised to go on, or back again, to Anderson's own writings. As I have discovered for myself, the best way to understand and evaluate *Winesburg, Ohio* or *Poor White* or *A Story Teller's Story* or such tales as "The Egg," "An Ohio Pagan," "The Man Who Became a Woman," and "Death in the Woods" is to read them for what they can tell you, not just about Anderson, but about yourself.

# Emerging Greatness
## (Review of *Windy McPherson's Son*)

### *by Waldo Frank*

We do not expect an Apocalypse, here in America. Out of our terrifying welter of steel and scarlet, a design must come. But it will come haltingly, laboriously. It will be warped by the steel, clotted with the scarlet. There have been pure and delicate visions among us. In art, there has been Whistler; and Henry James took it into his head to write novels. But the clear subtlety of these men was achieved by a rigorous avoidance of native stuff and native issues. Literally, they escaped America; and their followers have done the same, though in a more figurative meaning. Artist-senses have gone out, felt the raw of us, been repulsed by it, and so withdrawn to a magnificent introversion. So, when we found vision in America, we have found mostly an abstract art—an art that remained pure by remaining neuter. What would have happened to these artists, had they grappled with their country, is an academic question. But I suspect that the true reason for their *ivory tower* was lack of strength to venture forth and not be overwhelmed. This much is sure, however—and true particularly of the novel—that our artists have been of two extremes: those who gained an almost unbelievable purity of expression by the very violence of their self-isolation, and those who, plunging into the American maëlstrom, were submerged in it, lost their vision altogether, and gave forth a gross chronicle and a blind cult of the American Fact.

The significance of Sherwood Anderson whose first novel, "Windy McPherson's Son," has recently appeared (published by The John Lane Company), is simply that he has escaped these two extremes, that he suggests at last a presentation of life shot through with the searching color of truth, which is a signal for a native culture.

Mr. Anderson is no accident. The appearance of his book is a gesture of logic. Indeed, commentators of tomorrow might gauge the station at which America has arrived today by a study of the impulses —conscious and unconscious—which compose this novel. But it is

"Emerging Greatness," by Waldo Frank. Originally published in *The Seven Arts*, November 1916, pp. 73–78. Reprinted by permission of Jean Frank.

not a prophetic work. Its author is simply a man who has felt the moving passions of his people, yet sustained himself against them just enough in a crude way to set them forth.

His story has its beginning in an Iowa town. His hero, with a naive unswervingness from type, is a newsboy. His passion is money and power. He goes to Chicago. He becomes rich. He marries the daughter of his employer. And then, he becomes powerful. There is nothing new in this; although the way of telling it is fresh and sensitive. This is the romance of inchoate America. Like the Greek fables, it is a generic wishfulfillment to be garbed by each poet in his own dress. It has been done in a folk way by Horatio Alger; with a classic might by Theodore Dreiser. But so far, it has been the entire story. With Mr. Anderson, it is only the story's introduction.

When Sam McPherson, by a succession of clumsy assaults, charges to the control of the Arms Trust of America, he does not find there, like his novelistic brothers, a romantic and sentimental and overweening satisfaction. He finds a great disgust, a great emptiness. And he becomes interested in his soul! He learns that what he has done is spiritually nothing; that it has left him as helpless before the commands of life, as in the old days when he amassed pennies in Caxton, Iowa. It dawns on him, that if man is a measurer of truth, he has paralyzed competition, enslaved wealth, disposed of power without really growing at all. So Sam McPherson puts aside his gains; and pilgrimages forth, searching for truth.

This is the second part of the novel; and in it lies the book's importance. McPherson's quest of the grail is an awkward Odyssey indeed. It has the improbability of certain passages of Dostoëvski—the improbability of truth poorly or clumsily materialized. Moreover, in it we find an unleashed and unsophisticated power that we have all along awaited in the American novel. The resemblance to the Russian is, I am convinced, a consequence of a like quality in the two men. It is a temperamental, not a literary thing.

The abdicated millionaire works as a bartender in Ohio, as a builder in Illinois; he joins a threshing crew in the West and a mining camp in the South. He knows prostitutes and working-girls. He tries to help and seeks truth. He learns that labor-unions are more concerned over the use of scab machinery than by the prospect of losing a righteous strike; that the men are more interested in a raise of wages than in preventing a private band of grafters from stealing the town's waterworks. He becomes very miserable over the lot of the street-walkers. He asks the drinkers in the saloon where he is employed why they get drunk, and is discharged with an oath. Puerile, fumbling stuff it is— its efficiency of presentment about on a level with McPherson's method of gaining the light. Yet through it all, is a radiant glow of the truth.

Read the newspapers and the Congressional reports; read the platitudes of investigating commissions, of charity organizations, of revivalists and mushroom mysticisms—and you have the same helpless thing in extension. Sam McPherson, bewildered with his affluence and power, seeking the truth in the fair plains and the cancerous cities, ignorant and awkward and eager—is America today. And Sam McPherson, the boy, arrogant and keen and certain, hiding from himself his emptiness with the extent and occupation of the materials that his land floods upon him, is the America of our fathers.

For a feel of the America of tomorrow, do not look to this book. I am sure that Mr. Anderson will conduct himself better in subsequent works than he has in the conclusion of "Windy McPherson's Son." As we find the faint footprints of Horatio Alger at the book's beginning, so at the end is the smirch of Robert W. Chambers. (But after all, Balzac could not so wholeheartedly have swallowed France, had he not taken Pixérécourt and Madame de Scudéry along.) When Sam marries Sue Rainey, it is with the understanding that they are to have children and that they are to live gloriously for them. For a while, the magnate's money-madness slackens. But the pact fails, for the children can not come. Coolness between the two, with the goal of their creed denied them:—and at length, when Sam sacrifices his wife's father in his grapple toward dominion, she flees to New York. The man over whose fat body he has stepped to power shoots himself. And, sick of his tawdry, superficial kingdom, McPherson wanders off.

He gains nothing from his experiments, and this is well enough. He hunts in Africa, leisures in Paris, canoes in Canada and sentimentalizes in New York. All this we forgive him. But one day, he finds himself in St. Louis. He encounters a drunken mother, buys her three children, packs them into a train and drops them at the feet of his wife who, like some diluted Penelope, has been awaiting his return in a villa on the Hudson. "Not our children, but just *some* children is our need," he pronounces. And so, walks "across the lighted room to sit again with Sue at his own table, and to try to force himself back into the ranks of life." This is the last sentence of the book; the one episode that is *made* and insincere. I hope Mr. Anderson is ashamed of it. I hope he does not really believe that all man has to do, to find God, is to increase and multiply more helpless creatures like himself. This pretty surcease to trouble that comes from transferring the problems of life to the next generation is a biological fact. But it is not art. For with it is dimmed all the voluptuous speculation which flushes the novel as a sunrise transfigures a plain. Let life be happy, if it can. The sacred duty of art is to remain sorrowful, when it has challenged a consciousness of sorrow; to abide in the uncertain search of truth so long as the movement of mankind is hazardous. Let our heroes be joyous; but by conquering themselves, not by adopting children. The virtue of Mr. Anderson's book is that it is dynamic. His static ending is bad, because it breaks the rhythm. But it is worse since it slams the door on the vista of passionate inquiry which the book unfolds. Up to the end, we have a clear symbol of America's groping. At the end, we have nothing—in lieu of the suggested everything. But, of course, we may ignore the end. Or, in its fatuous simplicity, we may read still another symbol of America—a token of what might happen to us, if we sought at this stage to read our lives as a conclusion, rather than a commencement.

I was not certain that Theodore Dreiser was a classic, until I had read this novel of Mr. Anderson. Its first half is a portal from which emerges an American soul. This portal is the immediate past, and in the works of Mr. Dreiser we find its definite expression. Beside their magnificent mass-rhythms, the opening chapters of Mr. Anderson are paltry. One feels, indeed, that the uneasy spirit of Sam McPherson has come forth, not from his own youth, not from his own pages, but from the choking structures of Mr. Dreiser.

Mr. Dreiser may of course yet surprise us by the sudden discovery of a new spiritual light. He has not stopped writing. But I feel in his work the profound massiveness of a completed growth. Mr. Dreiser has caught the crass life of the American, armoring himself with luxury and wealth that he misunderstands, with power whose heritage of uses he ignores. The tragedy of his hero is that of a child suddenly in possession of a continent; too unknowing to know that he is ignorant; too dazzled to be amazed. His books are a dull, hard mosaic of materials beneath which one senses vaguely a grandiose movement—like the blind shifting of quicksands or the imperceptible breathing of a glacier. This is Mr. Dreiser, and this is enough. But with Mr. Anderson, the elemental movement begins to have form and direction; the force that causes it is being borne into the air.

Before Mr. Dreiser, there was "Huckleberry Finn"—there was, in other words, a formless delirium of color and of tangent. These are pre-cultural novels. And in the book of Mr. Anderson, I still find much of them. Indeed, the wandering of Sam McPherson has more than a superficial kinship with Huck Finn's passage down the Mississippi. The land that McPherson walks is still a land marred by men and women "who have not learned to be clean and noble like their forests and their plains." But Huck Finn is an animal boy, floating rudderless down a natural current, avid for food and play. And McPherson is a man, flung against his stream, avid for the Truth. . . .

In conclusion, let us not forget that this is Mr. Anderson's first book, and that a succession of them are already written and will appear in their turn. The fact that Mr. Anderson is no longer young is no hindrance to our hope of his growth. Genius in America, if it does not altogether escape America, rises slowly. For it has far to come. The European is born on a plateau. America is still at a sea-level. The blundering, blustering native was thirty-seven before he became Walt Whitman.

# How Sherwood Anderson Wrote
## *Winesburg, Ohio*

### *by William L. Phillips*

### I

Probably the most illuminating of the Sherwood Anderson papers recently made available for study is the manuscript of *Winesburg, Ohio*.[1] There on several pounds of yellowed paper lie the answers to questions which have been only hazily answered by critics content to draw their discussions of Anderson's literary habits from his own highly emotionalized accounts. The manuscript reveals Anderson's methods of work and, as a consequence, the limited extent to which his writing may be called "artless." With particular reference to *Winesburg* itself, moreover, it indicates that the book was conceived as a unit, knit together, however loosely, by the idea of the first tale, "The Book of the Grotesque," and consisting of individual sketches which derived additional power from each other, not, as anthologists of Anderson repeatedly suggest,[2] a collection of short stories which can be separated from each other without loss of effect.

The manuscript, first of all, makes possible a rather accurate dating of the writing itself, a matter not unimportant in the discussion of influences upon Anderson's fiction. In this connection, Anderson's

"How Sherwood Anderson Wrote *Winesburg, Ohio*," by William L. Phillips. From *American Literature*, 23 (March 1951), 7–30. Copyright 1951 by Duke University Press, Durham, North Carolina. Reprinted by permission of the publisher and the author.

[1] The Sherwood Anderson Papers, Newberry Library, Chicago. Excerpts from unpublished letters and manuscripts in the Newberry collection are here printed with the generous permission of Mrs. Sherwood Anderson and Dr. Stanley Pargellis, Librarian of the Newberry Library.

[2] The most recent, Horace Gregory, in his introduction to the *Portable Sherwood Anderson* (New York: Viking, 1949), p. 42, states the prevalent view in justifying his omission of "The Book of the Grotesque": "The loose construction of *Winesburg, Ohio* makes it possible to present the best of its stories without loss to the reader, and it should be remembered that the tales of *Winesburg, Ohio* were conceived and written as short stories before they appeared under the title of a book."

own accounts in his *Memoirs* of the writing of the tales need to be examined as to accuracy. There he said:

> I had been published. Books, with my name on their backs standing on a shelf over my desk. And yet, something eating at me.
>
> "No. I have not yet written."
>
> . . . upon the particular occasion I am speaking of . . . it was a late fall night and raining and I had not bothered to put on my pajamas. I was there naked in the bed and I sprang up. I went to my typewriter and began to write. It was there, under those circumstances, myself sitting near an open window, the rain occasionally blowing in and wetting my bare back, that I did my first writing.
>
> I wrote the first of the stories, afterwards to be known as the Winesburg stories. I wrote it, as I wrote them all, complete in the one sitting. I do not think I afterwards changed a word of it. I wrote it off, so, sitting at my desk, in that room, the rain blowing in on me and wetting my back and when I had written it I got up from my desk.
>
> The rest of the stories in the book came out of me on succeeding evenings, and sometimes during the day while I worked in the advertising office. At intervals there would be a blank space of a week, and then there would be two or three written during a week. I was like a woman having my babies, one after another but without pain.[3]
>
> I had been working so long, so long. Oh, how many thousands hundreds of thousands of words put down. . . .
>
> And then, on a day, late in the afternoon of a day, I had come home to that room. I sat at a table in a corner of the room. I wrote.
>
> There was the story of another human, quite outside myself, truly told.
>
> The story was one called "Hands." It was about a poor little man, beaten, pounded, frightened by the world in which he lived into something oddly beautiful.
>
> The story was written that night in one sitting. No word of it ever changed. I wrote the story and got up. I walked up and down in that little narrow room. Tears flowed from my eyes.
>
> "It is solid," I said to myself. "It is like a rock. It is there. It is put down. . . ."
>
> In those words, scrawled on the sheets of paper, it is accomplished.[4]

The romantic subjectivity of these two accounts indicates the importance of the *Winesburg* stories as a turning point in Anderson's

[3] *Sherwood Anderson's Memoirs* (New York: Harcourt, Brace, 1942), pp. 286–88. Reprinted with the permission of the publishers.

[4] *Ibid.,* pp. 279–80. For two similar accounts, both of which specifically mention "Hands" as the story the writing of which marked the turning point in his career, see "A Part of Earth" in the *Sherwood Anderson Reader,* ed. Paul Rosenfeld (Boston: Houghton Mifflin 1947), pp. 321–28, probably a rejected variant of one of the *Memoirs* passages quoted above, and a letter from Anderson to Roy Jansen, April, 1935, Newberry Library Collection.

writing career, at least as he saw it; but the same subjectivity suggests that the facts surrounding the composition of the stories should be studied in the light of other evidence. Indeed the mention of the type-written story in the first account and of the "words, scrawled on the sheets of paper" in the second should warn Anderson's biographers of his lack of interest in fact when invention would make a better story.[5]

If we assume that in the first account when Anderson speaks of "the first of the stories, afterwards to be known as the Winesburg stories" he is referring to "The Book of the Grotesque," the time indicated by the first paragraph is incorrect. This story, actually the first of the *Winesburg* tales to be written and the first to be published, appeared in the *Masses* in February, 1916,[6] and thus must have been written at least as early as November, 1915. In November, 1915, Anderson could not have had "books with [his] name on their backs" on his shelf, since his first book, *Windy McPherson's Son*, was not published until September, 1916, and since his second book, *Marching Men*, was not published until the autumn of 1917.[7] If, on the other hand, Anderson in the first account is speaking of the story "Hands," specifically mentioned in the second account, the paragraph still is inaccurate, since "Hands" was published in the *Masses* in March, 1916,[8] six months before the publication of his first novel and a year and a half before that of his second.

Furthermore, although Anderson insisted that after writing the story "Hands," "no word of it ever changed," the manuscript shows that the tale underwent extensive revisions of words and phrases after it had been written. And in addition to the manuscript revisions, the first five paragraphs of the *Masses* version of "Hands" are a re-arrangement of the corresponding first two paragraphs of the manuscript version, indicating that Anderson reworked the first part of the story before submitting it to the *Masses*.[9]

Two more accounts of the writing appear in Anderson's unpublished papers. On April 21, 1938, he wrote to his friend Roger Sergel that he

---

[5] Cf. *Memoirs*, p. 7: "Facts elude me. I cannot remember dates. When I deal in facts, at once I begin to lie. I can't help it. I am by nature a story teller."

[6] *Masses*, VIII, 17. The magazine publication of this story was not noticed by Raymond B. Gozzi in his "Bibliography of Anderson's Contributions to Periodicals, 1914–1946," *Newberry Library Bulletin*, pp. 71–82 (December 1948); Paul Rosenfeld erroneously gave its date of composition as 1918 in the *Sherwood Anderson Reader*, p. v.

[7] Cf. Harry Hansen, *Midwest Portraits* (New York: Harcourt, Brace and Company, 1923), p. 121, which includes statements from the publisher of the books.

[8] *Masses*, VIII, 5, 7.

[9] According to Floyd Dell, then coeditor of the *Masses* with Max Eastman, any changes not made by the author would have been made by Dell or Eastman; each in a letter to the writer has denied changing any of the tales. The only result of the *Masses* revision is a slightly more abrupt opening to the story.

had recently found a complete manuscript of *Winesburg, Ohio* in an old box of papers; and, explaining the fact that the manuscript was on cheap newsprint paper, he said:

> When I wrote the book I was employed in the copy department of an advertising agency and used to cop print paper. The mms is [*sic*] partly on the back of earlier attempts at novels and is mostly in long hand . . . pen, partly pencil.[10]

Anderson's statements in the letter to Sergel agree with the note which Anderson attached to the manuscript which he had found. There he said:

> At the time these stories were written, the author was employed as a copy writer in a Chicago advertising agency and the paper is no doubt that used for roughing up advertisements. It is likely the stories were written two or three times, in the writer's room, in a rooming house in Cass Street in Chicago, or in hotels as he traveled about, visiting clients of his employers. It is the author's notion that the manuscripts which only showed up after many years in a box of old manuscript, is the one prepared for the making of a fair copy by a stenographer. At the time these stories were written the author had already published two novels and had made beginnings and sketches for others and some of this manuscript is on the back of sheets covered with these abandoned efforts.

This last account again raises the problem as to when the stories were written. But, as we have shown earlier, Anderson had not "already published two novels" at the time of the writing of the first two stories, and there is good evidence that, as Anderson has indicated in the *Memoirs* passage quoted earlier, many of the stories were written in a short space of time.

The surviving manuscript consists of drafts of each of the *Winesburg* stories, seven of which are written on the cheap, now yellowed print paper used in blocking out advertisements. The other eighteen tales (counting the four parts of "Godliness" as individual tales) are written on the backs of twenty-one separate fragments of early writing, which are, in the main, parts of a novel concerning a character named Talbot Whittingham and variously called "The Golden Circle," "Talbot the Actor," and "Talbot Whittingham." [11]

Since most of the stories are written on the backs of these earlier attempts, and since several *Winesburg* narratives may appear on the

10 Newberry Library Collection.

11 This was a novel parts of which Anderson brought with him to Chicago from Elyria, Ohio, in early 1913, and which he worked on intermittently until his death. Several large bundles of "Talbot Whittingham" are now in the Newberry Library Collection. For comment concerning the merits of the novel, see Hansen, *op. cit.*, pp. 117, 122.

back of one fragment, it is possible to set up a chain of the composition of this draft of the tales. The supposition is that if a pile of scrap manuscript were to be used for writing, the entire pile would be turned over, and what was the last page of the abandoned fragment would appear as the first page of the new story. Thus, for example, when pages 2 to 12 of the manuscript "The Book of the Grotesque" appear on the backs of pages 15 to 5 of an earlier penciled story about a boy named Paul Warden, and the first four pages of the manuscript "Hands" continue down through the pile of the Paul Warden story to complete pages 4 to 1 of the fragment, it seems clear that Anderson wrote the two stories without a delay which would disturb the order of the pile of abandoned attempts.

By the use of such a chain of manuscripts, the order of composition for three groups of tales may be established.[12] In the first group the following stories appear on the backs of manuscripts the pages of which interlock:

| | |
|---|---|
| 1 "The Book of the Grotesque" | 7 "Surrender (Part Three)" |
| 2 "Hands" | 8 "Nobody Knows" |
| 3 "Paper Pills" | 9 "Respectability" |
| 4 "Tandy" | 10 "The Thinker" |
| 5 "Drink" | 11 "Terror (Part Four)" |
| 6 "Mother" | |

The second group begins a second chain of manuscripts, beginning with pages removed from the fragment on which "Mother" (Number 6 above) was written, and continuing on the back of another manuscript:

1 "Godliness (Part One)"
2 "Godliness (Part Two)"

The third group consists of five tales written on the backs of nine fragments, the pages of which do not follow an exact chain but which indicate that the tales were all written on the same small pile of abandoned manuscript. The probable order of these tales is:

| | |
|---|---|
| 1 "Adventure" | 4 "Loneliness" |
| 2 "The Strength of God" | 5 "An Awakening" |
| 3 "The Teacher" | |

This third group has connections to the pages of manuscripts on the backs of "The Thinker," "Surrender," and "Terror" in the first group.

---

[12] For a detailed description of the process, see William L. Phillips, "Sherwood Anderson's *Winesburg, Ohio*: Its Origins, Composition, Technique, and Reception" (unpublished doctoral dissertation, University of Chicago, 1949), Appendix.

Since the first three of the *Winesburg* tales ("The Book of the Grotesque," "Hands," and "Paper Pills" in Group 1) were published in magazines in February, March, and June of 1916 in that order,[13] it seems reasonable to assume that the drafts of all the stories written on the backs of abandoned manuscripts were written in the fall of 1915 and the winter of 1916. It seems proper to assume that over anything but a short period of time, the pile of manuscripts would have been disturbed to such an extent that a grouping like that above would not have been possible, and thus it seems clear that Anderson has correctly indicated that "the rest of the stories came out of me on successive evenings, and sometimes during the day while I worked in the advertising office. At intervals there would be a blank space of a week and then there would be two or three written during a week."

The remaining seven stories, written on the print paper, may well be the stories composed "in the advertising office" or "in hotels as he traveled about visiting clients of his employers." These are "The Philosopher," "A Man of Ideas," "Queer," "The Untold Lie," "Death," "Sophistication," and "Departure." Since two of the seven were published in magazines in December, 1916, and January, 1917,[14] at least those two may be placed with the stories jotted on the backs of manuscripts; some of the other five, as we shall see, were written later.

Anderson's statement that the manuscript represents "one prepared for the making of a fair copy by a stenographer" suggests that he felt that the manuscript was a late one, prepared just before the collection of the tales into a volume. This, however, is not the case. The preparation of a fair copy for a stenographer would probably have followed the order of the tales in the volume, whereas the order of the manuscripts suggests rather the order of *composition* of the tales. Furthermore, each manuscript contains evidence of extensive revision on the manuscript itself, the results of which revision appear in the magazine version of the tale. A manuscript prepared for the gathering of the tales into a volume might contain revisions from the magazine version to a final version, but could hardly contain revisions from an earlier writing to a magazine version.

Finally, Anderson's statement that "it is likely that the stories were written two or three times" needs to be examined. The revisions on the manuscripts indicate that Anderson was thinking his way through

13 "The Book of the Grotesque" in *Masses*, VIII, 17; "Hands" in *Masses*, VIII, 5, 7; and "Paper Pills" under the title of "The Philosopher" in *Little Review*, III, 7–9. An entirely different story appeared as "The Philosopher" in *Winesburg, Ohio*, a point which has been overlooked in Gozzi, *op. cit.* Rosenfeld in the *Sherwood Anderson Reader* erroneously dates "Paper Pills" as written in 1918.

14 "Queer," *Seven Arts*, I, 97–108 (December 1916); "The Untold Lie," *Seven Arts*, I, 215–21 (January 1917).

the stories as he wrote them, and that if there were earlier versions, they were mere outlines. Unless this kind of writing were considered a first draft and the revisions made on the manuscripts themselves considered a third draft, Anderson's *Memoirs* statement that "I wrote it, as I wrote them all, complete in one sitting," is closer to the actual manner of composition, although not wholly accurate, as we shall see when we come to consider the revisions themselves. Thus, from Anderson's varying accounts and from the evidence of the manuscripts we may conclude that the *Winesburg* stories were written during a relatively short period of time, one leading to another, and that this period of time was late 1915 and early 1916.

## II

The first *Winesburg* story, as we can see from Anderson's own accounts of its composition, was a starting-point for a career in short story writing which was to lead Anderson to international fame in the genre. One is naturally curious about the conception of the first tale, how its basic idea and the details of its rendering came about. Such a scene as this can be reconstructed: on a late fall day in 1915 Anderson had come home from his desk at the advertising office of the Critchfield Company to the third floor of a rooming house at 735 Cass Street in Chicago, just a few blocks away from the offices of Harriet Monroe's *Poetry* and Margaret Anderson's *Little Review*. He had perhaps stopped on a bridge over the Chicago River to try to fathom the expression on a face he had passed in the street, and then he had gone up to his room to write at a long table with a bare electric light over it. For nights before, figures had been passing before his eyes as he lay on the bed which he had had built up for him so that he could look out over the Loop.[15] Concerned for his own future as a writer, feeling himself one who "had known people, many people, known them in a peculiarly intimate way," he searched himself by throwing himself into the imagined life of another. That other, an old man with a white mustache, lay on *his* raised bed and watched in a half-dream the procession of figures before his eyes. They were all grotesques, and the old man wrote a book which he called "The Book of the Grotesque."[16]

Whether the conception of Anderson's own book of grotesques came

[15] For information concerning Anderson's circumstances in Chicago in 1915–16 I am indebted to Mr. George Daugherty, Mr. Max Wald, and Mr. Mitchell Dawson, all of Chicago, and to Mr. Marco Morrow, of Topeka, Kansas. For Anderson's accounts, see *Memoirs*, pp. 227–33, 277–80.

[16] *Winesburg, Ohio* (New York: B. W. Huebsch, 1919), pp. 1–5. This edition will be referred to throughout this paper; since the Modern Library reprint was printed from the original plates, the page numbers noted also apply to it.

before or immediately after he wrote this first *Winesburg* story, "The Book of the Grotesque," his own gallery of imaginary figures offered him more than enough characters for his book. For the past several years he had been writing novels about a Talbot Whittingham who had lived in a town called Winesburg, Ohio, so far as Anderson knew not a real Ohio town, but one which had the characteristics of Clyde, Ohio, where he had spent his boyhood.[17] The name of the town had perhaps been suggested by Wittenberg, the academy which he had attended, or perhaps there had remained in the back of his mind, lost to consciousness, the real town of Winesburg, to which he may have sent "Roof-fix" from his Elyria paint factory. The name of George Willard was similar in sound to the names of George Bollinger, Joe Welliver, and Trigant Williams which appeared on the pages of the rejected manuscript on which he wrote the *Winesburg* stories. Now he could tell how Tandy Hard got her name; he had told his friends in the rooming house that he was writing a trilogy about a woman named Tandy Hard; and Max Wald, the musician, had said that the name reminded him of nothing but hard candy.

The first figure to be clothed was that of the frightened little man who seemed to be afraid of his hands. Anderson once suggested that the impulse to write about Wing Biddlebaum came from his jokingly calling a friend "Mabel" in a bar and watching the knowing looks of the other men at the bar,[18] but the idea of writing about a man "in whom the force that creates life is diffused, not centralized" must have occurred to him earlier when he questioned a group at the Floyd Dells' parties about Freud's views on homosexuality, two years before.[19] After he had lifted Wing Biddlebaum of Winesburg from the life of imagination into the life of reality, the other "figures on the doorstep of his mind" stood "waiting to be clothed." There was the figure of Dr. Reefy, who, like the father of Talbot Whittingham in the pile of rejected attempts at novels, was a small-town doctor with radical ideas;

17 For Anderson's life in Clyde, drawn on in the *Winesburg* stories and others, cf. Evelyn Kintner, "Sherwood Anderson: Small Town Man" (unpublished M.A. thesis, Bowling Green State University, 1942), and William Alfred Sutton, "Sherwood Anderson's Formative Years (1876–1913)" (unpublished doctoral dissertation, Ohio State University, 1943).

18 *Sherwood Anderson Reader*, pp. 325–27.

19 *Memoirs*, pp. 243–44. The matter of Anderson's knowledge of Freudian psychology is a complicated one, and it has been made no less so by Frederick J. Hoffman's discussion of it in his *Freudianism and the Literary Mind* (Baton Rouge: Louisiana State U. Press, 1945), pp. 230–55. Although the proof cannot be reproduced here, it may however be said that Anderson first encountered Freudian terminology at the apartment of Floyd Dell in the late summer of 1913, and that by the time the *Winesburg* stories were written he was intimately acquainted with at least one practising psychiatrist, Dr. Trigant Burrow, to whom he had been introduced by his second wife, Tennessee Mitchell Anderson.

there was Tandy Hard, the girl whose strange name needed explanation; there were the friends of George Willard, his mother, his father.
All of these people were grotesques, suffering from the universal illness of isolation and frustration, and they all belonged in "The Book
of the Grotesque."

Here was an opportunity for the novel writer who had not been
published; the manuscripts of *Windy McPherson's Son* and *Marching
Men*, almost wholly written before he had left his Elyria paint factory
in late 1912, were still being peddled from publisher to publisher by
Floyd Dell.[20] Perhaps already Anderson was aware of the faults of
these books, difficulties which he had not been able to overcome. In a
gallery of portraits, a book of grotesques, there would be an opportunity to search back into his boyhood to exploit the material which
had provided the most appealing parts of his two early novels. Here
was an opportunity to allow the center of the stage to the characters in
episodes who had kept intruding into the plots of his earlier novels;
here he could build a series of incidents like the tale of Windy
McPherson's attempt to blow a bugle in the Fourth of July parade,[21]
an episode much more appealing as a portrait of Windy than as a
contribution to the growth of Windy's son, the chief character of the
novel. Windy really belonged in a "book of the grotesque."

One other factor helped to crystallize Anderson's conception of a
"book of the grotesque"—Edgar Lee Masters's *Spoon River Anthology*.
When the reviewers of *Winesburg, Ohio* in 1919 made the obvious
comparison between the two books, Anderson's publishers replied with
an announcement that "Mr. Anderson's 'Winesburg' stories appeared
in magazines before Mr. Masters's work appeared," clearly a misstate-
ment of the facts.[22] But Anderson himself, despite the critics' suggestions of influence, kept silent on the matter, while he strongly denied
the influence of "the Russians" and Theodore Dreiser. Fortunately,
some new evidence has appeared which helps to determine the facts of
the matter. Mr. Max Wald, one of the "Little Children of the Arts"
who lived with Anderson in the Cass Street rooming house, recently
recalled in an interview that shortly after *Spoon River Anthology*
appeared in book form (April, 1915), he bought a copy, read it, and
spoke admiringly of it to Anderson. Anderson, after remarking that

20 See Floyd Dell, *Homecoming* (New York: Farrar, 1933), pp. 253–54, for the
most accurate account.

21 *Windy McPherson's Son* (New York: John Lane Company, 1916), pp. 22–23.

22 The statement was reported in the *Bookman*, L, x (September 1919). Masters's
*Spoon River* portraits had begun to appear in *Reedy's Mirror* in the issue of May 29,
1914, and had been collected into a book published in April, 1915; the first
*Winesburg* story was not published until February 1916. Thus it is at least *possible*
for Anderson to have had a copy of *Spoon River Anthology* before him as he wrote
the *Winesburg* tales in the winter of 1915–16.

Tennessee Mitchell (soon to become his wife) knew Masters, took the book to his room and returned it in the morning, saying that he had stayed up all night reading the poems and that he was much impressed by them.[23] Very probably this reading of Masters's book just six months before the writing of the first *Winesburg* story helped shape the "book of the grotesque" into a collection of sketches in which the characters would be related in their environment and treated as a cross section of village life. It may be suggested furthermore that Anderson's reticence to discuss Masters's work in print may have resulted from his awareness of the past relationship of Tennessee Mitchell (his wife by the time of the book publication of *Winesburg*) and Edgar Lee Masters. Tennessee Mitchell was the "Deirdre" of Masters's *Across Spoon River,* scathingly denounced by him in that work; she had, apparently, been his mistress for eighteen months in 1909 and 1910, and, according to Masters, had been responsible for widening the breach between Masters and his first wife.[24] If Anderson had been aware of the extent of Tennessee Mitchell's alleged involvement with Masters,[25] he could hardly have failed to identify the original of "Georgine Sand Miner" and "Tennessee Claflin Shope" in *Spoon River Anthology* and "Deirdre" in the later *Across Spoon River,* and he may very well have preferred not to open the subject of his relations with Masters. In any event, it seems extremely likely that Anderson's admiration for Masters's portraits and his knowledge of their enthusiastic reception by the Chicago critics may have hastened his development from *Windy McPherson's Son* to "The Book of the Grotesque," later to be called *Winesburg, Ohio.*

The manuscript shows that from the first the *Winesburg* stories were conceived as complementary parts of a whole, centered in the background of a single community. In the first individual story,

[23] Statements in interview with the writer, Chicago, June 24, 1949.

[24] *Across Spoon River* (New York: Farrar, 1936), pp. 295–313. Masters verified the identification of Tennessee Mitchell as "Deirdre" in a letter to the writer, May 25, 1949. It must be said that the authenticity of the "Deirdre" episode rests solely on Masters's testimony; those close to Anderson at the time—Dr. Trigant Burrow, Mr. Karl Anderson, Mr. Max Wald, Mr. George Daugherty, Mr. Marco Morrow, and others—recall only that Anderson first met Masters through Tennessee Mitchell, who had known him before Anderson came to Chicago. Masters wrote of his acquaintance with Anderson: "After meeting I do not remember how often we saw each other; not often. I do remember he came to my house one night. I never discussed *Spoon River* with him, but I do think it had influence upon his *Winesburg, Ohio.*"

[25] In his *Memoirs,* p. 453, one of the few instances in which Anderson wrote of Tennessee Mitchell, he said: ". . . Tennessee—someone away back in your childhood had done you a great wrong. You could never quite tell of it, although you wanted to. Or perhaps it was some man later—some poet—you had a passion for poets."

"Hands," Anderson had called his town "Winesburg, Ohio"; in "Paper Pills," the next tale to be written, only "Winesburg" appears on the manuscript as the name of the town. In the second story he introduced "the Heffner Block," an actual group of buildings in the Clyde, Ohio, of his boyhood, and "John Spaniard," the disguised nurseryman French of Clyde.[26] In the first story he had mentioned that George Willard was the son of the proprietor of the New Willard House; the third story to be written, "Tandy," might well take place on the steps of the New Willard House. Tandy lives on a road leading off Trunion Pike, a new geographical detail added to the growing conception of the town of Winesburg; in the fourth story to be written, "Drink," the opening paragraph contains a reference to Trunion Pike, and added in this story to the physical picture of the town are Duane Street, the name of a Clyde street, and "Hern's Grocery," the disguised name of Hurd's grocery where Anderson worked as a boy in Clyde. Much of the action of this story takes place in the office of the *Winesburg Eagle,* which had been mentioned earlier in "Hands." One can see how each scrap of description tended to fill in the environment of Winesburg— its stores and its streets—and how after Winesburg was furnished with a Main Street, it would be easy to have a Duane Street, a Buckeye Street, and a Maumee Street branching from it.

As the streets led to each other, and all branched from Main Street, so one scrap of action led to another, and each had some reference to George Willard. In "Drink" it was mentioned in passing that George Willard, like Tom Foster, had a "sentiment concerning Helen White" in his heart. From this brief casual reference must have grown the conception of George Willard's love affair with Helen White which furnishes part of the interest in "The Thinker" and the entire interest in "Sophistication," both later stories, and which in turn suggested George Willard's adventures with the two other girls of the town, Louise Trunnion and Belle Carpenter, in "Nobody Knows" and "An Awakening." George's walk with Belle Carpenter in "An Awakening" provided a beginning for Wash Williams's lecture on women to George in "Respectability." The outbreak of George's schoolteacher in "The Teacher" led Anderson to wonder what effect she had on others of the town, and in "The Strength of God" he described her impact upon the Presbyterian minister. Kate Swift's naked form at prayer beside her bed suggested to him another sexually frustrated spinster, Alice Hind-man, who runs naked into the street in "Adventure." Reading the

26 The most convincing evidence that Anderson was thinking of Clyde characters as he filled out the *Winesburg* stories is his use of "Skinner Leason" for the name of the Winesburg grocer (*Winesburg, Ohio,* p. 28). There was a Skinner Letson in Clyde, and the name on the manuscript appears as "Letson" crossed out, with "Leason" substituted.

stories in the order of their composition, one can watch Anderson follow the excursions of his own imagination, while the town of Winesburg becomes completed in its physical setting and the people of Winesburg become tangled in their relations to each other, in either their awareness of each other or their significant unawareness of each other.

## III

A study of the manuscript furthermore reveals something of the way in which the individual *Winesburg* tales were written. No outlines or early half-formed versions of the stories exist, although there may have been some for a few of the tales. On the backs of the Newberry manuscripts of "Mother" and "Drink," however, is an earlier story which has been preserved in an early draft. The manuscript begins with eighteen words and phrases scrawled in a column down a page, forming a brief outline, one which might have been jotted down in a few seconds in an attempt to catch the characteristics of a figure in Anderson's fancy. Following this outline are thirty pages of a story, never completed, about a George Bollinger and his love affair with an Alice Hassinger.

Such brief outlines may or may not have been used for the *Winesburg* tales; with such a story as "Hands" it is likely that the story was written in one frenzied rush of the pencil. Anderson once said:

> I am not one who can peck away at a story. It writes itself, as though it used me merely as a medium, or it is n.g. . . . The short story is the result of a sudden passion. It is an idea grasped whole as one would pick an apple in an orchard. All of my own short stories have been written at one sitting.[27]

Let us examine for evidence of his working habits the manuscript of "Hands," which Anderson most admired and which he singled out for mention as one that had never been changed in a word.

The manuscript of this story consists of twenty-seven pages written in a penciled scrawl on the backs of three fragments of earlier stories. The handwriting is legible only with difficulty, and it becomes less legible toward the end of the story and in several sections in which the ideas apparently flowed more rapidly than the hand could put them down. Nowhere in the manuscript is there a rearrangement of the parts of the story, the deletion or addition of a paragraph, or even the deletion or addition of a complete sentence, indicating that Anderson followed the order of narration which came most natural to him, in some instances an order which violated the usual chronology of a

27 *Memoirs*, pp. 286, 341.

short story. There are no revisions so far as major changes in the story are concerned, and in this respect Anderson's comment that "no word of it ever changed" is correct; the story was "grasped whole."

There are, however, almost two hundred instances in which earlier words and phrases are deleted, changed, or added to, to provide the readings of the final published version of the story. The larger part of these revisions were apparently made after the story had been written through once, since they are made over the lines and in the margins. But about one-tenth of the revisions were made during the first writing, since they appear on the line of writing before it continues.

Such revisions as were made during the first writing provide an interesting picture of Anderson's habits, his manner of working through a story. He can be seen taking great care in the selection of the exact word for the idea to be expressed, sometimes rejecting one word for another only to reinsert the first one before the rest of the sentence was finished.[28] Occasionally the creative process was stopped while Anderson, always a bad speller, corrected his misspelling of a simple word.[29] One can observe the consolidation of ideas, and in some instances the dawning of new ideas which were then incorporated into the story and developed. Indeed, the entire idea regarding the need for a poet to tell the story of Wing Biddlebaum's hands may have come from Anderson's dissatisfaction with a word used in the first writing and immediately changed. In the first passage mentioning the need for a poet, the story of Biddlebaum's hands originally was called merely "strange"; then for "strange" (a word much used by Anderson and often deleted) was substituted "worth a book in itself." The sentence about the need for a poet then followed: "The story of Wing Biddlebaum's hands is ~~strange~~. worth a book in itself. Sympathetically set forth it would tap many strange, beautiful qualities in obscure men. It is a job for a poet." [30] It is not too fanciful to suggest that in searching for a better word than "strange" Anderson hit upon the idea of the need for a poet to write the story, a motif repeated later[31] which adds to the frequent intrusion of the author into this tale.

The revisions which Anderson made *during* the first writing, however, are greatly in the minority; about nine-tenths of the changes were made after a first draft had been completed. And it seems clear that the

[28] For example, "With a shiver of ~~dread~~ ~~fear~~ dread the boy arose. . . ." The final reading may be found in *Winesburg, Ohio*, p. 12. In notes following, the location of only the final reading will be indicated; each revision considered is representative of others which cannot be reproduced for lack of space.

[29] ". . . a part of the ~~towhn~~ town where . . ." (*ibid.*, p. 8).

[30] *Ibid.*, p. 10.

[31] *Ibid.*, pp. 12–13.

story, although first drafted in a "sudden passion," was reworked several times, since occasionally words which were added above the line of writing of the first draft were later themselves deleted. Most of the revisions of words and phrases were made only once, however. Of these it is significant that while there were 99 *substitutions* of words and phrases for earlier expressions and 58 *additions* of expressions, there were only 21 instances in which expressions were deleted and not replaced by others. Anderson's first writing of the story must have seemed to him sufficiently economical in its treatment, so that instead of paring the story further he was concerned with filling it out.

In the main his deletions simply removed overworked or awkwardly used words, although in one instance he added to the universality of the story by deleting the single word "his": "The story of Wing Biddlebaum is a story of ~~his~~ hands." [32] But the substitutions and additions which he made to the story show more clearly his attempts to give an accurate rendering of the fanciful figure of Wing Biddlebaum and his hands. Anderson was first of all aware that he would have to avoid any details about Wing's case that would disgust the "normal" reader if he were to treat the homosexually inclined character with sympathy. He must avoid the suggestion that Biddlebaum's attraction to George Willard is wholly erotic in nature. Thus he added the qualifying "something like" in "With George Willard . . . he had formed something like a friendship";[33] instead of "he still hungered for the boy" he wrote "he still hungered for the presence of the boy";[34] and he replaced "[Biddlebaum's hands] stole to George Willard's shoulders" with "[Biddlebaum's hands] stole forth and lay upon George Willard's shoulders." [35]

Often his revisions increased the suggestiveness of the tale with symbolic details. Instead of an ordinary veranda, Wing's porch was made a "half-decayed veranda," suggesting the state not only of the veranda but of the man who walked upon it; and the field which stood near Biddlebaum's house, originally a corn field grown with "weeds," was changed to "a field that [had] been seeded for clover but that had produced only a dense crop of yellow mustard weeds." [36] Wing Biddlebaum's hands were described as beating like "the wings of an *imprisoned* bird," and were made to appear as something outside him-

---

32 *Ibid.*, p. 9. One cannot, of course, be certain *why* Anderson made any of the revisions. It must be assumed that when a change achieves a new effect Anderson by his revision intended that effect.

33 *Ibid.*, p. 8.

34 *Ibid.*, p. 16.

35 *Ibid.*, p. 12.

36 *Ibid.*, p. 7. The book version and its later reprints read "*has* been seeded for clover," a typographical error; the manuscript has the more grammatically proper "had."

self, uncontrollable, unattached to himself by the change of *"his* hands" to *"the* hands."

>           the
> Again he raised ~~his~~ hands to caress the boy. . . . Again and again the fathers of the boys had talked of ~~his~~ the hands.[37]

Some of the stylistic traits that have been noticed in Anderson's prose —colloquialisms, repetitive patterns, and frequent auctorial intrusions—can be seen to have arisen in the revisions. He can be seen changing a more formal, Latinate expression to a colloquial, Anglo-Saxon one: "At times an almost overwhelming curiosity had taken ~~possession~~ hold of him." [38] He added the last name of Wing Biddlebaum three times and of George Willard twice in the story, so that neither of the men is ever called by a single name. This repetitive trick, probably learned from Gertrude Stein's "Melanctha," [39] achieves the simple, casual effect of language comparatively free of pronominal antecedents. Although in "Hands" there are no passages with marked patterns of repetition of the kind to be found elsewhere in the tales,[40] the revisions of the story indicate that Anderson tended to select a descriptive detail for a character or place which he repeated whenever the character or place was again mentioned. For example, in the opening sentence of the story Wing Biddlebaum is pictured walking upon the "veranda of a small frame house that stood near the edge of a ravine"; near the end of the story when Wing continues to walk "upon the veranda of his house," Anderson added "by the ravine," and a few lines later he changed the original "he went again to walk upon the porch" to "he went again to walk upon the veranda." [41] Finally, the intrusions of the author into this story, characteristic of oral storytellers and of Anderson's borrowing of their technique, did not go unnoticed by him; they were not merely the slips of an untrained fiction writer. Although the intrusions appear in the first writing of the story and were not added later, Anderson in several instances smoothed off his entrance into the tale and made his intrusion seem less blunt. For example, "We will look briefly into the story of the hands. It may be our talking of them will arouse the poet . . ." was softened to "Let us look briefly into the story of the hands. Perhaps our talking of

37 *Ibid.*, pp. 9, 12, 15. Italics mine.

38 *Ibid.*, p. 10.

39 In a letter to Gertrude Stein preserved in the Yale University Library, Anderson expressed his admiration for "the first thing of yours I read—in the Three Lives—about the nigger woman." Such repetitive patterns are also characteristic of the King James Version of the Bible and *Huckleberry Finn,* both of which Anderson much admired.

40 Cf. *Winesburg, Ohio,* pp. 4–5, 38–39, 168–69, 206–7, 219.

41 *Ibid.*, p. 16.

them will arouse the poet . . ." [42] as though the storyteller realized that he might offend his audience by directing their attentions too obviously.

The process of writing "Hands," then, was much as Anderson suggested; the story was "an idea grasped whole as one would pick an apple in the orchard." But, to continue his figure, the manuscript indicates that after Anderson had picked the apple he examined it carefully for bad spots and polished its minor imperfections.

## IV

When a number of the *Winesburg* stories had been written and revised, Anderson set about getting the individual tales into print. Because of their unconventional subject matter and treatment, they were not likely to be acceptable to the popular magazines; but Anderson was known to the editors of several "little magazines." Since Floyd Dell still had the manuscript of *Windy McPherson's Son* and was still convinced that Anderson was a writer who should be published, he was likely to accept some of the tales for the *Masses,* of which he and Max Eastman were co-editors. Anderson apparently sent the early tales to Dell in the order that he wrote them, since "The Book of the Grotesque" and "Hands," the first two of the tales to be written and published, appeared in that order in the February and March, 1916, issues of the *Masses.* Later in the year Dell published "The Strength of God," but soon a dissatisfaction with the stories arose in the editorial offices of the *Masses,* and the later tales were voted down by the editors.[43]

In the meantime one of the stories, "Paper Pills," had appeared in Margaret Anderson's *Little Review.* Anderson had contributed articles to the first two issues of this magazine in 1914, and he continued to publish sketches there during 1915 and 1916. Since the magazine was at this time still being published in Chicago, and since Anderson was a frequent visitor to Margaret Anderson's North Shore gatherings, it was not surprising that one of the early *Winesburg* tales should have been published in the *Little Review.*[44]

The beginning of plans in the winter of 1915–16 for a new "little magazine," the *Seven Arts,* offered another outlet for the stories. Edna Kenton had met Anderson in Chicago in the early winter of 1916 and

---

42 *Ibid.,* p. 12.

43 Letter to the writer from Floyd Dell, December 12, 1948. Cf. Hansen, *op. cit.,* p. 123, and Dell, *op. cit.,* p. 256.

44 Cf. n. 13. For an account of Anderson's relations with the *Little Review,* see Margaret Anderson, *My Thirty Years' War* (New York: Covici, Friede, Inc., 1930), pp. 90–91.

had read several of his stories. She sent Anderson's name to Waldo Frank, one of the men who was slated to become an editor of *Seven Arts* when it began publication. Anderson and Frank corresponded during the winter and spring of 1916, and Frank was enthusiastic about a number of the *Winesburg* stories which Anderson sent him. In the summer of 1916 Anderson invited Frank to come to Lake Chateaugay in upper New York for a vacation, and the two spent much time during June and July discussing Anderson's work. By that time, Frank has recently remarked, Anderson had "already written at least a majority of the Winesburg tales." [45] Frank's admiration for Anderson's work grew during this summer, so that for the first issue of *Seven Arts*, in November, 1916, he wrote the commendatory article, "Emerging Greatness," concerning Anderson's first novel (which by this time had been published). The second issue of *Seven Arts* had as its leading story "Queer," by Sherwood Anderson; the third issue printed "The Untold Lie" and announced that other *Winesburg* tales would follow. Two other tales did follow—"Mother" and "The Thinker"—before *Seven Arts* lost its subsidy and ceased publication. [46]

Except for "An Awakening" and "A Man of Ideas," which were printed in the *Little Review* some months later, [47] these were all of the *Winesburg* tales which appeared in magazines before their publication in book form in 1919. For the ten stories, Anderson later remembered, he received only $85, since of the three magazines in which they had appeared, only *Seven Arts* paid for its material. [48] But for a writer who had published only three short stories before, [49] the reception of the *Winesburg* tales by Floyd Dell, Margaret Anderson, and Waldo Frank must have led Anderson to believe that in such tales as these he had found his medium of expression.

Certain changes in the stories were made before Anderson submitted them to the magazines. Most of these were minor changes—revisions of punctuation and occasional changes of wording—but two were extensive. One was the rearrangement of the story "Hands" in the version published in the *Masses* mentioned earlier, [50] noteworthy only since

---

[45] Letter to the writer, March 23, 1949.

[46] "Mother," *Seven Arts*, I, 452–61 (March 1917), and "The Thinker," II, 584–97 (September 1917). With its next issue, the journal ended.

[47] "The [*sic*] Man of Ideas," *Little Review*, V, 22–28 (June 1918); "An Awakening," *Little Review*, V, 13–21 (December 1918). The latter story has been omitted from Gozzi, *op. cit.*

[48] *Memoirs*, p. 288.

[49] "The Rabbit-pen," *Harper's*, CXXIX, 207–10 (July 1914); "Sister," *Little Review*, II, 3–4 (December 1915); and "The Story Writers," *Smart Set*, XLVIII, 243–48 (January 1916). These do not include Anderson's contributions during 1902–5 to *Agricultural Advertising*, the house organ of the Chicago advertising firm for which he worked, some of which were fictional sketches.

[50] See n. 9, above.

this is the story of which Anderson said, "No word of it ever changed." But the second, involving the *Seven Arts* version of "The Untold Lie," is more striking. In *Seven Arts,* the story opens:

> When I was a boy and lived in my home town of Winesburg, Ohio, Ray Pearson and Hal Winters were farm hands employed on a farm three miles north of us. I cannot for my life say how I know this story concerning them, but I vouch for its truth. I have known the story always just as I know many things concerning my own town that have never been told to me. As for Ray and Hal I can recall well enough how I used to see them on our Main Street with other country fellows of a Saturday afternoon.[51]

The first-person narrator continues, telling the story exactly as it is told in the book version, except for frequent intrusions like "as I remember him" and "I myself remember." Since in the book version the only entrance into the tale of characters in earlier tales is a brief mention of "boys like young George Willard and Seth Richmond," [52] which might easily have been added to tie this tale loosely to the others, one might think that the *Seven Arts* version was an earlier one which had been reworked to fit into the collection of tales. This possibility has been seized upon by a student of Anderson who has recently suggested that not only did Anderson revise the magazine version of "The Untold Lie" to make it conform to the focus of narration of the other tales, but that the frequent intrusions of the author into the other tales are the results of faulty revisions of *their* earlier "I" (first person) versions. This writer concludes:

> It is quite likely, I should say, that some of these stories were originally written from a first-person observer focus and then revised to tone down the "I"; others were written from the omniscient author focus. . . . The impression that one gains of most of the *Winesburg* stories is that they were written with the author doing the telling as an "I," and that this "I" appeared wherever it was necessary for him to do so. Later the number of "I's" was cut down either by direct elimination (and making the necessary changes) or by substitution of "George Willard." [53]

This ingenious theory is, however, disproved by the manuscripts of the stories which are now available for study. None of the manuscript versions is of the "I" variety; and the manuscript of "The Untold Lie," like the others an omniscient author version, contains frequent

51 I, 215 (January 1917).

52 *Winesburg, Ohio,* p. 245.

53 Jarvis A. Thurston, "Sherwood Anderson: A Critical Study" (unpublished doctoral dissertation, State University of Iowa, 1946), pp. 98–99, 110. The unpublished material in the Newberry Library Collection was not available at the time of Mr. Thurston's study.

revisions the *results* of which appear in the magazine version. Thus, as he revised "Hands" before submitting it to the *Masses,* Anderson must have revised "The Untold Lie" immediately before sending it to Waldo Frank for publication in *Seven Arts;* the "I" version was not the first but a revised one, and the original omniscient author version stayed in the pile of manuscripts to be used in *Winesburg, Ohio.*[54]

## V

Most of the *Winesburg* stories must have been written, as Anderson said, in a short period of time with one providing the germ for another. But a few of the stories seem surely to have been written later. We have seen that eighteen of the twenty-five tales were written on the backs of the interlocking earlier manuscripts and thus must have been composed together. Of the seven stories on the yellow advertising copy paper (and therefore suspect of being later) two, "Queer" and "The Untold Lie," were published in the first two issues of *Seven Arts* and thus must have been written before, or at the latest, during Anderson's correspondence with Waldo Frank in the spring of 1916. A third, "A Man of Ideas," was published in the *Little Review* soon after the *Seven Arts* ceased publication, and before the publication in the *Little Review* of "An Awakening," one of the early tales. The remaining four—"The Philosopher," "Death," "Sophistication," and "Departure"—are the only ones which seem to have been written later.

There are two indications that "The Philosopher" was a later addition to the group of tales. The story written as "Paper Pills" and published under that title in the 1919 volume was first published in the *Little Review* as "The Philosopher" in June, 1916, when, according to Waldo Frank, a majority of the tales had been written.[55] It is not likely that Anderson would take the title of a story which was waiting to be published and put it on another story. Furthermore, it will be noticed that as the tales were written more and more details of setting were added, so that in contrast to "Hands" and "Paper Pills,"

[54] It is difficult to see, nevertheless, why Anderson should have made such a change. The awkwardness with which "I" has to account for his knowledge of the story detracts from the plausibility of the tale itself. The "I" character is not affected by the events which he tells about; "I" is not anxiously thinking "I Want to Know Why," or explaining why "I'm a Fool." He is rather telling a story which could more plausibly have been told by an omniscient author. The only reasons for the change which may be suggested are admittedly questionable ones. Perhaps Anderson wished to achieve some variety of telling in the four stories which appeared in *Seven Arts,* or perhaps he was hesitant about including George Willard in all the stories which he published in magazines, thinking that George's appearance as a connecting force in the final collection would dissipate its novelty in magazine appearances.

[55] Letter to the writer, March 23, 1949. Cf. n. 13 above.

which have only modest references to Main Street or the New Willard House, the later stories are filled with names of streets, business houses, and minor characters. "The Philosopher" is such a story; here, although half of the comparatively short story is taken up by Dr. Parcival's tale of his earlier life away from Winesburg, the rest of the narrative is filled with allusions to the *Winesburg Eagle*, its editor Will Henderson, Tom Willy's saloon, the baggage-man Albert Longworth, Main Street, Biff Carter's lunch room, and the railroad station, all of which had been mentioned in earlier stories.

"Death," "Sophistication," and "Departure," the remaining tales of those written on the advertising copy paper, are the last three tales in the *Winesburg* volume. None was published in a magazine, and all are filled with allusions to names and places which had been mentioned earlier. "Death" is actually two stories, the account of the love affair of Dr. Reefy and Elizabeth Willard and the story of George Willard's reaction to the death of his mother. It is preceded in the *Winesburg* volume by "The Untold Lie" and "Drink," tales which have their chief interest in characters outside the Willard family. But in "Death" the interest shifts back abruptly to Elizabeth Willard and her struggle with her husband over George's future. Dr. Reefy had not been mentioned since the early story "Paper Pills," but here he becomes Elizabeth Willard's lover just before her death, as the two most sympathetically treated of the mature characters in the book are brought together in a brief moment of escape from isolation. It seems as if Anderson realized that his "Book of the Grotesque" had become filled, and that to keep the novelistic quality of the work he would have to bring his chief characters to some end. Just as in *Windy McPherson's Son* and *Marching Men* it is the deaths of the mothers of Sam McPherson and Beaut McGregor which stir them to leave their villages permanently, so Elizabeth Willard's long-awaited death is the event which sends George Willard out of Winesburg and which prepares for the short résumé of his career in "Departure."

"Sophistication" is the culmination of the George Willard-Helen White affair which had been touched upon in several earlier stories, but which had not been given a full treatment. In it Anderson was able to show not only the final stage of George Willard's feeling for Helen White but also the growing sophistication which had resulted from his listening to the stories of the grotesques of Winesburg. Thus in the last two tales George Willard's affairs in Winesburg are brought to a close with the death of his mother and the establishment of a more mature relation with Helen White; he is ready for "Departure."

Whether a publisher suggested that the last stories be written to round out the career of George Willard or whether Anderson felt that they were needed to make his "Book of the Grotesque" something more than a mere collection of short stories cannot be determined. It is probable that the latter was the case. Anderson later said that although he had secured publication in magazines for some of the tales he wanted them put together in a single volume. "The stories belonged together," he said. "I felt that, taken together, they made something like a novel, a complete story [which gave] . . . the feeling of the life of a boy growing into young manhood in a town." [56]

But getting the items in "The Book of the Grotesque," as Anderson then spoke of it to Floyd Dell, published in a volume was a difficult matter. Anderson submitted the stories to John Lane, the English publisher of his first two novels, but the Lane firm had lost confidence in Anderson after the weak sales of his early books, and they refused the *Winesburg* stories on the ground that they were "too gloomy." [57]

Anderson's early work, however, had found admirers in people like Waldo Frank, Floyd Dell, Theodore Dreiser, Ben Hecht, Margaret Anderson, and Francis Hackett. And it was Francis Hackett, then literary editor of the *New Republic,* who showed the manuscript of "The Book of the Grotesque" to Ben Huebsch, owner and editor of a small publishing house in New York which had already published Joyce's *Dubliners* and *A Portrait of the Artist as a Young Man* and Lawrence's *The Prussian Officer* and *The Rainbow.* Huebsch became interested, obtained Anderson's release from John Lane, and suggested the title *Winesburg, Ohio* for the stories.[58] Finally, in April, 1919, fully three years after most of them had been written, the episodes which had begun with the conception of a "Book of the Grotesque," written (in the main) as a connected series, were published as *Winesburg, Ohio.*

[56] *Memoirs,* p. 289.

[57] Letter to the writer from B. W. Huebsch, June 22, 1949. For an account of the poor sales of the early books, see Hansen, *op. cit.,* pp. 121–22.

[58] *Ibid.*

# *Winesburg, Ohio*: Art and Isolation

## *by Edwin Fussell*

In 1915–16, when the sketches collected in *Winesburg, Ohio* were written, American culture was in the process of making its way from muck-raking to depth psychology; they have in common the discovery of hidden truth behind false appearances, and no one is going to be much surprised at the fact that such a deeply representative work of the time is likewise organized around the prevailing idea of "revelation" ("The people of the town thought of her as a confirmed old maid. . . . In reality she was the most eagerly passionate soul among them").[1] Anderson called attention to this aspect of the book's method when he dedicated it to the memory of his mother, "whose keen observations on the life about her first awoke in me the hunger to see beneath the surface of lives." All observation of the book is more or less constrained to begin from this primary motivation—"to see beneath the surface of lives"—and to proceed to admit the improbability of there arising from this motivation fiction of the kind that we call realistic or naturalistic (those kinds being much less in a hurry to leave the surfaces behind). Recent readings are thus rightly concerned with revision of the 1920s' picture of a "realistic" Anderson —in the 1920s anyone who tried to tell the truth was a "realist"—and with the elucidation of Anderson's more lyric achievement: they are properly concerned with defining the emotions that sustain *Winesburg, Ohio,* for example, and with observing the means by which Anderson was occasionally able to render these emotions with such sweetness and clarity.

It goes without saying that the emotions are loneliness and incompletion, particularly as these emotions take their source from some failure of affection or of creative expression. There is no disagreement on this score: the new criticism takes up where the old criticism left off. Whether viewed as a writer of "exposé" or as a minor poet

"*Winesburg, Ohio*: Art and Isolation," by Edwin Fussell. From *Modern Fiction Studies,* vol. 6, no. 2 (Summer 1960), 106–14. Copyright 1960 by Purdue Research Foundation, West Lafayette, Indiana. Reprinted by permission of the publisher and the author.

1 *Winesburg, Ohio* (New York: Modern Library, 1919), p. 191.

in prose, Anderson is indisputably the man who writes about discontinuity among persons and about the behaviors and feelings that
spring from that discontinuity. Stated so baldly, it does not perhaps
at once strike us as a theme capable of supporting a very ambitious
fictional *oeuvre* (though it is not quite fair to imply that Anderson
has nothing else to say); and we may even feel that without some act
of judgment entered by the participating intelligence, or alternatively
some connections made with other and more general truths, this
vision of isolation may not be capable of supporting more than a
static description of a pathetic situation. Yet it is particularly the
possibility of such an act of judgment on Anderson's part, or of such
a general extension of meaning, with respect to the pathos of his
materials, that is most persistently ignored (perhaps because the
pathos is in its own way so good); so that readers who come to
*Winesburg,* or who come back, fresh from the criticism of it—and
who reads even the minor classics these days entirely apart from the
offices of criticism?—are likely to see in it mainly a reflection of the
passivity of its critics and their easy satisfaction with its pathos.
Meanwhile its original impact becomes every year more difficult to
recapture or explain.

But upon the possibility of there really being in *Winesburg* such
a contribution of intelligent judgment consonant with truths of broad
applicability and thus qualifying and refining the vision of grotesque
isolation, would seem to depend the book's chances of survival as
more than a landmark in literary history. It is this question that the
present essay seeks to engage, if not definitively to answer. Obviously
the answer can be neither unassailable nor triumphant: *Winesburg*
has been repeatedly read, and if its acts of judgment were conspicuous
they would have been found out. We must be prepared to accept a
modest result and to content ourselves with remembering that the
addition of a single note can change the character of a chord.

We may make a beginning by noticing how ambivalent, if not confused, Anderson's feelings were toward the usual substance of his
fiction. The ambivalence could doubtless be documented from a
variety of fictional and biographical records; but a single passage from
*Poor White* (the novel immediately following *Winesburg*) is entirely
adequate to the outline and dimensions of Anderson's dilemmas.

> All men lead their lives behind a wall of misunderstanding they them-
> selves have built, and most men die in silence and unnoticed behind
> the walls. Now and then a man, cut off from his fellows by the
> peculiarities of his nature, becomes absorbed in doing something that
> is impersonal, useful, and beautiful. Word of his activities is carried
> over the walls.[2]

2 *Poor White* (New York: B. W. Huebsch, 1920), p. 227.

Perhaps the most obviously glaring anomaly in this passage is the way it envisages the artist, like all other men, living in isolation and working out of it, yet sees in his case the isolation mysteriously leading to creation instead of destruction. The distinction is not explored, nor even, apparently, recognized. Moreover, there is curious uncertainty in the phrase "cut off from his fellows by the peculiarities of his nature," which seems to imply that the "fellows" (whom Anderson has been describing in *Winesburg* as almost universally "grotesque") are somehow less "peculiar," more "normal" perhaps, than this artist who devotes himself to the "impersonal, useful, and beautiful." Finally, there is a contradiction which if we notice it at all must strike us as even more bewildering than the creation-destruction confusion, and which is equally unresolved: in the second sentence the artist is described as one "cut off from his fellows," as if the "fellows" were in happy communion with each other and therefore to be regarded as a homogeneous group from which *his* peculiarities have alienated him; yet in the first sentence Anderson tells us, sounding a little like Thoreau and at the same time echoing both doctrine and metaphor from *Winesburg,* that "all men lead their lives behind a wall of misunderstanding they themselves have built."

It will be said that of course Anderson is not skillful in expository prose and that it is therefore quite beside the point to submit to rational analysis a piece of writing so murky as the passage from *Poor White.* That would be true if the criticism were undertaken for any other purpose than to locate a center of tension in Anderson's feelings about this theme. That center of tension may now be broadly defined as the polarity of artist and society (and from Anderson's biography we should expect no less), particularly as both terms are illuminated (or muddied) by the shifting values that it is possible to attach to the words "normal" and "isolated." In order to see *Winesburg* clearly and as a whole, it is essential to bear in mind both ends of the polarity and not allow ourselves to be tempted, either by Anderson's ability to "see beneath the surface of lives" or by the fantastic pathos of the *Winesburg* victims, to focus all our attention on the grotesques. To do so is at a stroke to give up half the book; worse than that, to give up the half which furnishes perspective and therefore significance to the other.

If we approach the novel from the direction of George Willard, the young reporter presumably on the threshold of his career as a writer, instead of from that of the *subjects* of the sketches, *Winesburg* composes as a *Bildungsroman* of a rather familiar type the "portrait of the artist as a young man" in the period immediately preceding his final discovery of *métier.* In order to arrive at the rare excellence of *Winesburg,* we must first see that it is a book of this kind;

and then we must go on to see in what ways it is not typical of the *genre,* for it is in the differences that Anderson's merits are revealed. An initial formulation of this difference would mainly call attention to Anderson's almost faultless holding of the balances between his two terms, artist and society, a delicacy that was perhaps made easier for him by the genuine uncertainty of his feelings. To put it bluntly, there are few works of modern fiction in which the artist's relations with ordinary men are seen with such a happy blend of acuity and charity, few works of any age in which the artist and ordinary men are seen so well *as fitting together* in a complementary union that permits us to make distinctions of relative value while at the same time retaining a universally diffused sense of equal dignity. We need look no further for the cause of the remarkable serenity of tone of *Winesburg.*

This balancing of forces is the thing to hang onto; and it thus seems to me a mistake for Irving Howe, in his beautifully written description of *Winesburg,*[3] to call so much attention to the grotesques' pathetically eager need to draw sustenance from George Willard without equally emphasizing how many of them come to him convinced that it is *they* who have something to give. It is only a superficial irony that so few of the gifts (like the mother's $800) can possibly have for the young writer the same values that have been assigned to them by the givers. Their understanding is inevitably not the same as his, which is one of the general truths *Winesburg* readily enforces; but another is that without their gifts there would be no writer at all.

Everyone is ready to give George Willard good advice. Doctor Parcival urges him to write a book saying that all men are Christ and that all are crucified. Wash Williams is anxious to save him needless pain and trouble by putting him on his guard against "bitches." Joe Welling is pleased to confide in him a few secrets about the art of writing. Kate Swift, his former English teacher, tries to tell him to "know life" and "stop fooling with words." Perhaps none of this advice, in the form in which it is offered, is wholly sound. But it is well-intentioned, and one of the most engaging things in *Winesburg* is the way George Willard, on his part, is always ready to credit the local talkers with more wisdom than they may strike us as having. " 'I have missed something,' " he says, " 'I have missed something Kate Swift was trying to tell me' " (196); and he might as well be saying it of them all.

His mother has a more intimate and more comprehensive understanding of his needs and is thus appropriately the one who is able

3 *Sherwood Anderson* (New York: William Sloane Associates, 1951), pp. 102–6.

to articulate the representative prayer of all the grotesques: that " 'this my boy be allowed to express something for us both' " (26). For finally what the characters want of George Willard is to have their stories told (they are quite literally characters in search of an author); at the same time, they wish to have a stake in the way the stories are going to be told. Or say that they insist on having some share in the making of the artist whose task will be to expose them as they really are. Each in turn comes forward to offer his secret (the material of art) and to give up whatever fragmentary wisdom he may possess toward the development of the artist who will be the spokesman for everyone. Each one implicitly expects a reward for his contribution: the "release" into expressiveness which each needs but which only the artist may in real life encompass. Seen this way, the book begins to take on some of the formal quality of a procession, imbued like a ritual pageant with silent and stately dignity.

It has other kinds of motion, too; the relationship between writer and subject may, for instance, also be put in terms of an antithesis between development and fixity, an antithesis which we may not notice at first because George Willard's progress is so easygoing compared with the more explosive gestures of the grotesques. But throughout *Winesburg* runs the slow and often hidden current of George Willard's growth toward maturity; often the stream is subterranean and we are surprised to see where it comes out; sometimes it appears to lose itself in backwaters of irrelevance or naiveté. But all the time the book's current is steadily setting toward the ultimate "Departure." The torpidity of that stream is best taken as an expression of Anderson's humility, his refusal to sentimentalize the figure of the writer.

But we must not ignore the drift, for Anderson is equally clear (novelistically speaking) that the artist's essential quality must be defined as a capacity for the growth which he refuses to attribute to any of the grotesques. It is indeed the very description of their grotesqueness that each of them is forever frozen somewhere below the level of a full and proper development. Sometimes this incompletion is "their fault," sometimes not (unless it be more true to say that such a question of ultimate responsibility is meaningless); but there can be no doubt about Anderson's clear perception of the *fact*.

It is not enough, however, to see these figures as incomplete and to sense the pathos of their plight. It is not enough even to see that it is the glimmering awareness of their inadequacy that drives them to their futile efforts at revelation and communion. Ultimately it is only a sentimental reading of *Winesburg, Ohio* that fails to recognize that the grotesques' anxiety to escape their isolation is in itself excessive and truly symptomatic of their grotesquerie. It is of the utmost importance that their counterweight, George Willard, is almost alone among the inhabitants of *Winesburg*[4] in being able to accept the fact of human isolation and to live with it. His willingness to do so is at once the sign of his maturity and the pledge of his incipient artistic ability.

The view of the artist presented in *Winesburg* is that of a man who joins sympathy and understanding to detachment and imperturbability. Anderson obviously sees the relation of art and life as from one point of view illuminated by an opposition between the freedom and flexibility which are necessary to the creative role and, on the other hand, the extremes of static and rigid over-commitment instanced by the grotesques. This is undoubtedly the distinction—flexibility versus rigidity—which Anderson rather unsatisfactorily tries to explain with a modern "humours" theory in the introductory "Book of the Grotesque." This book is clearly not unrelated to *Winesburg, Ohio* and is like it built on the "notion that the moment one of the people took one of the truths to himself, called it his truth, and tried to live his life by it, he became a grotesque and the truth he embraced became a falsehood" (5). Anderson rather implies that what saved the old writer from becoming a grotesque himself (he is endangered by his obsession with his notion) is that he didn't publish the book. The clarity of Anderson's argument here is scarcely helped by his views about non-publication nor by his eccentric use of the word *truth;* but his general intention, a contrast between obsession and freedom, is plain enough. For the distinctions made in this introductory sketch are entirely continuous with the distinction made throughout *Winesburg* between George Willard and his fellow citizens, and are referable finally to one of those broad general truths or paradoxes about art and life that pervade the book, and in which Anderson's charity most winningly shows itself: namely, that the artist, in order to express the common passion, must remain free from entanglements with it, while those who actually *live* the common passion are by the very fact of their involvement prevented from coming to the threshold of complete self-realization and are thereby deprived of the release inherent in expression.

To remember that the "grotesques" are thus distorted and mis-shapen by their insistent involvement with life itself is to share Anderson's realistic perception of "normal" or "ordinary" people (as distinguished from the artist, who is "normal" in a different way);

---

4 A possible exception is Alice Hindman in "Adventure," who at the end of the story "began trying to force herself to face bravely the fact that many people must live and die alone, even in Winesburg" (134). But her unmarried state, although desolate, is not the quintessential loneliness.

it is to participate imaginatively in Anderson's remarkable vision of humanity, a vision tender without sentimentality, tough without rancor. The grotesques must not be thought of as necessarily unattractive, for the truths that distend them include "the truth of virginity and the truth of passion, the truth of wealth and of poverty" (4), properties or conditions either good or neutral, and not wholly unlovely even when carried to the excess that lays the grotesques open to the charge of "abnormality." Actually it is almost useless to attempt to retain any usual conception of "normality"—except in the sense of more or less "developed"—when dealing with Anderson (we have seen how he confused himself trying to use the word), for at the heart of his feeling is his uncommon ability to like people for what they are instead of for what they might be (a common failing among minor writers) while in the very act of seeing them as they are. And even if the grotesques are not, by virtue of their inability to develop into full and various normality, quite like other people, there still remains a question whether their lopsidedness does not especially endear them; and I think we must finally say that it does, that they are like Doctor Reefy's "twisted apples": "into a little round place at the side of the apple has been gathered all of its sweetness" (20). What Anderson could never articulate in expository prose he manages so easily with the most commonplace image.

And so easy is it to allow one's attention to be monopolized by the grotesques! Their problem is presented first and their bizarre revelations continually keep it at the forefront of our perception. Meanwhile, as I have said, the current of the book is setting away from them toward the final story, "Departure," and, before that, the climactic tale, "Sophistication," wherein George Willard's maturity is to be realized and the final opposition between artist and society drawn. The placing of this climactic story is important: it immediately precedes "Departure," which is pointedly *anti*-climactic, and immediately follows "Death" (Elizabeth Willard). And it is in significant contrast with an earlier story, "Loneliness," about the artist *manqué* Enoch Robinson who "never grew up."

In "Sophistication" we may find—or infer—an attitude about art and loneliness sufficiently complex and sufficiently clear to enable us to read *Winesburg* without those distortions of meaning that follow upon the loss of any important part of an organic entity. It is one of the few stories in the book which has a happy ending and it concludes with what is for *Winesburg* a startling statement: "For some reason they [George Willard and Helen White] could not have explained they had both got from their silent evening together the thing needed. Man or boy, woman or girl, they had for a moment taken hold of the thing that makes the mature life of men and women in

the modern world possible" (298). It would be difficult to imagine
a passage more explicitly pointing to the presence of the book's over-
arching meaning; but this is not to say that that meaning is very easy
to grasp or to conceptualize without offering violence to a story of
incomparable tact and delicacy (stylistic qualities happily matching
the virtues it recommends).

George Willard's maturity has of course been coming on for a long
time. In "An Awakening" (his), for instance, he has been shown
(1) trying to get " 'into touch with something orderly and big that
swings through the night like a star' " (219), (2) "muttering words"
into the darkness, and (3) feeling himself "oddly detached and apart
from all life" (221). But these inchoate impulses, although more or
less in the right direction, are quickly brought to an end by his
foolish involvement with the milliner Belle Carpenter. By the time
of "Sophistication" he is older and wiser. His mother's death has
intervened. It is this death, no doubt, that enables him now "for the
first time [to] take the backward view of life," to realize with the
"sadness of sophistication" that "in spite of all the stout talk of his
fellows he must live and die in uncertainty." The point of passage
from adolescence to maturity is thus defined as the moment one "hears
death calling"; and the universal response to an awareness of this
moment is to "want to come close to some other human" (286–87).
But not too close; wherein lies the moral of the story.[5]

"Sophistication" is nocturnal, but not that nightmare climate common to so many of the *Winesburg* stories, and as pleasantly informal
as the evening stroll that provides its slight framework. First we see
George Willard alone, "taking the backward view of life," and
anxiously waiting for the hour when he can share his new sense of
maturity with Helen White and perhaps compel her admiration of
it. Helen White is undergoing a rather parallel transformation into
womanhood, a transformation only vaguely felt by George Willard,
and comparatively unfocused for us, since her imputed maturity—
real or not, significant or not—is presented less for its own interest
than as a complementary background for George Willard's achievement of tranquility. ("The feeling of loneliness and isolation that

----

[5] The best possible gloss for "Sophistication," and for this aspect of *Winesburg*
generally, would be the following passage from D. H. Lawrence, "Poe," *Studies in
Classic American Literature* (1922):

> The central law of all organic life is that each organism is intrinsically
> isolate and single in itself. . . .
> But the secondary law of all organic life is that each organism only lives
> through contact with other matter, assimilation, and contact with other
> life. . . . Men live by love, but die, or cause death, if they love too much.

(Quoted from Edmund Wilson, ed., *The Shock of Recognition*, Garden City, N.Y.:
Doubleday, 1947, pp. 967–68).

had come to the young man . . . was both broken and intensified
by the presence of Helen. What he felt was reflected in her") (294).
Finally the two young people come together (each one from an atmosphere of "noise," meaningless superficial talk), and walk silently
through the streets of Winesburg to the deserted grandstand at the
fair grounds. So far as the story informs us, they never say anything
to each other.

In the grandstand they are confronted by "ghosts, not of the dead,
but of living people." One paradox leads to another: "The place has
been filled to overflowing with life . . . and now it is night and the
life has all gone away. . . . One shudders at the thought of the mean-
inglessness of life while at the same instant, and if the people of the
town are his people, one loves life so intensely that tears come into the
eyes" (295). This is perhaps the climax of the story—and thus of
*Winesburg, Ohio*—for at this point Anderson's own ambivalent attitude toward experience, and toward the art that arises from it to pro-
claim its ineradicable dignity, is fully embodied, not in terms of ideas
(which Anderson never learned to manipulate) but in terms of their
corresponding emotions encompassed in images.

Now that the summit of George Willard's emotional and aesthetic
development has been attained, we have a final look at the artist's
social role. It is all comprehended in a single sentence, again paradoxical: "He wanted to love and to be loved by her, but he did not
want at the moment to be confused by her womanhood" (296).
(Presumably she feels the same.) The point is that they recognize and
respect the essential privacy (or integrity) of human personality: "In
that high place in the darkness the two oddly sensitive human atoms
held each other tightly and waited. In the mind of each was the
same thought. 'I have come to this lonely place and here is this other,'
was the substance of the thing felt" (296). The loneliness is assuaged
—there is no other way—by the realization that loneliness is a universal condition and not a uniquely personal catastrophe; love is
essentially the shared acceptance by two people of the irremediable
fact, in the nature of things, of their final separateness. But these
are truths beyond the comprehension of the grotesques, and one
reason why they, who will not accept their isolation, are so uniformly
without love; like Enoch Robinson, they never grew up.

The artist, then, is not necessarily different from other people,
after all. Primarily, he is defined in terms of maturity and in terms
of the practical mastery of his craft (throughout *Winesburg*, George
Willard has been busy as a reporter, learning to fit words to life felt
and observed). The craft is his special secret, and it is not required
that "normal" or "ordinary" people have it. They will have other
skills, other secrets. But what they might all share, ideally, is that

mixture of participation and detachment, love and respect, passion and criticism, which is, Anderson tells us, the best privilege offered by the modern world to those who wish to grow up, and toward the attainment of which the writer's case—at first glance special, but ultimately very general—may serve as an eminently practicable pattern of virtue.

# Introduction to *Winesburg, Ohio*

## *by Malcolm Cowley*

Rereading Sherwood Anderson after many years, one feels again that his work is desperately uneven, but one is gratified to find that the best of it is as new and springlike as ever. There are many authors younger in years—he was born in 1876—who made a great noise in their time, but whose books already belong among the horseless carriages in Henry Ford's museum at Greenfield Village. Anderson made a great noise too, when he published *Winesburg, Ohio* in 1919. The older critics scolded him, the younger ones praised him, as a man of the changing hour, yet he managed in that early work and others to be relatively timeless. There are moments in American life to which he gave not only the first but the final expression.

He soon became a writer's writer, the only story teller of his generation who left his mark on the style and vision of the generation that followed. Hemingway, Faulkner, Wolfe, Steinbeck, Caldwell, Saroyan, Henry Miller . . . each of these owes an unmistakable debt to Anderson, and their names might stand for dozens of others. Hemingway was regarded as his disciple in 1920, when both men were living on the Near North Side of Chicago. Faulkner says that he had written very little, "poems and just amateur things," before meeting Anderson in 1925 and becoming, for a time, his inseparable companion. Looking at Anderson he thought to himself, "Being a writer must be a wonderful life." He set to work on his first novel, *Soldiers' Pay,* for which Anderson found a publisher after the two men had ceased to be friends. Thomas Wolfe proclaimed in 1936 that Anderson was "the only man in America who ever taught me anything"; but they quarreled a year later, and Wolfe shouted that Anderson had shot his bolt, that he was done as a writer. All the disciples left him sooner or later, so that his influence was chiefly on their early work; but still it was decisive. He opened doors for all of them and gave them faith in themselves. With Whitman he might have said:

"Introduction to *Winesburg, Ohio*," by Malcolm Cowley. From *Winesburg, Ohio,* by Sherwood Anderson. Copyright 1960 by The Viking Press, Inc. Reprinted by permission of The Viking Press, Inc., and Jonathan Cape Limited.

I am the teacher of athletes,
He that by me spreads a wider breast than my own proves the
width of my own,
He most honors my style who learns under it to destroy the
teacher.

As the disciples were doing, most of Anderson's readers deserted
him during the 1930s. He had been a fairly popular writer for a few
years after *Dark Laughter* (1925), but his last stories and sketches,
including some of his very best, had to appear in a strange collection
of second-line magazines, pamphlets, and Sunday supplements. One
marvelous story called "Daughters" remained in manuscript until
six years after his death in 1941. I suspect that the public would
have liked him better if he had been primarily a novelist, like Dreiser
and Lewis. He did publish seven novels, from *Windy McPherson's
Son* in 1916 to *Kit Brandon* in 1936, not to mention the others he
started and laid aside. Among the seven *Dark Laughter* was his only
best-seller, and *Poor White* (1920), the best of the lot, is studied in
colleges as a picture of the industrial revolution in a small Midwestern town. There is, however, not one of the seven that is truly
effective as a novel; not one that has balance and sustained force;
not one that doesn't break apart into episodes or nebulize into a vague
emotion.

His three personal narratives—*A Story-Teller's Story* (1924), *Tar:
A Midwest Childhood* (1926), and *Sherwood Anderson's Memoirs*
(1942)—are entertainingly inaccurate; indeed, they are almost as
fictional as the novels, and quite as deficient in structure. They reveal
that an element was missing in his mature life, rich as this was in other
respects. It does not give us, and I doubt that Anderson himself
possessed, the sense of moving ahead in a definite direction. All the
drama of growth was confined to his early years. After finding his
proper voice at the age of forty, Anderson didn't change as much as
other serious writers; perhaps his steadfastness should make us
thankful, considering that most American writers change for the
worse. He had achieved a quality of emotional rather than factual
truth and he preserved it to the end of his career, while doing little
to refine, transform, or even understand it. Some of his last stories—
by no means all of them—are richer and subtler than the early ones,
but they are otherwise not much different or much better.

He was a writer who depended on inspiration, which is to say that
he depended on feelings so deeply embedded in his personality that
he was unable to direct them. He couldn't say to himself, "I shall
produce such and such an effect in a book of such and such a length";
the book had to write or rather speak itself while Anderson listened as

if to an inner voice. In his business life he showed a surprising talent for planning and manipulation. "One thing I've known always, instinctively," he told Floyd Dell, "—that's how to handle people, make them do as I please, be what I wanted them to be. I was in business for a long time and the truth is I was a smooth son of a bitch." He never learned to handle words in that smooth fashion. Writing was an activity he assigned to a different level of himself, the one on which he was emotional and unpractical. To reach that level sometimes required a sustained effort of the will. He might start a story like a man running hard to catch a train, but once it was caught he could settle back and let himself be carried—often to the wrong destination.

He knew instinctively whether one of his stories was right or wrong, but he didn't always know why. He could do what writers call "pencil work" on his manuscript, changing a word here and there, but he couldn't tighten the plot, delete weak passages, sharpen the dialogue, give a twist to the ending; if he wanted to improve the story, he had to wait for a return of the mood that had produced it, then write it over from beginning to end. There were stories like "Death in the Woods" that he rewrote a dozen times, at intervals of years, before he found what he thought was the right way of telling them. Sometimes, in different books, he published two or three versions of the same story, so that we can see how it grew in his subconscious mind. One characteristic of the subconscious is a defective sense of time: in dreams the old man sees himself as a boy, and the events of thirty or forty years may be jumbled together. Time as a logical succession of events was Anderson's greatest difficulty in writing novels or even long stories. He got his tenses confused and carried his heroes ten years forward or back in a single paragraph. His instinct was to present everything together, as in a dream.

When giving a lecture on "A Writer's Conception of Realism," he spoke of a half-dream that he had "over and over." "If I have been working intensely," he said, "I find myself unable to relax when I go to bed. Often I fall into a half-dream state and when I do, the faces of people begin to appear before me. They seem to snap into place before my eyes, stay there, sometimes for a short period, sometimes longer. There are smiling faces, leering ugly faces, tired faces, hopeful faces. . . . I have a kind of illusion about this matter," he continued. "It is, no doubt, due to a story-teller's point of view. I have the feeling that the faces that appear before me thus at night are those of people who want their stories told and whom I have neglected."

He would have liked to tell the stories of all the faces he had ever seen. He was essentially a story teller, as he kept insisting, but his art was of a special type, belonging to an oral rather than a written tradition. It used to be the fashion to compare him with Chekhov and say that he had learned his art from the Russians. Anderson insisted that, except for Turgenev, he hadn't read any Russians when the comparisons were being made. Most of his literary masters were English or American: George Borrow, Walt Whitman, Mark Twain (more than he admitted), and Gertrude Stein. D. H. Lawrence was a less fortunate influence, but only on his later work. His earliest and perhaps his principal teacher was his father, "Irve" Anderson, who used to entertain whole barrooms with tales of his impossible adventures in the Civil War. A great many of the son's best stories, too, were told first in saloons. Later he would become what he called "an almighty scribbler" and would travel about the country with dozens of pencils and reams of paper, the tools of his trade. "I am one," he said, "who loves, like a drunkard his drink, the smell of ink, and the sight of a great pile of white paper that may be scrawled upon always gladdens me"; but his earlier impulse had been to speak, not write, his stories. The best of them retain the language, the pace, and one might even say the gestures of a man talking unhurriedly to his friends.

Within the oral tradition, Anderson had his own picture of what a story should be. He was not interested in telling conventional folk tales, those in which events are more important than emotions. American folk tales usually end with a "snapper"—that is, after starting with the plausible, they progress through the barely possible to the flatly incredible, then wait for a laugh. Magazine fiction used to follow—and much of it still does—a pattern leading to a different sort of snapper, one that calls for a gasp of surprise or relief instead of a guffaw. Anderson broke the pattern by writing stories that not only lacked snappers, in most cases, but even had no plots in the usual sense. The tales he told in his Midwestern drawl were not incidents or episodes, they were *moments,* each complete in itself.

The best of the moments in *Winesburg, Ohio* is called "The Untold Lie." The story, which I have to summarize at the risk of spoiling it, is about two farm hands husking corn in a field at dusk. Ray Pearson is small, serious, and middle-aged, the father of half a dozen thin-legged children; Hal Winters is big and young, with the reputation of being a bad one. Suddenly he says to the older man, "I've got Nell Gunther in trouble. I'm telling you, but keep your mouth shut." He puts his two hands on Ray's shoulders and looks down into his eyes. "Well, old daddy," he says, "come on, advise me. Perhaps you've been in the same fix yourself. I know what everyone would say is the right thing to do, but what do you say?" Then the author steps back to look at his characters. "There they stood," he tells us, "in the big empty field with the quiet corn shocks standing in rows behind them and the red and yellow hills in the distance, and from being just two indifferent workmen they had become all alive to each other."

That single moment of aliveness—that epiphany, as Joyce would have called it, that sudden reaching out of two characters through walls of inarticulateness and misunderstanding—is the effect that Anderson is trying to create for his readers or listeners. There is more to the story, of course, but it is chiefly designed to bring the moment into relief. Ray Pearson thinks of his own marriage, to a girl he got into trouble, and turns away from Hal without being able to say the expected words about duty. Later that evening he is seized by a sudden impulse to warn the younger man against being tricked into bondage. He runs awkwardly across the fields, crying out that children are only the accidents of life. Then he meets Hal and stops, unable to repeat the words that he had shouted into the wind. It is Hal who breaks the silence. "I've already made up my mind," he says, taking Ray by the coat and shaking him. "Nell ain't no fool. . . . I want to marry her. I want to settle down and have kids." Both men laugh, as if they had forgotten what happened in the cornfield. Ray walks away into the darkness, thinking pleasantly now of his children and muttering to himself, "It's just as well. Whatever I told him would have been a lie." There has been a moment in the lives of two men. The moment has passed and the briefly established communion has been broken, yet we feel that each man has revealed his essential being. It is as if a gulf had opened in the level Ohio cornfield and as if, for one moment, a light had shone from the depths, illuminating everything that happened or would ever happen to both of them.

That moment of revelation was the story Anderson told over and over, but without exhausting its freshness, for the story had as many variations as there were faces in his dreams. Behind one face was a moment of defiance; behind another, a moment of resignation (as when Alice Hindman forces herself "to face bravely the fact that many people must live and die alone, even in Winesburg"); behind a third face was a moment of self-discovery; behind a fourth was a moment of deliberate self-delusion. This fourth might have been the face of the author's sister, as he describes her in a chapter of *Sherwood Anderson's Memoirs*. Unlike the other girls she had no beau, and so she went walking with her brother Sherwood, pretending that he was someone else. "It's beautiful, isn't it, James?" she said, looking at the wind ripples that passed in the moonlight over a field of ripening

wheat. Then she kissed him and whispered, "Do you love me, James?"
—and all her loneliness and flight from reality were summed up in
those words. Anderson had that gift for summing up, for pouring a
lifetime into a moment.

There must have been many such moments of truth in his own
life, and there was one in particular that has become an American
legend. After serving as a volunteer in the Spanish-American War;
after supplementing his one year in high school with a much later
year at Wittenberg Academy; and after becoming a locally famous copywriter in a Chicago advertising agency, Anderson had launched into
business for himself; by the age of thirty-six he had been for some
years the chief owner and general manager of a paint factory in
Elyria, Ohio. The factory had prospered for a time, chiefly because of
Anderson's talent for writing persuasive circulars, and he sometimes
had visions of becoming a paint baron or a duke of industry. He had
other visions too, of being sentenced to serve out his life as a businessman. At the time he was already writing novels—in fact he had four
of them under way—and he began to feel that his advertising circulars were insulting to the dignity of words. "The impression got
abroad—I perhaps encouraged it," Anderson says, "—that I was
overworking, was on the point of a nervous breakdown. . . . The
thought occurred to me that if men thought me a little insane they
would forgive me if I lit out, left the business in which they invested
their money on their hands." Then came the moment to which he
would always return in his memoirs and in his fiction. He was dictating a letter: "The goods about which you have inquired are the
best of their kind made in the—" when suddenly he stopped without completing the phrase. He looked at his secretary for a long time,
and she looked at him until they both grew pale. Then he said with
the American laugh that covers all sorts of meanings, "I have been
wading in a long river and my feet are wet." He went out of the
office for the last time and started walking eastward toward Cleveland along a railroad track. "There were," he says, "five or six dollars
in my pocket."

So far I have been paraphrasing Anderson's account—or two of
his many accounts, for he kept changing them—of an incident that his
biographers have reconstructed from other sources. Those others give a
different picture of what happened at the paint factory on November
27, 1912. Anderson had been struggling under an accumulation of
marital, artistic, and business worries. Instead of pretending to be a
little crazy so that investors would forgive him for losing their money,
he was actually—so the medical records show—on the brink of

nervous collapse. Instead of making a conscious decision to abandon his wife, his three children, and his business career, he acted as if in a trance. There was truly a decision, but it was made by something deeper than his conscious will; one feels that his whole being, pysche and soma together, was rejecting the life of a harried businessman. He had made no plans, however, for leading a different life. After four days of aimless wandering, he was recognized in Cleveland and taken to a hospital, where he was found to be suffering from exhaustion and aphasia.

Much later, in telling the story time after time, Anderson forgot or concealed the painful details of his flight and presented it as a pattern of conduct for others to follow. What we need in America, he liked to say, is a new class of individuals who, "at any physical cost to themselves and others"—Anderson must have been thinking of his first wife—will "agree to quit working, to loaf, to refuse to be hurried or try to get on in the world." In the next generation there would be hundreds of young men, readers of Anderson, who rejected the dream of financial success and tried to live as artists and individuals. For them Anderson's flight from the paint factory became a heroic exploit, as memorable as the choice made by Ibsen's Nora when she walked out of her doll's house and slammed the door. For Anderson himself when writing his memoirs, it was the central moment of his career.

Yet the real effect of the moment on his personal life was less drastic or immediate than one would guess from the compulsive fashion in which he kept writing about it. He didn't continue wandering from city to city, trading his tales for bread and preaching against success. After being released from the hospital, he went back to Elyria, wound up his business affairs, then took the train for Chicago, where he talked himself into a job with the same advertising agency that had employed him before he went into business for himself. As soon as he had the job, he sent for his wife and children. He continued to write persuasive circulars—corrupting the language, as he said—and worked on his novels and stories chiefly at night, as he had done while running a factory. It would be nearly two years before he separated from his first wife. It would be ten years before he left the advertising business to support himself entirely by writing, and then the change would result from a gradual process of getting published and finding readers, instead of being the sequel to a moment of truth.

Those moments at the center of Anderson's often marvelous stories were moments, in general, without a sequel; they existed separately and timelessly. That explains why he couldn't write novels and why, with a single exception, he never even wrote a book in the strict sense of the word. A book should have a structure and a development, whereas for Anderson there was chiefly the flash of lightning that revealed a life without changing it.

The one exception, of course, is *Winesburg, Ohio,* and that became a true book for several reasons: because it was conceived as a whole, because Anderson had found a subject that released his buried emotions, and because most of the book was written in what was almost a single burst of inspiration, so that it gathered force as it went along. It was started in the late autumn of 1915, when he was living alone in a rooming house at 735 Cass Street, on the Near North Side of Chicago, and working as always at the Critchfield Agency. Earlier that year he had read two books that set his mind to working. One was *Spoon River Anthology,* by Edgar Lee Masters, which may have suggested the notion of writing about the secret natures of people in another Midwestern town. The other was Gertrude Stein's *Three Lives,* which pointed the way toward a simpler and more repetitive style, closer to the rhythms of American speech, than that of Anderson's first novels, *Windy McPherson's Son* and *Marching Men.* These had recently been accepted by an English publisher, but Anderson was beginning to feel that neither of them expressed his inner self. He searched, brooded, and wrote advertising circulars.

Then came another of his incandescent moments, one that he called "the most absorbingly interesting and exciting moment in any writer's life . . . the moment when he, for the first time, knows that he is a real writer." Twenty years later he described the experience in a letter, probably changing the facts, as he had a weakness for doing, but remembering how he felt:

> . . . I walked along a city street in the snow. I was working at work I hated. Already I had written several long novels. They were not really mine. I was ill, discouraged, broke. I was living in a cheap rooming house. I remember that I went upstairs and into the room. It was very shabby. I had no relatives in the city and few enough friends. I remember how cold the room was. On that afternoon I had heard that I was to lose my job.
>
> . . . There was some paper on a small kitchen table I had bought and brought up into the room. I turned on a light and began to write. I wrote, without looking up—I never changed a word of it afterwards— a story called "Hands." It was and is a very beautiful story.
>
> I wrote the story and then got up from the table at which I had been sitting, I do not know how long, and went down into the city street. I thought that the snow had suddenly made the city very beautiful. . . . It must have been several hours before I got the courage to return to my room and read my own story.
>
> It was all right. It was sound. It was real. I went to sit by my desk. A great many others have had such moments. I wonder what

they did. For the moment I thought the world very wonderful, and I thought also that there was a great deal of wonder in me.

"Hands" is still sound and real; as Henry James said of *The Scarlet Letter*, "it has about it that charm, very hard to express, which we find in an artist's work the first time he has touched his highest mark." It was, however, the second of the Winesburg stories to be written, since the first was "The Book of the Grotesque," which serves as a general prologue. "Paper Pills" was the third, and the others followed in roughly the same order in which they appear in the book. All the stories were written rapidly, with little need for revision, each of them being, as Anderson said, "an idea grasped whole as one would pick an apple in an orchard." He was dealing with material that was both fresh and familiar. The town of Winesburg was based on his memories of Clyde, Ohio, where he had spent most of his boyhood and where his mother had died at the same age as the hero's mother. The hero, George Willard, was the author in his late adolescence, and the other characters were either remembered from Clyde or else, in many cases, suggested by faces glimpsed in the Chicago streets. Each face revealed a moment, a mood, or a secret that lay deep in Anderson's life and for which he was finding the right words at last.

As the book went forward, more and more of the faces—as well as more streets, buildings, trades, and landscapes—were carried from one story to another, with the result that Winesburg itself acquired a physical and corporate life. Counting the four parts of "Godliness," each complete in itself, there would be twenty-five stories or chapters in all. None of them taken separately—not even "Hands" or "The Untold Lie"—is as effective as the best of Anderson's later work, but each of them contributes to all the others, as the stories in later volumes are not expected to do. There was a delay of some months before the last three chapters—"Death," "Sophistication," and "Departure"—were written with the obvious intention of rounding out the book. First George Willard is released from Winesburg by the death of his mother; then, in "Sophistication," he learns how it feels to be a grown man; then finally he leaves for the city on the early-morning train, and everything recedes as into a framed picture. "When he aroused himself and looked out of the car window," Anderson says, "the town of Winesburg had disappeared and his life there had become but a background on which to paint the dreams of his manhood."

In structure the book lies midway between the novel proper and the mere collection of stories. Like several famous books by more recent authors, all early readers of Anderson—like Faulkner's *The Unvanquished* and *Go Down, Moses*, like Steinbeck's *Tortilla Flat* and

*The Pastures of Heaven,* like Caldwell's *Georgia Boy*—it is a cycle of stories with several unifying elements, including a single background, a prevailing tone, and a central character. These elements can be found in all the cycles, but the best of them also have an underlying plot that is advanced or enriched by each of the stories. In *Winesburg* the underlying plot or fable, though hard to recognize, is unmistakably present, and I think it might be summarized as follows:

George Willard is growing up in a friendly town full of solitary persons; the author calls them "grotesques." Their lives have been distorted not, as Anderson tells us in his prologue, by their each having seized upon a single truth, but rather by their inability to express themselves. Since they cannot truly communicate with others, they have all become emotional cripples. Most of the grotesques are attracted one by one to George Willard; they feel that he might be able to help them. In those moments of truth that Anderson loves to describe, they try to explain themselves to George, believing that he alone in Winesburg has an instinct for finding the right words and using them honestly. They urge him to preserve and develop his gift. "You must not become a mere peddler of words," Kate Swift the teacher insists, taking hold of his shoulders. "The thing to learn is to know what people are thinking about, not what they say." Dr. Parcival tells him, "If something happens perhaps you will be able to write the book I may never get written." All the grotesques hope that George Willard will some day speak what is in their hearts and thus re-establish their connection with mankind. George is too young to understand them at the time, but the book ends with what seems to be the promise that, after leaving Winesburg, he will become the voice of inarticulate men and women in all the forgotten towns.

If the promise is truly implied, and if Anderson felt he was keeping it when writing "Hands" and the stories that followed, then *Winesburg, Ohio* is far from the pessimistic or destructive or morbidly sexual work it was once attacked for being. Instead it is a work of love, an attempt to break down the walls that divide one person from another, and also, in its own fashion, a celebration of small-town life in the lost days of good will and innocence.

# A Novel of Becoming

*by Blanche Housman Gelfant*

In his introduction to the Modern Library edition of *Poor White,*
Sherwood Anderson wrote: "There was a town in the state of Ohio.
The town was really the hero of the book. . . . What happened to the
town was, I thought, more important than what happened to the
people." [1] Anderson's main strategy for dramatizing what happened
to the town, as industrialism hit it and it became a city, is to identify
the process of urbanization with his central character, Hugh McVey.
Hugh is not merely the inventor who brings social change to Bidwell;
he is the human counterpart to the historical process of change. What
happens to him, as he becomes something he was not, is, conversely,
what happens to the town. The changes within Hugh are set against
the background of shifting relationships among the people of Bidwell.
Their actions represent the dynamics of urbanism as a way of life.
What happens to them, as they accommodate their values, relationships, and manners to the demands of a new mechanical age, is again
a dramatization of the process of social change. The subplots (like
the short fables Anderson introduces into the narrative) reinforce,
through particularized incidents, the theme of becoming. The story
of the harness-maker and his helper summarizes the tensions and conflicting values that arose with the transition from craftsmanship to
machine production; and the marriage between Hugh and Clara
implies the wider failure of love, which is thematic to the novel. All
of the action is heightened by the changes in setting, as the large lovely
landscapes, the apple orchards, and farm fields disappear to make room
for factories and crowded shoddy houses. With the change in landscape
comes also the disintegration of the old way of life of rural America.
The most lyrical and evocative passages in *Poor White,* passages that
are implicit judgments upon the new life, re-create the quiet mood and

"A Novel of Becoming." From Chapter Four of *The American City Novel,* by
Blanche Housman Gelfant, pp. 99–106. Copyright 1954 by the University of
Oklahoma Press. Reprinted by permission of the publisher.

1 Sherwood Anderson, Introduction, *Poor White* (New York: Modern Library,
1925), vi. *Poor White* was originally published in 1920.

pace of the town, the satisfying activities, both arduous and joyous, of the farm folk, and the freshness and sensuous beauty of the natural scene. Against this harmonious past are set the tensions and conflicts of the growing city; and the nostalgic mood of the novel reinforces the theme of loss.

The condition of modern man, as Anderson sees it, is summarized in the character of Hugh McVey. Hugh is necessarily one of Anderson's grotesques, for he is less a human being than the human equivalent to a state of social change. His early stupor is hardly credible; yet his lethargic state of vague dreaming is evocative of America's slow sleepy towns. His complete isolation and fumbling inarticulateness are also unbelievable; yet they too become a satisfactory projection of man's inner dissociation in the world of machines. As Hugh changes from the lazy giant who slept by the mudbanks of the Mississippi to a busy inventor always making "definite" things, he embodies the *process* of urbanization. And it is significant that he is prodded out of his dreamy lethargy by a woman from New England. The driving practicality, enterprise, and shrewdness that overtake and transform the Midwest have come from the bustling centers of the East, where industrialism first took hold. In his own slow awakening to the consequences of industrialism, Hugh embodies a *moral attitude* towards the process of social change. At first, he had lacked any moral referents by which to judge the growth of cities: "he had seen towns and factories grow and had accepted without question men's word that growth was invariably good." [2] But as he catches the "disease of thinking," he begins to question the value of what he has helped to bring to Bidwell; and his awakening to the social and personal implications of the machine age is representative of a collective growing awareness. In his own failure to establish satisfactory human relationships, Hugh also embodies the *human consequences* of industrial urbanism. The hope behind his activities as inventor was that he could make for himself a place within the community. Isolated by his grotesqueness and inarticulateness, he had always been "seeking a place where he was to achieve companionship with men and women." [3] But his isolation is not broken by his success with the machine. Rather it is consolidated, for the place he makes for himself is in the shop, in the midst of machinery parts, and not in the community among friends and family. Indeed, his mechanical achievements destroy not only his own chances for human companionship: they destroy the very community of the town. "The people who lived in the towns," says Anderson, ". . . [had been] like mem-

2 *Ibid.*, 369.
3 *Ibid.*, 32.

bers of a great family." [4] That family is disintegrated under the impact of industrialism and the competitive codes it imposes.

The larger collapse of the community is represented through the gallery of townspeople, all of whom undergo a change as Bidwell becomes industrialized. While the secondary characters are more credible as human beings than the grotesque hero, they too are human correlatives to a process of social change. Steve Hunter, once just a "noisy boastful youth," embodies the new spirit of business enterprise, exploitation, and individualism. Ben Peeler, who no longer has time to chat with his neighbors now that he has become a capitalist, represents the uncertainties and insecurities of the business man. He is "nervous and irritable," always worried about the security of his property. Tom Butterworth turns away from the farm that had sustained him, leaving it in hired hands, while he attends to matters of money-making. Ed Hall, "who had been a carpenter's apprentice earning but a few dollars a week . . . [and] was now a foreman," [5] betrays the workers. Having been one of them, he knows how fast they can work and on how little they can live, and he uses this knowledge strategically by imposing a speed-up system and fighting the demand for fair wages. As these people move with accelerated pace, as they become avid for money and indifferent to human values, and as they grow apart from family and community, they incorporate the attitudes and relationships of urbanism as a way of life. They live by a new business ethic, which permits them to cheat and exploit each other. They establish new relationships of inequality, of capitalist and worker, employer and employee. They become strangers moving in a strange new world, for as they transform the country into an ugly, smoke-clouded, mechanized cityscape, they lose their relationship with nature—and they grow frightened, silent, and haggard. Their situation is summarized in Anderson's fable of the country mice who come to the city and grow weak and afraid under their unnatural conditions of life. "Modern men and women who live in industrial cities," Anderson says, "are like mice that have come out of the fields to live in houses that do not belong to them." [6]

The total change within Bidwell is pictured in miniature in the subplot of the harness-maker and his helper. Jim Wainsworth represents the craftsmanship which the machine destroys. As Wainsworth is being displaced, the personal rewards of craftsmanship—integrity, independence, pride, self-respect, and honesty—are also disappearing. Significantly, Wainsworth is "the first man in Bidwell to feel the

4 *Ibid.*, 46.
5 *Ibid.*, 213.
6 *Ibid.*, 114.

touch of the heavy finger of industrialism." [7] This fatal touch turns him into "a silent disgruntled man," for it is, in reality, the opening blow against the age of craftsmanship that he represents. When Joe Gibson, a worthless drunkard, comes into the shop to be Wainsworth's helper, the full weight of industrialism is thrown upon the harness-maker, and he is never to lift himself from it. Gibson has the one faculty worshipped above all others in the new Bidwell—"the faculty for making money." His pleasure lies in the process of money-making; the money itself means little to him. In his indifference to the end of money-making and his excitement over the means, Gibson is the personification of the irrational drive for profit that seemed to Anderson a peculiar madness of the modern age. Gibson introduces the harness-maker to the new way of doing business: for honesty and neighborliness, he substitutes shrewdness and impersonality; for integrity, promotive skill; for the pleasure in creative work, the sterile pleasure in mere money-making. Under the strain of trying to readjust to Gibson's modern ways—if only in order to survive—Wainsworth cracks. He makes a wild and futile attempt to murder the new age by attacking the people who symbolize it, Steve Hunter, the business organizer, and Hugh McVey, the practical inventor. The failure of his attempt suggests the futility of trying to turn back twentieth-century "progress."

Just as the harness-maker represents the passing age of the craftsman, the farm hand, Jim Priest, represents the dying past of rural America. This past is recaptured in beautiful genre paintings of country life that are enframed within the narrative. These picture the awakening of life at dawn, the men washing at the pump, the women stirring in the kitchen, the animals grunting in their sheds and contentedly eating; the family working in the fields, and the "great hay wagons loaded with children, laughing girls, and sedate women" [8] going out to the fields for picking; the quiet Sunday afternoons in town, made colorful with the young folk dressed in their courting clothes; the tired gathering of family and farm hands around the great supper table at night; and the slow growth of the small boxlike farmhouses that "became almost beautiful in their humanness." [9]

One of the most memorable folk scenes is the wedding celebration for Hugh and his wife. The union of man and woman calls for elemental joy—for dancing, eating, drinking, and love-making. Jim Priest dominates the scene as the animated (and slightly inebriated) spirit of the folk. Here, in its color, gay action, and crowdedness is a verbal equivalent to a Breughel genre painting:

7 *Ibid.*, 134.

8 *Ibid.*, 45.

9 *Ibid.*, 131.

He began to dance a heavy-footed jig on a little open place by the kitchen door and the guests stopped talking to watch. They shouted and clapped their hands. A thunder of applause arose. The guests who were seated in the parlor and who could not see the performance got up and crowded into the doorway that connected the two rooms. Jim became extraordinarily bold, and as one of the young women Tom had hired as waitresses at that moment went past bearing a large dish of food, he swung himself quickly about and took her into his arms. The dish flew across the floor and broke against a table leg and the young woman screamed. A farm dog that had found its way into the kitchen rushed into the room and barked loudly. Henry Heller's orchestra, concealed under a stairway that led to the upper part of the house, began to play furiously. A strange animal fervor swept over Jim. His legs flew rapidly about and his heavy feet made a great clatter on the floor. The young woman in his arms screamed and laughed. Jim closed his eyes and shouted. He felt that the wedding party had until that moment been a failure and that he was transforming it into a success. Rising to their feet the men shouted, clapped their hands and beat with their fists on the table. When the orchestra came to the end of the dance, Jim stood flushed and triumphant before the guests, holding the woman in his arms. In spite of her struggles he held her tightly against his breast and kissed her eyes, cheeks, and mouth. Then releasing her he winked and made a gesture for silence. 'On a wedding night some one's got to have the nerve to do a little love-making,' he said.[10]

The irony of Jim Priest's comment is that the newlyweds are incapable of "a little love-making." The failure of love is the corollary in the novel to the rise of industrialism. The bizarre relationship between Hugh and Clara externalizes man's inner state of dissociation in the machine age. Modern man and woman do not know how to move towards the consummation of their desires. Clara's search for love is frustrated by an antecedent failure in man. She cannot find a lover and husband; only her mannish woman-friend can give her the understanding and companionship she needs. Thus, *Poor White* anticipates the theme of Anderson's later novel *Perhaps Women* by showing that man has become incapacitated and the hope for the future lies in and with the woman.

The end of *Poor White* reveals Hugh and Clara groping towards a union, but the solution to the problem of the failure of love is not a facile one; and the novel leaves the situation still unresolved. The central purpose of the novel does not require, of course, that the problems raised should be solved. One could hardly expect Anderson to present a solution to the problems that emerged with the rise of industrial urbanism, especially since they are so manifold and com-

10 *Ibid.,* 303.

plex. One of the remarkable things about *Poor White* is that it does state almost every problem involved in this transition from agrarianism to urbanism: the growing struggle between workers and capital, the increasing inequality of wealth, the rise of an amoral business code, the growing mania to produce (as symbolized by Clara's aunt who knits hundreds of pairs of socks which no one will ever wear), the mushrooming of ugly crowded cities whose shoddy houses are to become the nation's slums, the breakdown of community spirit and the growing sense of individualism and alienation, the aesthetic loss in the transformation of the large undulating orchards into harsh, smoke-ridden cityscapes, the loss of man's independence and pride as he is transformed from craftsman to machine-hand, and finally, the failure of man's inner world.

These are the problems central to the whole body of twentieth-century city fiction. But the mere exposition of social problems is not the achievement of *Poor White*. The achievement of the novel lies in its dramatization of a historical moment of transition. The past that *Poor White* re-creates provides a perspective upon the present; it is also a judgment of what America has become with the emergence of industrial urbanism. Perhaps this past of small towns and rural countrysides was never as lovely as Anderson creates it. But his image has the quality of a collective memory, for in moods of nostalgia or dissatisfaction, we evoke an image of yesterday such as that captured and made timeless in the novel—the image of an endless American landscape of fresh beauty and quiet charm, of people walking peacefully in the fields, drawing their strength from the soil, of men living in social harmony and at one with their community and with themselves. The meaning of the city lies not only in the tensions and disharmonies of the present as the novel portrays them emerging in Bidwell but also in the loss of a romantic past as the town succumbs to the forces of history and becomes the city.

# The Promise of Sherwood Anderson
## (Review of *The Triumph of the Egg*)

### *by Robert Morss Lovett*

Sherwood Anderson's published work now includes three novels, two volumes of short stories, and one of poems or chants. It is strikingly alike in substance; it is amazingly uneven in execution; but it is animated by a singular unity of intention. It is all a persistent effort to come to close grips with life, to master it, to force it to give up its secret. It suggests a wrestling match in which the challenger is thrown again and again, and yet each time comes back with thews and sinews braced and muscles hardened to try another fall. In his persistence Mr Anderson is like Jacob with the angel, crying through the night, "I will not let thee go except thou bless me." And like Jacob he waits until the breaking of day to triumph: "I have seen God face to face."

Let it be said at once that the morning is not yet. Mr Anderson has not completely subdued his material to form, has not thoroughly penetrated it with interpretation. It remains recalcitrant and opaque. But as his work has progressed he has shown constantly a firmer grasp on his problem, a more complete conception of the difficulties of approach, and the resources and limitations of his art. In this respect there is something final about The Triumph of the Egg. It by no means represents the attainment of the goal, but it marks a definite accomplishment beyond which the method he has tested may carry him on the next dash, but which remains for the time being a sort of "farthest north."

It is natural to speak of Sherwood Anderson's work in metaphors of physical achievement, for his struggle is first of all an athletic one with the crude stuff of life in a material world. Five years or more ago a former editor of THE DIAL persuaded him to set down his thoughts about American literature in a paper called An Apology for Crudity, in the light of which his fiction should be read.

"The Promise of Sherwood Anderson," by Robert Morss Lovett." From *The Dial*, 72 (January 1922), 79–83.

> For a long time I have believed that crudity is an inevitable quality
> in the production of a really significant present-day American literature.
> How indeed is one to escape the obvious fact that there is as yet no
> native subtlety of thought or living among us? And if we are a
> crude and childlike people how can our literature hope to escape
> the influence of that fact? Why indeed should we want it to escape? . . .
> We talk of writers of the old world and the beauty and subtlety
> of the work they do. Below me the roaring city lies like a great animal
> on the prairies, but we do not run out to the prairies. We stay in our
> rooms and talk. . . .
> I know we shall never have an American literature until we return
> to faith in ourselves, and to the facing of our limitations. We must
> in some way become in ourselves more like our fellows, more simple
> and real.

This is Mr Anderson's creed. He has tried always to work under
its sanctions. He has made it his first object to see American life as
it is, without illusion. It is a grim spectacle, and he confesses his inability to see it beautifully.

> As a people we have given ourselves to industrialism, and industrial-
> ism is not lovely. If any man can find beauty in an American factory
> town I wish he would show me the way. For myself, I cannot find it.
> To me, and I am living in industrial life, the whole thing is as ugly as
> modern war.

But this reality has interest. We are a crude people, but not dull.
In some strange way the human forms which this life assumes have
a grotesque quality which makes them as fascinating as gargoyles.
Over and over again Mr Anderson has drawn them for us—in Windy
McPherson, in Smoky Pete, in Melville Stoner. And the reality tempts
always with a demand for interpretation: What is the meaning of
it? The answer Mr Anderson seeks from the starting point of the
people to whom the reality belongs. Instead of using it in illustration
of themes already conventionalized in old world literature, he tries
to let it develop according to its own pattern. Instead of imposing
upon it an interpretation from old world philosophy he tries to draw
from it its own meaning.

It is true that Mr Anderson has been influenced by the technical
experiments of his predecessors, but in so far as he has yielded to
them he has failed. His first novel, Windy McPherson's Son, begins
with a transcript from middle-Western life so faithful that it seems
autobiographic; but having established a complete groundwork of
reality the author in an endeavour to maintain interest or to dis-
engage significance has recourse to the romantic formula. The point
is clearly perceptible at which his fact passes over into fiction. In
Marching Men the substance of the book is indubitably experience,

but the material is subordinated to a thesis which is more than a part of the psychology of the hero. Poor White is the best of the three novels. Here the realism in which Mr. Anderson works so confidently is raised to significance by a symbolism which is so immediate in its process that it seems unpremeditated and unconscious. But the large sweep and scope of the story somehow carry it beyond the author's control. Somewhere he loses his grasp on the meaning of events, the clue to their interpretation, and presents them with an emphasis which is misplaced, and with a conclusion which is mechanical and arbitrary. Winesburg, Ohio revealed Mr Anderson's true vehicle in the short story. As Mr Garland's Main Travelled Roads represented the early practice of realism, so Winesburg, Ohio will be cited as the embodiment of the severity and simplification of its later mode. The stories reveal by flashes the life, the activity, the character of the little mid-Western town as completely as the persistent glare of Mr Sinclair Lewis's searchlight upon Gopher Prairie. The Triumph of the Egg has, through greater diversity of material and wider variety of method and style, the same compelling unity, a unity not geographical, but cosmic.

Of the stories which compose this last volume it is not necessary to speak in detail. Several of them, including the longest, the novelette, Out of Nowhere Into Nothing, have already appeared in this magazine and are familiar to its readers. But of the impressive unity of their appearance in this volume much may be said. They fall together as if by predetermined arrangement, and answer to each other like the movements of a *symphonie pathétique*. They combine to give a single reading of life, a sense of its immense burden, its pain, its dreariness, its futile aspiration, its despair. Sometimes the theme is expressed in farce, the failure of a trick, as in The Egg; sometimes in grim comedy as in War: again in tragedy as in Brothers. Sometimes it sounds in the thin treble of childhood as in I Want to Know Why; sometimes in the cracking voice of old age as in Senility. And this hopelessness is not an interpretation playfully or desperately imposed on the phenomena of life from without by thought or reason; it springs implicitly from within; it is of the essence of being. It is pervading and penetrating, overwhelming and unescapable. It is as if, to use Cardinal Newman's words, man were implicated from birth in some "vast aboriginal calamity"; only instead of placing the fall of man historically in the Garden of Eden Mr Anderson traces it biologically to the egg.

It is characteristic of Sherwood Anderson's art that, instead of seeking escape from life and forgetfulness of it, he grapples with it in an effort to set the tortured spirit free from its servitude to matter. The Triumph of the Egg represents to the full that contest with elemental things which leads one to speak of him in terms befitting the wrestler or explorer. And of this struggle of art with nature he is entirely conscious. It gives the head-note to the volume in verses which under still another figure express so perfectly Mr Anderson's theory of the function of art towards its material that to quote them makes further exposition superfluous.

> Tales are people who sit on the doorstep of the house of my mind.
> It is cold outside and they sit waiting.
> I look out at a window.
>
> > The tales have cold hands,
> > Their hands are freezing.
>
> A short thickly-built tale arises and threshes his arms about.
> His nose is red and he has two gold teeth.
>
> There is an old female tale sitting hunched up in a cloak.
>
> Many tales come to sit for a few moments on the doorstep and then go away.
> It is too cold for them outside.
> The street before the door of the house of my mind is filled with tales.
> They murmur and cry out, they are dying of cold and hunger.
>
> I am a helpless man—my hands tremble.
> I should be sitting on a bench like a tailor.
> I should be weaving warm cloth out of the threads of thought.
> The tales should be clothed.
> They are freezing on the doorstep of the house of my mind.
>
> I am a helpless man—my hands tremble.
> I feel in the darkness but cannot find the doorknob.
> I look out at a window.
> Many tales are dying in the street before the house of my mind.

The futility of art is a part of the futility of life. It is a theme personal to the artist: and in Mr Anderson's case it is the source of that lyric strain which recurs like a thread of wistful beauty throughout his book. The first sketch, The Dumb Man, defines with uncanny precision the artist's dilemma in the face of his wavering, elusive, baffling subject matter—and his exasperating impotence. The last paragraph of Brothers is a lyric cry of the artist's soul. The Man with the Trumpet hurls in strident notes the defiance of the artist to his public. All this marks Sherwood Anderson as a thoroughly self-conscious as well as conscientious worker in literature. He will make no compromises with life and no false claims for himself. He has done with illusions. He has put behind him the conventional armour of fiction. He engages in his struggle naked and empty-handed. And in spite of the melancholy scene in which he finds himself, in spite of the darkness in which he gropes and the dimly discerned horrors which he grasps, he preserves in his enterprise the faith of the artist, the soul of a poet. It is in this evidence of a true vocation that one finds in largest measure the promise of Sherwood Anderson.

# The Artist as Prophet

## by Rex Burbank

Anderson made it evident in "Seeds," that he reprehended a detached or even a temporarily involved tampering with the inner life. In that story, which is based largely upon Anderson's talks in 1916, with Burrow at Chateaugay Lake, a crippled woman from Iowa makes grotesque efforts to entice the men of her Chicago rooming house into her rooms, going so far at one point as to stand naked before her hall door. Yet she is frigid and deathly afraid of men, and shrinks from them when they come near. In discussing her actions, the narrator and his psychologist acquaintance take opposite views of the extent to which one may probe clinically into the secret recesses of the inner life for the purpose of "curing" a psychic illness. The narrator, speaking for Anderson, maintains that the professionally induced love the psychologist practices upon his patients violates love by rationalizing it. "The thing you want to do cannot be done," he tells the psychoanalyst. "Fool—do you expect love to be understood?" But in rejecting the synthetic love of the psychoanalyst, the narrator embraces another "cure" for the woman: sex. And, when he tells his friend LeRoy, who had been the woman's neighbor, that he could have helped her by becoming her lover, LeRoy replies, "It isn't so simple. By being sure of yourself you are in danger of losing all of the romance in life. You miss the point. Nothing in life can be settled so definitely."

The point of this story is that the inner life is a myriad of often conflicting impulses—of love and hate, revulsion and attraction, beauty and ugliness. And the inner life has been choked by "old thoughts and beliefs—seeds planted by dead men," by efforts to control it, or understand it. What the woman needed was "to be loved, to be long and quietly and patiently loved. . . . the disease she ha[d] is . . . universal. We all want to be loved and the world has no plan for creating [our] lovers." Like the psychoanalyst, LeRoy wants "more than anything else in the world to be clean," to be free of the doctrines and formulas that have destroyed the spontaneity and the force of love and that have made men and women grotesque and emotionally crippled.

"The Artist as Prophet." From Chapter Six of *Sherwood Anderson,* by Rex Burbank, pp. 107–23. Copyright 1964 by Twayne Publishers, Inc. Reprinted by permission of the publisher.

In the complete spiritual exhaustion of both the scientist and the artist (LeRoy is a painter), we see Anderson's statement of the need for psychic rebirth; and the fact that the "disease" is universal indicates the need for a cultural rebirth. It is by no means coincidental that, at about the same time he called Burrow's attention to "Seeds," Anderson wrote to Brooks that he had "been reading *The Education of Henry Adams*" and felt "tremendously its importance as a piece of American writing." [1]

*The Education of Henry Adams* offered Anderson a rationale for the cultural and psychological reformation necessary to cure the "universal disease." Under the influence of Adams, Anderson found Chartres Cathedral a symbol of the power of sex as a civilizing force and a monument to the creative and unifying effects of a religion grounded in recognition of the mystery, fecundity, and beauty of the "dark blood." Adams saw the popular influence of the Virgin Mary in the twelfth century as being basically sexual,[2] and in her power he saw the fructifying effects of sex upon art. The art of the Middle Ages found in the Louvre and the hundreds of cathedrals built in the name of Mary were cultural testaments to the centrality of sex in human creativity. It followed that the absence of great art and literature—the symbols of a great culture—in America were the result of Puritanism. In the chapter "The Dynamo and the Virgin," Adams had lamented:

> The Woman had once been supreme; in France she still seemed potent, not merely as a sentiment, but as a force. Why was she unknown in America? For evidently America was ashamed of her, and she was ashamed of herself, otherwise they would not have strewn fig-leaves so profusely all over her. When she was a true force, she was ignorant of fig-leaves, but the monthly-magazine-made American female had not a feature that would have been recognized by Adam. The trait was notorious, and often humorous, but any one brought up among Puritans knew that sex was sin. In any previous age, sex was strength. Neither art nor beauty was needed. Every one, even among Puritans, knew that neither Diana of the Ephesians nor any of the Oriental goddesses was worshipped for her beauty. She was goddess because of her force; she was the animated dynamo; she was reproduction —the greatest and most mysterious of all energies; all she needed was to be fecund.

Adams provided Anderson with a symbol for his belief (previously derived from Brooks, Rosenfeld, and Frank) that Puritanism and industrialism were historically connected, and also for his conviction

---

1 Howard M. Jones and Walter B. Rideout, eds., *Letters of Sherwood Anderson* (Boston: Little, Brown, 1953), p. 43.

2 For a full discussion of Adams's primitivism see James Baird, *Ishmael: A Study of the Symbolic Mode in Primitivism* (New York: Harper & Row, Publishers, Inc., 1960), pp. 141–48.

that sexual repression meant death to art and beauty. Adams held that "sex was strength" for any age previous to the twentieth century. "The Venus of Epicurean philosophy survived in the Virgin of the Schools," but "all this was to American thought as though it had never existed. The true American knew something of the facts, but nothing of the feelings; he read the letter, but he never felt the law. Before this historic chasm, a mind like that of Adams felt itself helpless; he turned from the Virgin to the dynamo as though he were a Branly coherer. On one side, at the Louvre and at Chartres, as he knew by the record of work actually done and still before his eyes, was the highest energy ever known to men, the creator of four-fifths of his noblest art, exercising vastly more attraction over the human mind than all the steam engines and dynamos ever dreamed of; and yet this energy was unknown to the American mind. An American Virgin would never dare command; an American Venus would never dare exist."

This passage, one Anderson felt important enough to quote in *A Story Teller's Story*, is implicit in the themes of *Many Marriages* and of *Dark Laughter*. In *Many Marriages*, John Webster transforms his Puritanistically virgin daughter into a virgin cleansed of the notion, as Adams puts it, "that sex was sin"; she is ready to accept the "gift of life" (which, as in *Poor White*, is symbolized by some multi-colored stones he gives her). In *Dark Laughter* the hero slowly achieves understanding and acceptance of "the blood" as the central creative force in life. It was Adams, therefore, rather than D. H. Lawrence, who had the greatest influence upon Anderson's attitudes from 1920 to 1925. Despite Irving Howe's very persuasive argument that Anderson moved into "the Lawrencian orbit," Lawrence was for Anderson no more than a greatly admired fellow novelist who shared his general views on the importance of sex. Anderson found a kinship with Lawrence in their shared repugnance for bloodless spirituality and intellectualism; but Anderson, like Adams, was fighting primarily the repressiveness of American Puritanism and machine worship (Webster is a washing-machine manufacturer) rather than the more intellectually formidable European *haute monde* who populated Lawrence's works. It would no doubt have been well had Anderson taken lessons from Lawrence; for, if he had studied *The Rainbow* and *Women in Love* with care, he might have learned that symbols and symbolic acts alone are not enough to carry a thesis which purports to comprehend all the complex facets of life.

## I. Many Marriages

*Many Marriages* is shaped, from beginning to end, by the proposition that by lifting the lid of moral repression from the inner life one may release the manifold impulses of the subconscious and enjoy a multitude of beautiful relationships and "many marriages." A small-town businessman nearing forty, John Webster suddenly falls in love with his secretary and decides to leave his family and his business and to live with her in another city. Though there has been no love in his family since his marriage, he feels obliged to explain his decision to his daughter Jane and to try to save her from the kind of sterile, purposeless life he has renounced. Resolving to "bring life" to her by teaching her of "this other, this inner" life of love and of the finer feelings which demand sensual expression, he brings both Jane and his wife to his bedroom, and, standing naked before them, delivers a night-long lecture that is interlarded with soul-searching interior monologues containing reminiscences about his marriage and explanations for its failure, reflections about the social and historical causes behind the plight of modern men, and assertions about the necessity of freeing the sexual impulses in order to liberate the inner life. He observes: "If one kept the lid off the well of thinking within oneself, let the well empty itself, let the mind consciously think any thoughts that came to it, accepted all thinking, all imaginings, as one accepted the flesh of people, animals, birds, trees, plants one might live a hundred or a thousand lives in one life." At the end of the long night, Webster leaves; his wife poisons herself; and Jane, now awakened like Mary Cochran in "The Door of the Trap," is ostensibly free to receive all the impulses of life.

In the central episode of the story, Webster places a picture of the Virgin Mary on his bedroom dresser, flanks the picture with two candlesticks bearing figures of Christ on the cross, and paces naked before the picture. After several nights of this ritual exercise, he manages at last to draw Jane and his wife to the room, where they observe the ceremony in shocked bewilderment. As symbols, the Virgin and the two icons bring into association Webster's rite and the idea of the sanctity of sex, and his nakedness signifies his own purification and rebirth through acceptance of the senses. The picture has two rhetorical functions. First, it supports Webster's effort to persuade his daughter that the Puritan morality by which she was brought up is a denial of life; for, as he explains to her that his startling act was necessary to properly arrest and hold her attention, he declares: "I have a desire to in some way make the flesh a sacred thing to you." Second, the Virgin symbol suggests the notion of sex as a creative, unifying force. Anderson's thesis is that sex is the agency by which all the senses come to life and through which the inner creative life of the imagination is set free; the picture of the Virgin represents—to him as it did to Adams —the symbolic synthesis of physical and spiritual love that unites rather than separates people and ultimately expresses itself in the beauty of art.

The chief weakness of *Many Marriages* is that the symbols—of

which the picture of the Virgin is one of the most important—are made
to carry a greater rhetorical burden than they can bear, being used in
lieu of action to convey the themes. Anderson's thesis is not imaginatively realized through either symbols or action, and the novel lapses
therefore into mere rhetoric. Limited largely to Webster's reflections
about life, which begin in puzzled wonderment and end in compla-
cent, almost arrogant self-assurance, the narrative is hopelessly bur-
dened by direct assertion, which in the absence of action almost un-
dermines the thesis; for Webster confirms his own stupidity and egotism in his protracted soul-searching, his certainty that what he smugly
calls his insanity is really the only sanity, his cruel denunciation and
degradation of his wife in the presence of his daughter, and his ab-
surdly clinical erotic tampering with his daughter. The assertions
about his daughter in the following passage, for instance, have no
scenic support and betray Webster's vanity and self-satisfaction in his
new-found freedom: "His daughter was standing in the doorway leading to her own room, looking at him, and there was a kind of intense
half-insane mood in her as all evening there had been in him. He had
infected her with something out of himself. After all there had been
what he had wanted, a real marriage. After this evening the younger
woman could never be what she might have been, had this evening
not happened. Now he knew what he wanted for her."

*Many Marriages* is a thoroughly irresponsible work, both artistically
and intellectually; but we need not question Anderson's integrity of
purpose. The irresponsibility consists in his failure to condense his
material, to tighten the structure of the book, and to examine the nature and consequences of his themes and the assumptions behind them.
Above all, it is irresponsible because his mouthpiece, Webster, wins
his argument too easily; he has no articulate antagonist to challenge
his assumptions. In the absence of any discernible dialectic or narrative conflict, Webster's supposedly sophisticated ideas about life and
sex become the maunderings of a terribly ignorant man, and his
symbolic act of psychic and physical rebirth is reduced to absurdity.

## II.  Dark Laughter

*Dark Laughter*, which reveals Anderson's admiration for the stream-
of-consciousness techniques of James Joyce, is a somewhat more successful effort at a "sophisticated" treatment of the need for "blood
consciousness" than is *Many Marriages*. But *Dark Laughter* is thoroughly artificial in style and characterization and only slightly better
than the earlier book in dramatic enactment of its thesis. Like his
Adamic predecessors, the hero breaks with convention and tries to find
meaning in his own life by "entering into" the lives of others. A jour-

nalist and an aspiring writer, he abandons his newspaper job in Chicago and his wife. He is a writer and intellectual whose anti-conventionalist intellectualism is in itself conventional. He goes back to the small town of his youth, an Ohio River town in Indiana called Old Harbor, where he assumes the name Bruce Dudley and takes a job in a wheel factory owned by Fred Grey. Anderson's diagnosis of the social illness that drives Dudley to Old Harbor, and his use of primitivistic imagery are similar to those in his four earlier romances: "He [Dudley] had a vague notion that he, in common with almost all American men, had got out of touch with things—stones lying in fields, the fields themselves, houses, trees, rivers, factory walls, tools, women's bodies, sidewalks, men in overalls, men and women in automobiles."

At the factory he becomes friendly with Sponge Martin, a craftsman and a primitive who symbolizes instinctive self-fulfillment in the creativeness of his trade and in his frank, uninhibited response to the promptings of the flesh, particularly his sexual relations with his wife. Martin is contrasted with Fred Grey, a typically impotent Andersonian businessman whose emotional poverty is reflected in sexual inadequacy. Dudley and Grey's wife Aline, whom he sees waiting for Grey outside the factory gate, are instantly attracted to one another; and, when after a period of time he becomes her gardener and lover, she leaves Grey and goes away with Dudley.

The similarity between Anderson's Fred and Aline Grey and Dudley and D. H. Lawrence's Lord and Lady Chatterley and Mellors (Lawrence's work came later) is palpable enough, as is the theme that sex is at once the culmination of physical and spiritual love and the fountainhead of human self-fulfillment. The Joycean influence is apparent in the awkward stream-of-conscious style carrying the rambling thought of Dudley who, somewhat like Bloom and Dedalus in *Ulysses*, is searching for the source of his being. But *Dark Laughter* can hardly be compared qualitatively with either *Lady Chatterley's Lover* or with *Ulysses*, for, like *Many Marriages*, it consists largely of the reflections of the principal characters, Bruce Dudley and Aline Grey, about the complexity of life and the mess people make of it. Moreover, their wandering recollections and self-analyses impede rather than advance or generate action. Dudley is a dreamer and cannot, like his friend Sponge Martin, act upon his impulses. It is Aline who initiates their affair, secures him as her gardener, and takes the final steps to bring about their union. This weakness in the character of Dudley comprises the chief weakness of the book; for, lacking indirect expression through action, his reflections are obvious and affected and in fact represent an escape from rather than a movement toward the desired response to the natural impulses.

*The Torrents of Spring*, which was prompted by *Dark Laughter* and aimed most specifically at it, points among other things to the irrelevance of themes to action in the repeated scenes Hemingway draws involving incredibly literary and intellectual waitresses who cite Henry James and read the *Manchester Guardian* for no reason explainable in the narrative. *Torrents* also pillories those stylistic and structural affectations that accompany the paucity of action: absurd rhetorical questions about trivial matters, intended to invest those matters with "mystery"; frequent sentence fragments designed to render the fragmentary nature of the mind in operation but too often effecting a disingenuous tone; and the disjunctive structure, ostensibly conceived to further delineate the movement of a mind groping and searching back and forth in time but impressing the reader as an ostentious contempt for form.

*Dark Laughter* is an unsuccessful effort to combine a highly sophisticated Joycean stream-of-consciousness style and structure with the simple rhythms of New Orleans jazz and to bring two sophisticated people, Bruce Dudley and Aline Grey, to simple acceptance of the senses—as symbolized by the "dark laughter" of the Negroes who move in the background throughout the story. Once more, Anderson's solution to the problems of the individual in relation to society and to himself to oversimplified. We are left to wonder where Bruce and Aline go from Mudcat Landing and what they do in the face of the same problems that existed before they fell in love. Having shown the need to repudiate conventional values, Anderson is obligated to prove in authentic narrative terms that the alternatives his characters embrace are workable, as he indicates they are. He suggests that the union of Bruce and Aline brings an end to their problems, but the feeling remains that it merely represents a new beginning and that, while they may have achieved the uncomplicated response to the senses of Sponge Martin and the Negroes, they will hardly be able, in light of their conditioning by the refinements of cultivated society, to adopt the simple primitivism Martin and the Negroes symbolize.

More than anything else, *Many Marriages* and *Dark Laughter* demonstrate that a simple blood consciousness and freedom from sexual inhibitions can hardly solve the problems of a complex modern life for sophisticated, complicated people. And, when Anderson purports to portray the workability of such simplistic solutions, his "sophisticated" characters turn out after all to be simple-minded and confused.

### III.  *D. H. Lawrence and Freud*

In reference to Lawrence's *Studies in Classic American Literature*, Anderson commented to Alfred Steiglitz that "when [Lawrence] tells a story, he is fine; when he lays down his principles, I think him a pretentious fool. He dreams of being the great, dark animal. It is, after all, a neurotic wish." [3] With more temperate language, Anderson could just as well have said the same thing about himself. His cultural and psychological primitivism was based upon an even less critical anti-intellectualism and irrationalism than was Lawrence's. If Lawrence's rejection of reason as a guide to human conduct left him little to go by except the instincts—which he sanctified ("my religion is the blood")—he nevertheless had considerable first-hand acquaintance with ideas which enabled him to make distinctions necessary to a fairly tenable primitivistic position.

For one thing, Lawrence never regarded reversion to a less civilized state, which Anderson suggests in the simple sensuality of the Negroes, as an answer to contemporary cultural failure; and so Lawrence never fell into the impracticable cultural primitivism of *Dark Laughter*. Moreover, Lawrence read Freud, which Anderson claimed he never did; and he was able to come to grips with the complexities of sex as Anderson never could. As Frederick Hoffman has well demonstrated,[4] Lawrence was fully aware of the intricacies of the sex instinct as defined by Freud and was able to deal brilliantly—if not always defensibly—with Freudian descriptions of subtle relationships between the conscious and the unconscious. He was capable, after careful study of Freud, of accepting some of Freud's principles and rejecting others. With considerable self-assurance, he could affirm the vitalism of the unconscious and the centrality of sex as a life-generating force and reject Freud's conception of the ego as a desirable intellectual, moral and social deterrent to the excesses of the id, or unconscious, which Lawrence maintained was corrupted rather than moderated by the ego.

Anderson first learned his Freud on what Hoffman has called the summary or survey level, from articulate laymen, like Dell, who read Freud in translation and passed their general understanding on to others.[5] Anderson's introduction to the new psychology came shortly after his arrival in Chicago in 1913. At Chateaugay Lake in 1916—when he was writing the *Winesburg* tales—he met Burrow and had the discussions with him that culminated in "Seeds." While Burrow later told Hoffman that Anderson "very definitely" did not read Freud nor "draw any material from what he knew of Freud through oth-

[3] *Letters*, p. 144.

[4] Frederick J. Hoffman, *Freudianism and the Literary Mind* (Baton Rouge: Louisiana State U. Press, 1957), Chapter VI, "Lawrence's Quarrel with Freud." See also Trilling's *The Liberal Imagination* (New York: Viking Press, 1950), and Howe on this issue of Lawrence's acquaintance with ideas and Anderson's lack of intellectual background.

[5] *Ibid.*, pp. 89-90.

ers," [6] he subsequently corrected himself and conceded that "it would now appear that Anderson was not [un]influenced by my talks with him on psychonalysis." His own chief interest, Burrow went on, was in what seemed to him "the social implications of the neurosis and it was this aspect of our talk that took a strong hold with Anderson." [7] Burrow emphasized once more what he had told Hoffman: "that Sherwood Anderson was an original psychologist in his own right and, if he profited by any insights of mine, I also profited in no small measure by the exceptional insight of his literary genius." [8]

The truth of Burrow's comment in his letter to Hoffman that "Anderson was a man of amazing intuitive flashes but . . . like Freud, the chief source of his material was his own uncanny insight" is readily apparent when we once more regard *Many Marriages* and *Dark Laughter* in the light of "Seeds." In contrast to the romances—in which he develops a thesis about the "social implications" of neurosis —his theme in "Seeds" comes through in brief, penetrating insights into the needs of all men through portrayals of the psychoanalyst, the artist, and the woman from Iowa. In other words, he analyzes his characters in the story without setting forth in narrative terms his thesis that the ills of the world could be cured by a greater consciousness of the "dark blood." Anderson repeatedly rejected Freudian formulas, for he resisted what he regarded as the oversimplification of the human mind and heart. He resented the tendency of the popular psychoanalysis he was acquainted with to generate self-consciousness and inhibitions by labeling an individual's expressions and gestures with pat phrases. His steadfast refusal to accept such systematization and oversimplification is what Burrow found most engaging and brilliant in him, and his own artist's reliance on his imaginative projection into the inner lives of others and absorption of those lives finds its best expression in such great tales as "Seeds." Where Anderson develops a thesis, as he does in *Many Marriages* and *Dark Laughter,* he falls into the same oversimplification the psychoanalyst and narrator do in "Seeds"; and he becomes even more liable than Lawrence to the charge that he "dreams of being the great, dark animal," which is, "after all, a neurotic wish."

The romance was clearly not Anderson's form. When he wanted to deal with "ideas," he did his best work in the imaginative autobiog-

---

[6] *Ibid.*, p. 236. See Burrow's letter to Hoffman of October 2, 1942.

[7] See Burrow's letter to William L. Phillips, in Burrow, *A Search for Man's Sanity* (New York: Oxford U. Press, 1958), p. 559. In this letter Burrow corrects his earlier statement to Hoffman that Anderson had not been influenced by the ideas of Freud, saying that it was likely that Burrow's own comments on Freud probably had considerable influence on Anderson.

[8] *Ibid.*

raphy or "confession," a form admirably suited to his best narrative style of intimate, subjective commentary. Such a work is *A Story Teller's Story*.

## IV. A Story Teller's Story

In *The Anatomy of Criticism*, Northrop Frye terms one of his hybrid forms the romance-confession, which he defines as the fictionalized "autobiography of a romantic temperament." "Nearly always some theoretical and intellectual interest in religion, politics, or art plays a leading role in the confession," Frye writes. "It is his success in integrating his mind on such subjects that makes the author of a confession feel that his life is worth writing about." [9] He adds that the familiar essay bears the same formal relation to the confession that the tale has to the romance and that the short story has to the novel. *A Story Teller's Story* may best be defined as a romance-confession made up of familiar essays that are held together—like the tales in *Winesburg*—by a common theme and by a mythical rather than a chronological structural sequence. Because it remains close to Anderson's own experience, it is vastly superior both artistically and rhetorically to *Many Marriages* and to *Dark Laughter*.

In spite of the sometimes annoying tone of calculated naïveté interspersed with lapses into pretentious cultural sophistication; notwithstanding the occasionally digressive "Notes" that too often mar the internal coherence; and despite the superfluous epilogue about a corrupted American writer, *A Story Teller's Story* contains some of Anderson's finest writing. While it hardly deserves to be classed with *Walden* or with *Leaves of Grass*, it does share two qualities with those masterpieces. First, it has an intangible but pervasive quality which suggests the presence of an authentic person and of a vital, sensitive inner life moving through successive stages of struggle with the world of fact but left finally to nourish itself with rare "moments" of beauty of life and art. As in *Walden* and in *Leaves of Grass*, we are aware at all times of an immediate and sustained link with a personality who dominates his material but is inseparable from it and whose essential life has been fashioned out of the great struggle of his imagination to achieve integrity. Second, it shares with these two books a structural cohesion and movement which have unfortunately gone unappreciated by most critics but which make the book a significant expression of the "American myth." Admittedly—almost defiantly—an imaginative biography, it deliberately scorns the primacy of the world of fact and compels an imaginative, mythical interpretation.

[9] Northrop Frye, *The Anatomy of Criticism* (Princeton, N.J.: Princeton University Press, 1957), p. 308.

Because Anderson transforms the essence of both his imaginative and factual life into a fable that brings together the chief skeins of his own experience and the myth of the American Adam, he succeeds in doing what he could not do in any of his books except *Poor White*: he finds an intellectually defensible, if not practicable, attitude or thesis, based not on a course of social action or simple blood consciousness but on a state of mind. As Frederic I. Carpenter has ably shown, the American Adam myth has involved an imagined redemption as well as a fall.[10] The American Adam has helped destroy his great primitive paradise, but he has become wiser; and, in his new wisdom, he perceives his kinship with that paradise and pursues a course of wise innocence, glimpsing thereby a "paradise to be regained." In all his romances Anderson's heroes follow this course; but in *Windy, Marching Men, Many Marriages,* and *Dark Laughter* we are given to believe that in family life, in psychological collectivism, or in blood consciousness, a paradise of renewed innocence may be realized. *A Story Teller's Story* has a more defensible thesis than any of these novels because Anderson ends the book with the ambiguities and dilemmas implicit throughout the narrative.

The point of view is that of the self-confident, successful author who nostalgically recalls his development as a writer, recollects the factual and fanciful life of his youth, points to the facts of life which misdirected his imaginative endowment and sent him into the "ugly" world of fact, relates the struggle between his imaginative nature and the demands of a business society that led to his break from business, and tells of his quest for critical guidance and for esthetic and moral integrity in America. In typical Anderson fashion, the narrative sequence moves back and forth in time; but, overall, the book has a discernible development which is psychological and chronological as well as mythical.

Moving back and forth in a kind of psychological continuum, the narrative progresses by means of an accretion of concrete incidents that cluster about the four successively higher stages of the artist's psychic development: (1) his small-town youth, the time of fancy, sentience, and innocence; (2) his young manhood in Chicago, the awakening to "a consciousness of something wrong" and a reaching out for a meaningful connection with life; (3) his plunge into the world of fact, of business and the success ethic, and the rebellion of the inner life and purification ("a sweet clean feeling") and rebirth in the act of becoming a writer; (4) the construction of a new life, the "pilgrimage" of the artist, as the prototype of the "whole man," in search of psychic and sentient integrity and simplicity.

[10] Frederic I. Carpenter, "'The American Myth': Paradise (To Be) Regained," *PMLA*, LXXIV, 5 (December 1959), 599–606, p. 606.

Each stage of development is constructed loosely about a symbolic character or group who have contributed to his imaginative heritage or growth. In Book I we see the stage of youthful fancy and innocence. The natural demand of the fancy is for a role, an identity, a heroic conception of self, and for union with others. The symbolic figure in this section is his father, Irwin Anderson. In a series of parallels between himself as a boy and his father, Anderson discloses the glories and the dangers of the romantic fancy and concurrently frames his esthetic theories in narrative terms. The father's yarn-spinning, directed in one episode toward the farm girl Tillie, is a kind of love-making which takes both the storyteller and the listener out of themselves and unites them in an almost mystical embrace. "In the world of fancy . . . no man is ugly. Man is ugly in fact only." The demands of the fancy are for love and beauty, and in it "all morality . . . becomes a purely esthetic matter. What is beautiful must bring esthetic joy; what is ugly must bring esthetic sadness and suffering."

In the father's tale of his own heroism and tragedy during the Civil War, he illustrates the dangers inherent to the fancy. Where it has nothing in the real world upon which to fix itself, it becomes an instrument of escape; and, driven in upon itself, it causes grotesqueness, egocentricity, and disorder. The adult imagination comes into being when the youthful, romantic fancy is brought to bear upon the recalcitrant world of fact, when the youthful luxury of pure and innocent dreams gives way to a conscious effort to shape the world of fact and sense to its ideal of beauty. In his father's childish innocence, Anderson sees a symbol of America in its immaturity: a people still unable to bring the needs of the fancy for love and beauty to bear upon its material life.

Book II begins with his first experience in Chicago and is built upon a series of contrasts depicting the painful process of facing the facts of life. Plunged into the grim, factual world of Chicago, the narrator's mind moves nostalgically back in time to Clyde and to Judge Turner, who first awakened his imagination to the possibility of beauty in the life of actuality in telling him of Chartres Cathedral. At this stage of the artist's pilgrimage, the fancy shrinks away from "a world where only men of action seemed to thrive" and which was symbolized by the Ford.

In this section Anderson relates his growing sickness as his revulsion from industrial squalor and from the tired, dirty, defeated people broadened the chasm between his inner and outer life. "I lay on my back," he writes of his early days in Chicago, "trying to get up courage to face facts." The unsatisfied demands of the fancy drove him to writing, but "I was always trying to create in a world of my fancy and that was always being knocked galley-west by the facts of my life." He was drawn reluctantly into the difficult world of fact by Alonzo Berners, a young man crippled and beaten by life who "simply loved the people about him and the places in which they lived and . . . that [had] become a force in itself affecting the very air people breathed."

This Berners episode sets the stage for Book III, in which Anderson explains his entry into business as a kind of "fortunate fall" in which his imaginative life fixed itself upon the "unstated but dimly understood American dream" of making himself "a successful man in the business world." The central "character" in this book is the nameless, faceless mass of Americans who are grotesquely absorbed in their own affairs. Like the original Adam of the Old Testament, he discovers evil; and his moral life begins when psychological revulsion initiates an awareness that the great evil in life is egoism and that Puritanism, industrialism, and the success ethic are not only social manifestations but also causes of self-love. Supporting this moral discovery is consciousness of the historical myth of the garden and awareness of the failure of America to live up to its promise: "This vast land was to be a refuge for all the outlawed brave foolish folk of the world." There was to be a new beginning, a new chance for man: "The declaration of the rights of man was to have a new hearing in a new place." But "something went wrong."

> They built the cathedral of Chartres to the glory of God and we really intended building here a land to the glory of Man, and thought we were doing it too. That was our intention and the affair only blew up in the process, or got perverted, because Man, even the brave and the free Man, is somewhat a less worthy object of glorification than God. This we might have found out long ago but that we did not know each other. We came from too many different places to know each other well, had been promised too much, wanted too much. We were afraid to know each other.

Constructed around two climactic moments of discovery, Book III relates (1) Anderson's sudden realization that his life as a businessman was unclean, his "overwhelming feeling of uncleanliness," his abandonment of business—partly as a response to psychological necessity—and (2) his entry into a new world purified of egoism and demanding a new morality. Book IV presents the building of that new moral world. The chief symbols, the Virgin and the Dynamo, represent the culmination of his now-conscious quest for a symbol of the good life. This chapter traces his quest in the East among the intellectuals, whose absorption with ideas destroyed any sentient and emotional contact with life and art; the chapter ends with the climactic, epiphanous moment at Chartres, when with Rosenfeld he sat entranced before the great Cathedral and found at last the symbol of imaginative fulfillment in love and art, the symbol of a whole people welded together for the creation of beauty. "It was one of the best moments of my own life. . . . In the presence of the beautiful old church one was only more aware, all art could do no more than that—make people, like my friend and myself, more aware . . ." of the "tragic-comic sweet way" of life. Anderson had at last found his symbol of human perfection. It remained now to turn from the past to the future—with the qualities embodied by the Cathedral as the goal—to America with a new understanding of the nature and possibilities of art.

Students of American literature would do well to look more closely and favorably at *A Story Teller's Story*, particularly as a definition of the condition of the artist in America. As Anderson portrays it, that condition is scarcely encouraging, and yet a note of hope for the future of art in America persists as a kind of undertone which surges up during the moment at Chartres when Anderson decides that, for better or worse, "The future of the western world lay with America." Like its immediate predecessor, *The Education of Henry Adams*, *A Story Teller's Story* does not violate the ambiguities and self-contradictions its author encounters in his quest for an understanding of his world; rather, it maintains them, and as Anderson accepts without attempting to alter the conditions of American life—neither despairing nor affirming a cheap, accommodating optimism—we feel some of the tragedy that goes with being an artist in America.

# Reviews of *A Story Teller's Story*

## *by Ernest Hemingway and Gertrude Stein*

*A Story-Teller's Story*, by Sherwood Anderson.
New York. B. W. Huebsch. 1924. 442 pages.

In a review of Ernest Hemingway's "In Our Time" (The Three Mountain Press) the *Dial* recently said: "Mr. Hemingway's poems are not particularly important, but his prose is of the first distinction. He must be counted as the only American writer but one—Mr. Sherwood Anderson—who has felt the genius of Gertrude Stein's 'Three Lives' and has been evidently influenced by it. Indeed Miss Stein, Mr. Anderson and Mr. Hemingway may now be said to form a school by themselves." Two of these writers have consented to give *Ex Libris* their opinion in regard to the latest book written by the third.[1]

THE EDITOR

The reviewers have all compared this book with the "Education of Henry Adams" and it was not hard for them to do so, for Sherwood Anderson twice refers to the Adams book and there is plenty in the "Story Teller's Story" about the cathedral at Chartres. Evidently the Education book made a deep impression on Sherwood for he quotes part of it. He also has a couple of other learned quotations in Latin and I can imagine him copying them on the typewriter verifying them carefully to get the spelling right. For Sherwood Anderson, unlike the English, does not quote you Latin in casual conversation.

As far as I know the Latin is correct although English reviewers may find flaws in it, and all of my friends own and speak of "The Education of Henry Adams" with such solemnity that I have been unable

Reviews of *A Story Teller's Story*. From *A Lost Book Review*: A Story-Teller's Story, in *Fitzgerald/Hemingway Annual*, ed. by Matthew J. Bruccoli (Washington, D.C.: NCR Microcard Editions, 1969), pp. 71–75. The review appeared originally in *Ex Libris*, 2 (March 1925), 176–77. Reprinted by permission of Alfred Rice, Attorney, and the Estate of Gertrude Stein.

[1] *Ex Libris* was a publication of the American Library in Paris—Ed.

ever to read it. "A Story Teller's Story" is a good book. It is such a good book that it doesn't need to be coupled in the reviewing with Henry Adams or anybody else.

This is the Life and Times of Sherwood Anderson and a great part of it runs along in a mildly kidding way as though Sherwood were afraid people would think he took himself and his life too seriously. But there is no joking about the way he writes of horses and women and bartenders and Judge Turner and the elder Berners and the half allegorical figure of the poor devil of a magazine writer who comes in at the end of the book. And if Sherwood jokes about the base-ball player beating him up at the warehouse where he worked, you get at the same time, a very definite sharp picture of the baseball player, drunk, sullen and amazed, knocking him down as soon and as often as he got up while the two teamsters watched and wondered why this fellow named Anderson had picked a fight when he couldn't fight.

There are very beautiful places in the book, as good writing as Sherwood Anderson has done and that means considerably better than any other American writer has done. It is a great mystery and an even greater tribute to Sherwood that so many people writing today think he cannot write. They believe that he has very strange and sometimes beautiful ideas and visions and that he expresses them very clumsily and unsuccessfully. While in reality he often takes a very banal idea of things and presents it with such craftsmanship that the person reading believes it beautiful and does not see the craftsmanship at all. When he calls himself "a poor scribbler" don't believe him.

He is not a poor scribbler even though he calls himself that or worse, again and again. He is a very great writer and if he has, at times, in other books been unsuccessful, it has been for two reasons. His talent and his development of it has been toward the short story or tale and not toward that highly artificial form the novel. The second reason is that he has been what the French say of all honest politicians *mal entouré*.

In "A Story Teller's Story," which is highly successful as a piece of work because it is written in his own particular form, a series of short tales jointed up sometimes and sometimes quite disconnected, he pays homage to his New York friends who have helped him. They nearly all took something from him, and tried to give him various things in return that he needed as much as a boxer needs diamond studded teeth. And because he gave them all something he is, after the manner of all great men, very grateful to them. They called him a "phallic Chekov" and other meaningless things and watched for the sparkle of his diamond studded teeth and Sherwood got a little worried and uncertain and wrote a poor book called "Many Marriages." Then all the people who hated him because he was an American who could write and did write and had been given a prize and was starting to have some success jumped on him with loud cries that he never had written and never would be able to write and if you didn't believe it read "Many Marriages." Now Sherwood has written a fine book and they are all busy comparing him to Henry Adams.

Anyway you ought to read "A Story Teller's Story." It is a wonderful comeback after "Many Marriages."

—Ernest Hemingway

A Stitch in time save nine. Birds of a feather flock together. Chickens come home to roost.

There are four men so far in American letters who have essential intelligence. They are Fenimore Cooper, William Dean Howells, Mark Twain and Sherwood Anderson. They do not reflect life or describe life or embroider life or photograph life, they express life and to express life takes essential intelligence. Whether to express life is the most interesting thing to do or the most important thing to do I do not know, but I do not know that it is the most permanent thing to do.

Sherwood Anderson has been doing this thing from his beginning. The development of the quality of this doing has been one of steady development, steady development of his mind and character, steady development in the completion of this expression. The story-teller's story is like all long books uneven but there is no uncertainty in the fullness of its quality. In detail in the beginning and it does begin, in the beginning there is the complete expression of a game, the boys are and they feel they are and they have completely been and they completely are. I think no one can hesitate before the reality of the expression of the life of the Anderson boys. And then later, the living for and by clean linen and the being of the girl who has to have and to give what is needed is without any equal in quality in anything that has been done up to this time by any one writing to-day.

The story-teller's story is not a story of events or experiences it is a story of existence, and the fact that the story teller exists makes a story and keeps on making a story. The story-teller's story will live because the story-teller is alive. As he is alive and as his gift is the complete expression of that life it will continue to live.

—Gertrude Stein

# Sherwood Anderson

## by T. K. Whipple

Sherwood Anderson combines an unusual number of activities: he is at once observer, interpreter, creator, and critic. To begin with, he presents a picture, as do most of our writers, of that portion of the United States which he has known intimately. Yet, since he has not contented himself with rendering the surface, his picture is not mere mimicry: he has tried to get beneath the appearances and to understand, by imaginative penetration, the vital processes of American life. He has digested the crude matter of experience and converted it into the substance of art, so that it has become a new thing, though still also a likeness of the old—a process as baffling to analysis as man's psycho-physical parallelism, yet familiar to every good portrait-painter. Furthermore, Anderson has pondered over his experience, both actual and imaginative, and has tried to draw tentative conclusions, not only concerning American civilization but concerning human existence in general. Not only has he, like the others, made a diagnosis, but also, unlike them, he has a remedy to suggest. Therefore, to one interested in the relation of current literature to modern life, he is the most instructive of our contemporaries.

Since his world is a representation of the Middle West, it has many familiar features. The country is rich and fertile, and highly cultivated; it is a succession of cornfields, cabbage fields, berry fields, and always cornfields again, with here and there a bit of woodland. Many of its details are pleasant—a pool in a brook near a bridge, a cluster of wild flowers in spring beside an old log, the sound of wind in the growing corn, the smell of freshly turned earth. But it is monotonous; it is so flat and so full of things that the eye cannot carry far in any direction. Since it is all the same, there is no use in going from one place to another. Walking along one of the roads, one passes field after field of the same crops, the same groves of the same trees, the same farmhouses. The road never turns, there is never a view. On and on one goes, hemmed in by an eternity of repetition. Even the towns do not

"Sherwood Anderson." From Chapter Six of *Spokesmen: Modern Writers and American Life*, by T. K. Whipple (New York: D. Appleton and Company, 1928), pp. 115–37. Reprinted by permission of Hawthorn Books, Inc.

help, for they are all alike and all as void of distinction as the country. They have all a paltry, mean ugliness, as one walks down Main Street past the livery stable, the drugstore, the hardware store, the frame hotel, to the red frame railroad station. Nor is even the big city much better, for the city is simply one of the towns enlarged, with endless blocks of identical buildings, grimy, featureless. It is a gigantic anthill, as they are little anthills.

The inhabitants match the country, not in luxuriant vigor and fecundity, but in absence of distinction. To be sure, they have features, but there is nothing memorable in their features: one has a red nose and two gold teeth; another is a large man with a drooping mouth covered by a yellow mustache; one of the women is tall and gaunt, her face marked with smallpox scars; another is a gray, silent woman with an ashy complexion. In a week spent in Winesburg, Ohio, one would not see one person who could be remembered for two days. And at first the habits of these folk look commonplace enough, as they go about their business, for the most part silently, stopping to speak for a moment with Shorty Crandall, the clerk in Sylvester West's drugstore, or with Sid Green, who works in Myerbaum's notion store. For a time, these people seem like the country, pointless, monotonous.

But their behavior is not always so quiet. As they walk along the street, they sometimes mutter to themselves, and their hands twitch; now and then one of them breaks out and begins shouting a stream of incoherent words. And in private they are much less restrained. On rainy nights they walk endless miles alone through the country, or they run wildly through fields and woods, sometimes groaning and sobbing and rolling on the ground. And other of their ways are still odder. Evidently, their usual composure is only a mask worn with difficulty, and occasionally thrown off willy-nilly. For beneath the uniform flat surface seethes a life of extraordinary intensity, a life which manifests itself in periodic explosions. These inarticulate and unrational people, always brooding and always uncomprehending, have immortal longings in them, and they burst for brief instants into electric activity. By their outbreaks they vindicate their humanity and become real and living. The conflict of the submerged life with the meaningless surface produces drama and significance.

Anderson affords a key to the understanding of this country in his sentence, "The living force within could not find expression." The people are baffled because their lives offer no channel through which their vitality can discharge itself. That is why they are all, as he himself has more than once pointed out, grotesque, misshapen, deformed by their own bottled-up energy. They are uncomprehending because their world offers them nothing to comprehend; their existence is an interminable reiteration of meaningless detail, and the innate incapacity of man to be a vegetable makes the tragedy. This is the land, not of repressed, but of unfulfilled, desires. Nor, although sex plays an enormous rôle in this country, is it true that these desires are exclusively sexual. The drama is not chiefly the struggle of sex with convention, nor even the struggle of desire in general with convention or with inhibition of any sort. It is something vastly wider: it is the rebellion of all desire against the inanity of life. Like all other men and women, Anderson's are fired with longings, dreams, ideals, aspirations—but these they cannot even formulate, much less effectuate. Desire, in this land, instead of being a creative force, is destructive, devastating, thwarted and made futile by the lack of any means of realization, by the pointlessness of life. Over the whole scene broods the tragic pathos of futility and waste. Here, life is unbearable commonplace tempered by lunacy.

Because, in this country, everything important happens below the surface, Anderson does not often develop the setting to any great extent. His writing is not conspicuous for the sensuous imagination it evinces. His landscapes, for example, are much less fully visualized than those, say, of Miss Cather. He makes little appeal to eye and ear and nose. Solidity and density are not characteristic of his world; his background is given as fully as his theme requires, but no more: it is not dwelt on for its own sake. And so it is likewise with his characters: there are no complete, rounded-out portraits; they do not possess an independent, tri-dimensional existence of their own—compare them in this respect, for example, with the grotesques of Dickens. There is no one in Anderson's stories who is remembered as an individual like Quilp or Micawber. For Anderson's great faculty is not the imagination that bodies forth the form of things unseen, but rather the insight which probes and penetrates. Yet the process by which he works is not analytical dissection; he is not in the usual sense a "psychological" writer. That is, he does not take the motives of his people apart and explain them. Perhaps he could not if he wished. A man in *The Triumph of the Egg* says: "I have entered into lives. I have gone beneath the surface of the lives of men and women." Anderson might say the same; he has "entered into the lives of men and women" by an intuitive and imaginative process. It is as if he had witnessed or heard of an incident, and had then brooded over it until he had come to feel sympathetically and participate in the emotions of the people concerned—not at all by any conscious intellectual process. He truly "enters in," as if the experience had been his own. And he enables the reader to do the same —not to watch an experiment in vivisection, but to explore the depths of living personality by himself getting inside the skins of other men and women.

No wonder then if in his pursuit of the secret essence he tends to neglect the surface. Life in his rendering is stripped to the stark essentials. In his world, we are ever watching the interplay of elemental forces, as elemental as heat, magnetism, or gravitation. His people are dismantled energies, almost as abstract as the diagrams of a treatise on physics, as simple as a corked bottle half full of boiling water. The austere bareness of this art may displease readers accustomed to the more comfortably upholstered worlds of other novelists; yet it is a prime cause of his chief appeal—his intensity. Beneath the impersonality of his manner, a keen, a piercing sympathy makes itself felt. His pity is the prime motor of his work; the pressure of his compassion gives his world its potency and concentration. In some strange way—I suppose because his stories are conceived in passion—he has the power to convey feeling directly, as it is conveyed in lyric poetry. Drayton's sonnet, "Since there's no help, come, let us kiss and part," or Burns' song, "Ane fond kiss, and then we sever," is no bad parallel for some of Anderson's stories: there is the same absence of characterization, of explanation, of everything except the one sharp essential feeling. At his best, Anderson conveys precisely that sense of constriction about the heart and that difficulty of breathing which one gets from the finest lyrics.

How he does it is a mystery. His style is plain and bare, yet in the extremity of its simpleness lies this power, perhaps because it is so unforced and altogether natural. The author feels his people and his story so strongly and enters into them so fully that he is led instinctively to record the significant details, the significant speeches and actions; and when they are recorded in the most direct and honest of words, they convey what he wishes to convey. His writing has the quality of a well-scrubbed plank floor—its clean freshness, its frank homeliness, and its slight roughness and unevenness. He uses no subterfuges and no tricks. In part, his art consists in a remarkable freedom from artifice. He is the opposite of an "artful dodger"; he knows no smartness. Such utter straightforwardness as his is a triumph.

And it is as characteristic of his structure and narrative as of his diction. His stories are as devoid of plot as they are of all the devices taught by correspondence schools for producing salable fiction. His best stories seem to have no technique at all: each deals with an episode, a crisis in one or two lives, and Anderson first gives what information is needed concerning the participants, and then proceeds with his anecdote. As a writer, his outstanding trait is his integrity; to maintain such integrity against all the lures and pressures of twentieth-century America is a notable feat which speaks highly for his instinct as a workman. To possess not only the story-telling knack but also the critical sense and the severity of taste necessary for strict self-

discipline—for certainly he received no outside aid of consequence—
that is singular good fortune. Anderson must have been endowed with
the rigorous conscience of the true craftsman. He has repeatedly stated
that that is his ideal of writing: to deal with words with the same
honest skill and solid workmanship with which a good carpenter
treats wood or a mason stone. He wishes to make a handicraft of literature, and his success has not been small.

Although I have been speaking primarily of his short stories, much
of what has been said applies also to his novels. Yet as works of art
the latter are inferior. The more complex chain of incidents he
handles with less skill. Moreover, his novels all have a thesis to maintain or a theme to develop; they are not mere stories, mere presenta-
tions of human life, and what they may gain in significance they tend
to lose in intensity and actuality. The faculty which works well in the
lesser medium is apparently incapable of grappling with, shaping, and
sustaining a long work. The beginnings of *Windy McPherson's
Son* and of *Marching Men* have the excellences of the tales except
their final poignancy; but both novels in later portions lose the narrative and dramatic interest and become treatises. Much the same is
true of *Poor White,* although the hero, Hugh McVey, is the most
fully embodied of all Anderson's characters, and the treatise, if I may
call it that, takes the form of an extremely interesting sketch of the
coming of industrialism to Ohio. *Many Marriages* is a short-story
fantasy amplified into an essay in mystical philosophy. *Dark Laughter,*
in form the best of the novels, is too preoccupied with exemplifying a
theory to give much of any sense of character.

Some twelve years ago Anderson wrote:

> For a long time I have believed that crudity is an inevitable quality
> in the production of a really significant present-day American litera-
> ture. How indeed is one to escape the obvious fact that there is as
> yet no native sublety of thought or living among us? And if we are a
> crude and childlike people how can our literature hope to escape the
> influence of that fact? Why indeed should we want it to escape?

If his own work is taken as commentary, to explain what he means
by "crude and childlike," the statement holds good, and is especially
salutary when "sophistication" is all the vogue. American writers who
decide to be sophisticated produce the literary equivalent of those
wooden châteaux modeled on Blois and Amboise which were popular
half a century ago. On the other hand, the best of current fiction has
the quality of a well-built stone barn. The difficulty is that the ar-
tisan needs not only honesty and skill, but good material. He cannot do first-class work with rubble and shale, and Anderson's performance suffers from the sort of stuff he has had to deal with. Com-

pared with the imaginative worlds of any of the major British or French novelists, of Fielding or Balzac, say, the world of his making is a little poor, in the sense that it lacks variety, body, massiveness. He gets powerful effects with gray and drab and tan, but it is a pity that his palette is not fuller. As diet for the imagination, as aesthetic experience, his work is somewhat spare and lean—but the responsibility for this deficiency rests, not with Anderson, who has done the best he could, but with his environment.

When the verisimilitude rather than the creative qualities of Anderson's writing is considered, the first result is hesitancy. Can this scanty land, this penurious world, be the Middle West, notoriously dropping with fatness? Is not Anderson's country too different from Dreiser's or Sandburg's or Lewis's for them all to be true? On the contrary, these several accounts, so far from being contradictory, dovetail together into a complete picture. Sinclair Lewis provides the inert, thickly varnished surface; Sandburg the background of natural loveliness and of man's works, beautiful and ugly; both Sandburg and Dreiser the hurly-burly of city life, and Dreiser also something of the underlying economic processes and of the life lived by the victors in the struggle. Futrhermore, *Main Street* and *Babbitt, Sister Carrie* and *Jennie Gerhardt* have many points of contact with Anderson's work, in the stress they lay on helpless, fumbling unfulfillment; and Sandburg shows that he is not oblivious of this aspect of his world when he writes in "Halstead Street Car" of

> *Faces*
> *Tired of wishes,*
> *Empty of dreams.*

In his earlier novels Anderson deals with the bustle of the city and with prosperity and success and industrialism, but the reader tends to forget that side of Anderson's work because the author himself is comparatively little interested in it. He treats by preference not the enemies of life, but life itself, such as it is, going on below the surface, with random irruptions through the crust. Because he has penetrated more deeply than any one else into the submerged portion of mid-American life, one remembers chiefly that aspect and thinks of him as portraying only the type with which he is most successful.

No doubt Anderson's writing gives only one or two phases out of many, and gives those as seen through a highly individual temperament; yet that he has captured not only artistic but social truth any one may demonstrate to himself by standing on a favorable corner in any small town or industrial community and watching the faces that pass—faces commonplace, dull, apparently lifeless, yet touched with unspeakable pathos. That the reading of Anderson leads to a heightened realization and a new perception is the best proof that his transcript is faithful to its original. And what he leads one to perceive afresh is the old familiar tragedy which one encounters in almost all our contemporary writers—spiritual frustration. "The living force within could not find expression": could there be a better statement of that specific tragedy, of desire balked by the insignificance of life, of potentialities squandered in futility and waste? I do not know where a sharper feeling could be found than Anderson's of the senseless destructiveness, the inane wastefulness, the ugliness triumphant, of a life which wrecks and crushes the insubstantial wishes and aspirations of men, of a life in which the individual, in his struggle for spiritual existence, always goes down to defeat, overcome by an environment which is hostile to the very nature of life.

The difficulty is that the society which Anderson portrays was devised not for humane ends and is conducted without care for humane values. Historically, as he points out in *A Story-Teller's Story*, this society is the legacy of pioneering. Towns, cheap and ugly, were thrown together regardless, only to serve as way-stations or trading-posts where the newcomers might push their private fortunes. The pioneer's motive, in carrying out which he was willing to suffer any hardship or deprivation, was personal advancement; consequently, he created a world ill adapted to other motives—created, in brief, a practical society which his descendants have inherited, as they have inherited, at least in part, his point of view. If most of them lack his fierce practical ambition, yet they are the heirs and the victims of a tradition which they do not care to carry on and which they are unable to get rid of. They are at a standstill, for they would like to live, but, having no facilities for such an undertaking, do not know how to set about it. Except for the natural setting, their world is hideous, in material objects, in human appearances, and in human character. To borrow a phrase from Van Wyck Brooks, it "sends up to heaven the stench of atrophied personality." For that reason, these people are incapable of themselves remedying the defects of their surroundings; they have no source of beauty within themselves, nor even a conscious desire for it. Many interests—the secondary intellectual and aesthetic interests—are scarcely to be expected in a rural community, which can do well enough without them if it has the essentials—proper work and play, communal social life, religion. But, because it provides no outlets, this world is stagnant; it is devoid of amusement, of pleasure; it is joyless because its people have never known how to get joy out of working and playing together. Worse still, it is no social organism, and worst of all, it is destitute of religion. What passes as religion among a few is a debased fanaticism; the great majority have none of any sort, yet their lives are made bleak by the influence of a once lively faith which degenerated first into a timid constraint and then into a mere dead weight.

Though much of the foregoing is touched upon in Anderson's social criticism, most of his comment is devoted to another side of the situation, a side to which his novels are largely devoted. *Windy McPherson's Son, Many Marriages,* and *Dark Laughter* all deal with men who have made business successes and who have found themselves still dissatisfied with the futility of their lives. *Marching Men* and *Poor White* handle the question of industrialism. In Anderson's mind, industrialism and success-worship are intimately related, more intimately, I think, than the facts warrant, inasmuch as the practical ideal, as witness Benjamin Franklin, long antedated the Machine Age. However, there is no doubt that for half a century the two have been combined. Anderson's theory is that after the pioneer age a new civilization was beginning to develop, having as basis the work of craftsmen:

> . . . A slow culture growing up—growing as culture must always grow—through the hands of workmen.
>
> In the small towns artisans coming in—the harness-maker, the carriage-builder, the builder of wagons, the smith, the tailor, the maker of shoes, the builders of houses and barns, too.
>
> As Slade and James were to be the fathers of the modern gunmen, so these the fathers of the artists of the generations to come. In their fingers the beginning of that love of surfaces, of the sensual love of materials, without which no true civilization can ever be born.
>
> And then, like a great flood over it all the coming of the factories, the coming of modern industrialism.

In *Poor White* he says of this transition:

> . . . A sense of quiet growth awoke in sleeping minds. It was the time for art and beauty to awake in the land.
>
> Instead, the giant, Industry, awoke.

And he describes the Age of Exploitation in words reminiscent of Henry Adams:

> It was a time of hideous architecture, a time when thought and learning paused. Without music, without poetry, without beauty in their lives or impulses, a whole people, full of the native energy and strength of lives lived in a new land, rushed pell-mell into a new age.

Anderson hates the standardized inhumanity of machines and machine-slavery, as he hates that practical ambition which turns a young American into "a mere smart-aleck, without humbleness before the possibilities of life, one sure of himself" . . . "blind, deaf, and dumb, feeling and seeing nothing." There is nothing to add to Anderson's own words. Of our ten writers, he is by all odds the profoundest and most searching critic of American life.

One reason is that he has himself lived through the whole process more completely than any of the others. Born in 1876 in Camden, Ohio, he watched the coming of the factories, of which he writes; and furthermore, as he says, "I was to take up the cry myself and become one of the most valiant of the hustlers." He uses his own experience not only in his social criticism but in the themes of his novels: he himself at one time owned a small factory, but he grew dissatisfied and one day walked off and left it, as do Sam McPerson and John Stockton. He became a writer of advertisements, in which occupation he saw still more of the ways of the boosters. But he has also taken part in other kinds of American life; like Sandburg, he has been a day-laborer and a soldier; he has been a factory-hand; and he has drifted about doing odd jobs, especially in racing stables. He has seen much of the picaresque side of American life which rarely gets into books. He therefore knows from the inside many types of life which his contemporaries know if at all only as spectators. Sandburg, for instance, seems never to have been touched by the go-getter's philosophy, and Dreiser, who has framed his notion of the universe on what he saw as a reporter in slums and police-courts, has had a less wide experience than Anderson. Moreover, he is more critically minded than Sandburg, less confused than Dreiser, and more reflective than Sinclair Lewis.

Yet he has many of the traits of his own most typical characters: he too broods over what he cannot understand, and gropes for he knows not what; he too is puzzled and uncomprehending, so that he often gives the effect of being inarticulate, because he cannot translate his feelings and his intuitions into logical terms. He was long in coming to know his own mind; he published his first volume at the age of forty, after he had tried all sorts of other activities. Evidently, for him it was long true that "the living force within could not find expression." As he appears in his books, especially *A Story-Teller's Story,* he has no self-assurance, but is wistful and shy, full of humility, and above all of reverence. Nothing is plainer than that he is endowed with a strongly religious nature; one hears throughout his writing that cry of the heart which is the source of all religion. That this need has found no satisfaction is the explanation of much of his insatiate random seeking. He has not found life a friendly and easy medium in which to effectuate his desires. His environment has been blankly impervious to his wishes. Hence comes that sense of the pathos of life, of *lachrymæ rerum,* which pervades his work.

Anderson, I suspect, is more strongly oriented to the inner than to the outer life—not, of course, that he is detached from or indifferent to his surroundings, but that he cares more for the subjective than for the objective element in experience. According to this conjecture, he is in this respect at the opposite pole from Sandburg; he absorbs rather than is absorbed by what goes on about him; with a kind of reticence, he draws it into himself, but does not surrender himself to it. In his autobiography, he describes the extraordinary vividness which has always characterized the life of his fancy; a snatch of conversation overheard by chance, a person glimpsed on a street car, any occurrence however trivial, is enough to start a train of suggestions in his mind—and it is with these suggestions rather than with the people who initiate them that he is preoccupied.

If there be any truth in this guess, many peculiarities of his work can be accounted for. While to deny him a large capacity for experience would be wrong, yet to maintain that he is much more open to certain types of experience than to others is possible. This theory would explain why he shows comparatively little regard for sensations or sensuous beauty, and thus—since his chief interest is turned away from the external world of solid physical appearances—why his writing makes little appeal to the senses and also why he is most sensuous when he is most fanciful, as in John Webster's vision of the southern river with the negroes and their boats drifting through a forest. It would also explain his neglect of people's outsides—looks, behavior, mannerisms—in contrast with his uncanny insight and singularly direct feeling for obscure emotions and hidden motives. And finally it would account for the fact that his creation is not full-bodied, if not indeed slightly bloodless, a quality which betrays a certain lack of gusto and at times even the weariness of a spirit which has not been able to establish fruitful, invigorating contacts with the surrounding world.

Since Anderson's stories are the product of such a temperament as his working upon such surroundings as he has had, into the result must enter not only the peculiarities of his personality but the peculiarities of his environment. The comparative poverty of his imaginative world is due to the fact that the environment has been ill adapted to meet the needs of his particular mental bias. It has been rich in those qualities with which he is little concerned: in the beauty of nature, in the obvious commotion of city streets, in the achievements of a mechanic civilization, in all that spectacular pageantry with its violent contrasts of which Dreiser is enamoured, in all those external or non-human aspects which fascinate Sandburg. But it has been poor in the things for which Anderson cares, for his interest is in the human soul, in dramatic or poetic human values, and in the relations and interactions of men and women with one another. Here his world has failed him, for it has been most deficient in the riches of human nature, in emotion, aspiration, endeavor, achievement, reverence, integrity—in the human quality which comes from work well and lovingly done, and in all those results for the human spirit of full lives well lived. Therefore his imagination has had to feed upon a somewhat scanty fare; his misfortune has been to live in a society which, being by its constitution practical and by its profession repressively moralistic and thus adverse to the life of realization, has deprived its members of satisfaction in work, of emotional and religious experience, and of well ordered social life, and has consequently failed in the development of full-grown personalities.

Except for the signs it shows of undernourishment, Anderson's work is singularly free from the qualities which are to be expected of the literature produced in such a society. In his pamphlet *The Modern Writer* he discusses the prostitution and standardization and sentimentality which are imposed upon popular literature among a people who do not value the poetic temper, but he himself has never yielded to the pressure, as he himself, so far as his writing is concerned, is remarkably immune from the dominant point of view. His imagination may have been somewhat starved, but it has not been warped. In spite of his critical attitude, he has not developed that hatred of his environment which prevents experience and leads to fleeing from reality into weak romantic reverie; at most, he betrays now and then a perhaps undue self-distrust and self-consciousness. In his work he has shown no instability or uncertainty of aim; from the first he has known what he was about. His sense of fact and truth of feeling have survived unharmed. Unlike many contemporaries, he is not deficient in critical sense and discipline. Yet in this respect he has not escaped altogether unscathed; not only did he find no aid or guidance outside himself, but it was only in spite of everything that he finally found his proper vocation. Not until comparatively late in life did he come in contact with a current of living thought, with men who debated vital questions of art, literature, and society. The strengthening he felt from this outside corroboration of his purposes he has amply acknowledged. But had he encountered something of the sort a decade or two earlier, his work might have profited, and surely his thought would have benefited in that it would have been less fumbling and drifting, would have had a somewhat more assured central point of rest.

Even so, of course, Anderson is too much the seeker ever to have arrived at a hard-and-fast philosophy. Among our present writers, he is one of the few real mystics. At first glance, he may look like much the same sort of naturalist as the others. The world as shown in his portrayal is naturalistic, like the world of Henry Adams, Sandburg, and Dreiser—chaotic, unintelligible, purposeless, with man the sport and victim of forces he cannot understand or control. It is a futile and a tragic world; yet Anderson, unlike certain others, does not make the assumption that it has always been and must always continue to be futile and disordered. He does not first reduce American behavior to a theory of life and then erect it into a scheme of the universe. His standard is never quantitative, and he is never an uncritical worshiper of mere force. The law of the jungle is not for him eternal and immutable. He obscurely apprehends that there may be a solution and a remedy, and this solution he finds in a mystical relation between the human unit and the universe. His quest has always been for the source of a more abundant life, and such a source he discovers in a union or identification of the individual with something outside himself, a merging of the single personality in something larger. Hence his preoccupation with the breaking down of the walls and barriers that hem in and isolate each man and separate him from the world about him and from the others of his kind.

In *A Story-Teller's Story* there are records of two unmistakable mystical experiences. One is the magnificent episode of John Berners, than which Anderson has written nothing finer, which led him to ask himself whether one had "to come to the realization that oneself did not matter, that nothing mattered but a kind of consciousness of the wonder of life outside oneself," and which, in spite of his "having no God, the gods having been taken from me by the life about me, as a personal God has been taken from all modern men by a force within that man himself does not understand but that is called the intellect," ended thus:

> I had suddenly an odd, and to my own seeming a ridiculous, desire to abase myself before something not human and so stepping into the moonlit road I knelt in the dust.

The other experience, which is plainly the foundation of *Marching Men,* Anderson had while in the army.

> The constant marching and manœuvring was a kind of music in the legs and bodies of men. No man is a single thing, physical or mental. The marching went on and on. The physical ruled. There was a vast slow rhythm, out of the bodies of many thousands of men, always going on and on. It got into one's body. There was a kind of physical drunkenness produced. . . . One was afloat on a vast sea of men. There was a kind of music on the surface of the sea. The music was a part of oneself. One was oneself a part of the music. One's body, moving in rhythm with all these other bodies, made the music. . . . One's body was tired but happy with an odd new kind of happiness. The mind did not torture the body, asking questions. The body was moved by a power outside itself.

Since, as he says, he has no God, Anderson's is a nature-mysticism much like Whitman's. He advocates a return to a simpler and more primitive way of life, to the condition of savages and even of beasts and plants. In his first novel he wrote:

> American men and women have not learned to be clean and noble and natural, like their forests and their wide, clean plains.

This point of view is at the root of his affection and admiration for horses and negroes; it recurs again and again in his stories, and explains his choice of title for his novel *Dark Laughter*. Hence comes his hatred of the intellect, as a dividing, separating force which will not let man "just be, like a horse or a dog or a bird." That is why he usually joins "dry" and "sterile" with "intellectual." As a character in *The Triumph of the Egg* exclaims:

> What makes you want to read about life? What makes people want to think about life? Why don't they live? Why don't they leave books and thoughts and schools alone?

Even one who holds that the intellect need not be an impoverishing factor in experience and that to live like the animals is neither a feasible nor a desirable solution of the human problem may still concede that it would be better to live so than not to live at all, and be grateful to Anderson for the emphasis he lays on the importance of living.

The gist of all his philosophy is in these passages from *A Story-Teller's Story*:

> Could it be that force, all power, was a disease, that man on his way up from savagery and having discovered the mind and its uses had gone a little off his head in using his new toy? I had always been drawn toward horses and dogs and other animals and among people had cared most for simple folk who had no pretense of having an intellect, workmen who in spite of the handicaps put in their way by modern life still loved the materials in which they worked, who loved the play of hands over materials, who followed instinctively a force outside themselves they felt to be greater and more worthy than themselves—women who gave themselves to physical experiences with grave and fine abandon, all people in fact who lived for something outside themselves, for materials in which they worked, for people other than themselves, things over which they made no claim of ownership. . . .
>
> When you take from man the cunning of the hand, the opportunity to constantly create new forms in materials, you make him impotent. His maleness slips imperceptibly from him and he can no longer give himself in love, either to work or to women. "Standardization! Standardization!" was to be the cry of my age and all standardization is necessarily a standardization in impotence. It is God's law. Women who

choose childlessness for themselves choose also impotence—perhaps to
be the better companions for the men of a factory, a standardization age.
To live is to create constantly new forms: with the body in living children; in new and more beautiful forms carved out of materials; in
the creation of a world of the fancy; in scholarship; in clear and lucid
thought; and those who do not live die and decay and from decay
always a stench arises.

These passages make clear Anderson's reason for laying so great stress
on craftsmanship and sex: he conceives both as means by which man
escapes from his prison cell and joins himself to a larger life and a
larger world, as implements by which to destroy the partitions between man and nature, between man and man, and between man and
woman. He recognizes the mystical element in love of every sort, and he
ranks love of creative work and sexual love first. The theme of sex is
thus treated in *Many Marriages,* and in the most enigmatic and most
unusual of his tales, and also the most avowedly mystical, "The Man's
Story" in *Horses and Men.* I do not understand this story, but so far
as I can decipher a meaning it is that through the love and possession
of one woman a man may attain to a similar kind of union with the
whole world. If sometimes one is tempted to demur at what seems
Anderson's obsession with sex, one must remember that sex is for him a
key to a larger experience.

In his theory and thought, then, as well as in his practice, Anderson
is a thorough-going champion of the poetic temper and of the life of
realization against all their enemies. His work, for all its high merit
within its severe limitations, has quite as much social as literary importance. No other poet, novelist, or dramatist is so fully conscious of
the American situation or drives it home so forcibly as does Anderson,
both in his imaginative creation and in his critical comment. His
picture of human starvation and frustration, his historical explanation
of the condition he presents, his suggestions concerning the way to a
better and fuller life—all combine to lend him a unique significance
in present American letters. In this achievement, he has brought into
play all his faculties: he has used his insight into the natures of other
people; to communicate his discoveries, he has availed himself to the
best of his ability of his power as story-teller and worker in words; he
has thought over what he has experienced and discerned in an effort to
extract its import; in opposition to every outside influence, he has followed his bent and maintained his integrity. The appearance on the
literary scene of such a man is a heartening portent.

# The Short Stories

## by Irving Howe

Although there is a gap of more than a decade between Anderson's first two volumes of stories and his last one, chronology is of slight consequence to a study of his career as a story writer. *Death in the Woods,* which appeared in 1933, contains a few stories quite different in style and subject matter from those in the earlier books, but except for one or two sketches of Southern hillsmen none of these later innovations is particularly important. The one significant line of division in his stories cuts equally through all three books.

Some eight or ten of Anderson's stories, by far the best he ever wrote, can be considered a coherent group. Such stories as "I Want to Know Why," "The Egg," "Death in the Woods," "I'm a Fool," "The Man Who Became a Woman," and to a lesser extent "The Corn Planting," "A Meeting South," and "Brother Death" are similar in having as their structural base an oral narration, as their tone a slightly bewildered tenderness, and as their subject matter elemental crises in the lives of simple townspeople. In these stories the central figure is often an "I" who stands at the rim of the action, sometimes looking back to his boyhood and remembering an incident he now realizes to have been crucial to his life, a moment in which he took one of those painful leaps that climax the process of growth. The narrator tells his story in a manner that is an implicit rejection of literary naturalism: he cannot content himself with a catalogue of behavior for he realizes that in the word "behavior" are coiled the greatest enigmas; he stresses the strangeness of his remembered experience because he feels that the ordinary can best be perceived through the intense light cast by the strange; and though he now claims a partial understanding of the incident that persists in his memory, that understanding is itself a humility before the general problem of human experience. Life, as he conceives it, is buried in marshes of sloth and apathy, and only in a rare emergence into awareness does one find its epiphany, the *true moment.*

"The Short Stories." From *Sherwood Anderson,* by Irving Howe (New York: William Sloane Associates, Inc., 1951), pp. 147–77. Copyright 1951 by William Sloane Associates, Inc. Reprinted by permission of William Morrow & Company, Inc.

Anderson's narrator senses that in the seemingly simple act of telling his story he enters into a highly complex relation with his audience and that, as one able to shape both the materials of his narrative and the responses of his listeners, he is momentarily in a position of great power. The atmosphere of oral narration, deliberately created by Anderson, is the setting of his best stories, which can be read not merely as imaginative versions of human experience but as renderings of a pervasive pattern of story-telling. Part of the craft of oral narration consists in the narrator's working not only for the usual kinds of interest and suspense, but also to produce in his listeners a vicarious responsibility for the successful completion of the story. The audience quickly senses this relationship and, if the narrator is at all skilled, becomes emotionally involved with his struggle to tell his story almost as much as with the story itself.

The narrator is seen weighing his recollection in his mind, perplexed by the course it has taken and wondering whether it is merely of private significance or of larger emblematic value. As he turns to the memory that is his burden, he seems doubtful that he will be able to extract it from the chaos of the past and give it form. He becomes aware, as well, of the temptations that follow from his power as story teller, but it is a particular virtue of Anderson's short fictions that his narrator does not try to dominate or assert superiority over his audience. Respecting the community of narrator and listener, or writer and reader, Anderson establishes as his controlling point of view the voice of a hesitant human being, one who is anything but omniscient.

In choosing to simulate oral narrative Anderson was aware of the traditional resources he could thereby tap. Sensing that story-telling had once been a ceremony in which the listeners expected the narrator thoroughly to exploit his craft and thus fulfill his communal role, Anderson quite cannily tried to re-establish something of this atmosphere of ritual in his stories. He hoped to lend the act of story-telling a synoptic significance it could not otherwise have, to restore to the story teller a fraction of his role as tribal spokesman or, at least, public figure. But he also sensed, as had Conrad before him, that the most effective story teller is one who is felt to be not merely skillful but also deeply involved in the outcome of his own story. The Andersonian narrator therefore seeks to persuade his audience that the disburdening of his mind has a purpose other than the stimulation of its pleasure; he hints that for him, and perhaps through him for the audience, the recollection of the past provides an occasion for a symbolic cleansing and relief. And, in more private terms, he would certainly have agreed with D. H. Lawrence that "One sheds one's sickness in books—repeats and presents again one's emotions to be master of them."

In those of his stories that follow the oral narrative pattern, Anderson often resorts to a bold sort of artlessness. The narrator of "The Egg," for example, occasionally confesses his perplexity before the events he recalls. Such an intrusion of comment into a narrative is considered a heresy, or at least a fallacy, by certain severe critics; and, indeed, by derailing the story from its guiding point of view an intrusion can immediately destroy every shred of verisimilitude. But in those of Anderson's stories that live, artlessness is usually the veil of conscious craft, and the narrator's intrusion, precisely because it *is* the narrator's and not Anderson's, becomes an integral part of the story. Even while wandering from his narrative line, the oral story teller will drive his apparent divagations toward his climax—and this is exactly the strategy Anderson employs.

It is interesting that the untutored listener will often have a greater regard for this element of narrative contrivance than the sophisticated reader who has been educated to expect "naturalness" in art. The untutored listener realizes that he is supposed to discount, though not disregard, the narrator's claim to be baffled by his own story, for that claim is part of his craft. (This is particularly noticeable in an audience listening to a ghost story.) The listener instinctively senses what the modern critic strives to restate as doctrine: a story, being primarily a story, is not reproducible in any terms but its own, and after the work of exegesis is done there still remains a dimension of unexplicated wonder, to which the story teller will naturally direct his awe and thereby the audience's attention. The narrative device that might be called the protestation to perplexity is a traditional and almost an instinctive way of telling a story, used by Homer and Defoe, Conrad and Twain.

But it is the mark of the good story teller that, even as he confesses to bewilderment about the story's meaning, he is actually presenting the reader with the materials necessary for a total response. Sometimes, as in "The Egg," both Anderson and his narrator seem slightly bewildered by the story's terrible events, but the story is nevertheless there in its entirety and virtual perfection. Sometimes, as in "Death in the Woods," the narrator confesses that "the notes had to be picked up slowly one at a time," but Anderson himself has them all firmly in possession and control. In either instance, all that is important is that the reader not feel that he has been unduly deprived or overloaded; and there is surely no warrant for either feeling with regard to "The Egg" or "Death in the Woods."

A great deal of cant has been written to the effect that Anderson's stories are "moving" but "formless"—as if a work of art could be moving unless it were formed or form could have any end other than to move. Those who make such remarks are taking form to signify merely the executive plan or technical devices that go into the making of a work of art. But while form includes these it is not reducible to them—unless, of course, one prefers to take the scaffolding as the purpose of the construction. In modern literary discussion form is too often seen as a virtually autonomous and isolable characteristic of a work of art, too often equated with the conscious planning of a James or the elaborate structure of a Proust. And when one tends to think of form largely in terms of the complex and elaborate, one may soon deny it to the simple and primitive. Actually, however, form can be properly apprehended only by relating techniques and strategies to their organic context of emotion and theme, and it is consequently difficult to imagine a work of art with acknowledged authenticity of emotion to be simultaneously lacking in form. Valuable and finely formed fictions, such as some of Anderson's stories and Lawrence's novels, result not merely from the contrivance of skilled intention but also from the flow of released unconscious materials—which is to be taken not as a plea against the use of the blue pencil but as a statement of what it is used on.

In Anderson's best stories, form is achieved through two essential means: tone and perspective. Tone is the outward sign of the emotion resident in a work of art; it is the essence of what a writer communicates, undercutting and simultaneously uniting subject matter and character portrayal. The tone of love, as realized in the best stories and in *Winesburg,* is the ultimate quality for which Anderson should be read. One reason this tone is so fully present in his best stories is that the structure of the oral narrative, while itself simple, yet permits him a perspective on his material that is both consistent and complex. The consistency is largely derived from his use of the first person as narrator, while the complexity is enforced by an interaction of the four levels of movement in his stories: the events themselves; the feelings of the boy involved in them; the memory of the adult who weighs his involvement in the light of accumulated experience; and the final increment of meaning suggested by the story but beyond the conscious recognition of its narrator. The true action of these stories is thus not the events narrated but the narrator's response, not the perceived object but the perceiving subject. That is why Anderson's stories are so seldom dramatic in the usual sense of the term: their purpose is not to record a resolution of conflict but to refract an enlargement of consciousness.

Somewhat less complex than this abstract model of Anderson's "oral" narratives are his two most popular stories, "I'm a Fool" and "I Want to Know Why." Though both are written in the first person, their narrators speak, not as men looking back to boyhood, but as boys involved in the immediate present. The result is a rich quality of sensuousness, but also an absence of the irony and complication of vision possible in the stories where the narrator is an adult.

Anderson himself sensed that neither story could be considered in the same class as "The Egg" or "The Man Who Became a Woman," and of the excessively ingenuous "I'm a Fool" he wrote to Van Wyck Brooks that "its wide acceptance is largely due to the fact that it is a story of immaturity and poses no problem." "I'm a Fool" and "I Want to Know Why" are usually taken to be quite similar stories, perhaps because both are dramatic monologues of racetrack swipes, but actually the difference between them is so considerable that to specify it is to begin a properly discriminating judgment of Anderson's work as a story writer.

In intention "I'm a Fool" is patterned after Mark Twain, but in execution it is closer to Tarkington. The monologue of the boy who outsmarts himself through an excess of shrewdness is internally coherent and only occasionally disrupted by "literary" phrasing. But this coherence is not related to the boy himself; the monologue is inconceivable from the lips of "a big lumbering fellow of nineteen" who has learned to drink and "swear from fellows who know how." The surface of his musing is too coy for the character it is supposed to reflect, and no attribution of ironic intent can dispel the incongruity. Actually, the monologue comes from Anderson's own mouth, Sherwood masquerading as an adolescent in "dirty horsey pants" and improvising a remarkable imitation of adolescent reverie—while pointing with the elbows of his prose to how ingenious an act it is. Too ambitious in motivation to be taken as the ironic anecdote it might have been, "I'm a Fool" is insufficiently ambitious in execution to be a very good story. The boy's unhappiness is too local to what is merely adolescent in his experience, and hence cannot thoroughly involve the reader to whom the significance of adolescence is in its tension of "becoming."

This is precisely the effect Anderson does achieve in "I Want to Know Why," also a story in which an adolescent narrator describes a troubling experience at a race track. In the story's rambling opening, the boy is revealed through several neatly economical touches; he is "just crazy" about horses and he feels a strong sense of companionship with the Negro swipes. In the boy's feeling there is clearly more than hunger for adventure; his displaced sexual energy has an esthetic and moral dimension of which he is only dimly aware but which is a major spring of his behavior. He is no longer innocent, but he is still pure. In the life he sees at the training tracks—not, he carefully specifies, at the racing tracks—he senses a natural fraternity: "You hunch down on top of the fence and itch inside of you. Over in the sheds the niggers giggle and sing. Bacon is being fried and coffee made. Everything smells lovely. . . . It just gets you, that's what it does." This is a boy with a vision, and within the limits of what is possible to him it is an admirable vision.

When the boy notices that the trainer of the stallion Sunstreak is as moved as he at watching the horses run, he feels that "there wasn't anything in the world but that man and the horse and me"—a sense of communion that is the essence of the fineness for which he has yearned. But that same night the boy sees the trainer enter a brothel, and through a window watches him staring at a prostitute, "lean and hard-mouthed and . . . a little like the gelding Middlestride." The trainer has the same shine in his eyes as "when he looked at me and at Sunstreak. . . ." And now for the boy "things are different. . . ."

The story revolves around two moments of intense perception, one resulting in joy and the other in pain. The first moment is the boy's sudden awareness that he shares his love for horses with the trainer and the second his shock at discovering the trainer's lust for the prostitute. In this play of symbolic action he learns that the extremes of good and evil can coexist in the same person and can elicit a bewildering similarity of response. Not that the man can love both the pure horse and the contaminated woman, but that he can apparently love both in the same way, is the source of the boy's sorrow. As Cleanth Brooks and Robert Penn Warren have noted, the boy is undergoing an "initiation" into the adult world. Simultaneously, however, the boy, remembering his idealized though nonetheless sexual feeling for horses, fiercely rejects the degraded love between humans he has suddenly witnessed.

The degradation of the brothel is real enough and the boy's revulsion is certainly justified, but the degradation cannot be taken as the only cause of the revulsion. The boy fears the prospect of all adult sexuality, which can never be as "pure" as his relation to horses. So that even as he undergoes his "initiation" into the adult world, he is developing powerful and enduring resistances to it. Life can never again seem so simple and fraternal as it once was; he has entered the blighted arena of knowledge and judgment, he must now confront experience in terms of ambiguity and qualitative distinctions, he must choose rather than absorb. This, then, is Anderson's theme: the niceties of a boy's discriminations and the brutal need to apply them to what he will soon learn to call the real world.

Through the skilled use of a symbolically charged comparison and of a recurrent image, Anderson realizes this theme in dramatic action. The stallion is felt by the boy to be an agent of virility, while the prostitute he instinctively compares to a gelding—which reveals the essence of the story through symbols inherent in the perceptions of its major character. But this meaning is complicated and enriched by a recurrent image of cleanliness through which the boy refers to the sense of purity he had found at the training tracks. For adolescents an obsessive concern with cleanliness indicates a rejection of the "dirty things" grown-ups do. The boy is left with a highly troubled feeling: a realization that he will not be able to satisfy his wish to achieve surface sexual pleasures through his fondness for horses and simultaneously to reject human heterosexuality as unclean and sterile.

In "I Want to Know Why" Anderson completely identifies himself with adolescent feeling: that is, he achieves a triumph of tone. More than most of his stories, which too often tend to a paradigmatic bareness, it deserves Virginia Woolf's praise for creating "a world in which the senses flourish . . . dominated by instincts rather than ideas . . . [in which] race-horses make the hearts of little boys beat high. . . ." In language that reverberates with echoes of the authentic Twain, Anderson does justice to what is distinctly boyish in his boy: "More than a thousand times I've got out of bed before daylight and walked two or three miles to the track." Except for two minor intrusions by an adult voice and several badly superfluous sentences at its end, the story thoroughly maintains the tone and perspective native to its adolescent narrator.

The feeling at the core of "I Want to Know Why" receives several variations, usually more subtle and complex, in the best of Anderson's stories. And in such not wholly successful but still fine pieces as "The Corn Planting," "Brother Death," and "A Meeting South" the possibility of instantaneous and total rapport between two people or between man and nature is again the dominant theme.

"The Corn Planting" is one of Anderson's last stories, subdued and bare. It contains a powerful fable, but lacks sufficient surface representation to transform the fable into a full-bodied story. One evening an old farmer is told by friends that his only son has been killed in the war. Quietly the man returns to his house. A little while later he and his wife are seen walking mutely through their fields in the dead of night, the old man with a hand corn-planter and the old woman with a bag of seed corn. The climax of the story is sufficiently striking as a bit of symbolic grotesquerie to deserve a fuller context:

> They were both in their nightgowns. They would do a row across the field, coming quite close to us as we stood in the shadow of the barn, and then, at the end of each row, they would kneel side by side by the fence and stay silent for a time. The whole thing went on in silence. It was the first time in my life I understood something . . . I mean something about the connection between certain people and the earth—a kind of silent cry, down into the earth, of these two old people, putting corn into the earth. It was as though they were putting death down into the ground that life might grow again. . . .

In "Brother Death" the theme of rapport is presented through an intimate relationship between two children, brother and sister, who make a private circle of their lives because the boy, suffering from heart disease, may die momentarily and the girl alone understands that to confine him is to kill him before death. The figures of Ted and Mary Grey are drawn with lovely tenderness in the story's opening pages, the boy resisting with mute stubbornness all attempts to tame him and the girl, her sensibility inflamed to preternatural proportions, offering him in advance, as it were, what she can of the feminine responses he will never live to enjoy. The girl insists "that Ted be allowed to die, quickly, suddenly, rather than that death, danger of sudden death, be brought again and again to his attention." And the story boldly hints that in some obscure but essential way the parents are partly the agents of the boy's death: John Grey cuts down two shade trees near his house that have no utility but have given his children much pleasure—an act that is like a killing of luxuriant childhood. The story is muddied by an irrelevant middle, but in its final paragraph returns to the tone of gray somberness Anderson achieves so well:

> But while he lived, there was always, Mary afterwards thought, a curious sense of freedom, something that belonged to him that made it good, a great happiness, to be with him. It was, she finally thought, because having to die his kind of death, he never had to make the surrender his brother had made—to be sure of possessions, success, his time to command—would never have to face the more subtle and terrible death that had come to his older brother.

In "A Meeting South" the theme of rapport receives another variation. The first-person narrator, clearly Anderson himself, introduces David, a young Southern writer apparently modeled after William Faulkner. David has been in the First World War, suffers extreme pain from his wounds, and, as he tries to dull his pain by drinking heavily, has great difficulty in sleeping. The narrator brings David to Aunt Sally, a large old woman who had run a brothel in her youth but now sits at home chatting with young people. Instinctively she senses that David "lived always in the black house of pain. . . ." The narrator feels a throb of satisfaction, he has brought the sensitive young man to a mother. Secure in the unstated affection of the old woman, David tells of his efforts to sleep by drinking whisky to the rhythm of the Negroes who work in the fields by moonlight. In the end, the young writer manages to reach sleep on Aunt Sally's patio. "A Meeting South" occasionally skirts sentimentality and lacks dramatic incident, but if viewed simply as a character sketch it is a fine example of Anderson's gift for gravely lyrical expression.

In three stories, "The Man Who Became a Woman," "The Egg,"

and "Death in the Woods," Anderson reached the peak of his powers. Judged by no matter how severe standards, these stories are superb bits of fiction, the equal of anything of their kind done in America. Each of them is written in the first person, with the narrator looking back to an adolescent experience, but it would be a sad misreading to think of them only or mainly in terms of adolescence.

The theme of "The Man Who Became a Woman" is much like that of the earlier story, "I Want to Know Why," but to compare the two is to see how the materials of a good story can be reworked into a great one. "The Man Who Became a Woman" is richer in atmospheric texture than the earlier story, it is more certain in technique and consistent in point of view, it benefits greatly from its narrator's distance, and through the most dramatic incident in all of Anderson's fiction it establishes an aura of implicative terror.

Anderson introduces the racetrack milieu with authentic touches possible only to a writer in complete imaginative control of his materials ("when we had got through eating we would go look at our two horses again"). In this atmosphere Herman Dudley meets Tom Means, an educated swipe who hopes to write stories about horses. "To tell the truth I suppose I got to love Tom . . . although I wouldn't have dared say so, then." Through this sentence both the adolescent actor and the adult he has since become are concretely placed. The adolescent of the past and the adult of the present are not completely separated, as they never can be; and something of the adolescent's love for horses comes through in the adult's remark about Tom Means's effort to "write the way a well bred horse runs"—"I don't think he has," a statement that is less a judgment of Tom Means's literary ability than an offering of loyalty to the narrator's own youth. This narrator is not secure in his male adulthood, for the story he is trying to tell represents a threat he does not quite know how to cope with. At several points he interrupts his narrative to assure the reader, and himself, that the remembered incident was thoroughly unusual in his life. Each return to his narrative then brings another variation on its theme.

He loves Tom Means; he loves horses; he is fond of Negro swipes; and though he begins to dream of women, he is virginal. Precisely his extreme awareness of the affective values available in horses and men prevents him from moving toward full adult sexuality. When he walks his horse after a race, "I wished he was a girl sometimes or that I was a girl and he was a man."

One cold rainy night he is so overcome with loneliness that he wanders into a nearby mining town. In a saloon he sees his face in a mirror: "It was a girl's face . . . a lonesome and scared girl, too." He is afraid that if the men in the saloon see his "girl's face" there will be trouble. But, of course, the men do not notice it, and the only trouble

is a brutal brawl that leaves him "sick at the thought of human beings.
. . ." Back at the stables, the boy beds down happily in his horse's stall,
"running my hands all over his body, just because I loved the feel of
him. . . ." But suddenly the stall is invaded by two half-drunk Negroes
who mistake him, "my body being pretty white," for a girl. The boy is
too terrified to speak—perhaps the Negroes are right. He runs wildly
into nearby woods, feeling that "every tree I came close to looked like
a man standing there, ready to grab me." The story reaches its
grotesque climax when the boy falls across a horse's skeleton near an
old slaughterhouse. "And my hands . . . had got hold of the cheeks of
that dead horse and the bones of his cheeks were cold as ice with the
rain washing over them. White bones wrapped around me and white
bones in my hand."

Like "I Want to Know Why," this story is based on a contrast between horses and men, but here the action is less dependent on a naïve
moral polarity of animal goodness and human depravity. The horses
and men are not, as in the earlier story, independent agents whose
moral qualities are measured by an adolescent observer; they are rather
mental referents of the moment in adolescence when psychic needs and
moral standards clash. That moment is presented with commanding
skill: its meaning is extended by a skein of sexual images (horses, faces,
dreams, trees) unconsciously employed by the boy, and its alternation
between incident and reverie, with reverie mirroring the persistent
power of incident in the narrator's mind, results in a tightening clamp
of suspense. But the story's greatest power is released when the boy
stumbles over the horse's skeleton, a brilliant bit of gothic symbolism.
The horse is, of course, a love object of adolescence and, as the boy
falls over its skeleton, his hands clutching the bones that are the color
of his own girlish skin, he is actually tripping, in terror and flight,
over the death of his adolescent love. But his encounter with the
skeleton allows of another, yet congruent, reading: by a simple inver-
sion of color, the "white bones wrapped around me and white bones in
my hand," as well as the terror felt by the boy when he is enveloped
by these bones, may be seen as referring to a forbidden homosexual
fantasy. The diffused love of adolescence has been destroyed, but one
strand of it survives—and it is this which prompts the narrator to re-
hearse his experience.

One of the most beautiful qualities of the story is the way in which
the adolescent's natural affection for Negroes is seen ripening into the
adult's complex social understanding. Herman Dudley awkwardly but
movingly explains why Negro swipes, isolated from all social life,
might be tempted to molest the sort of white girl found near stables—
an explanation completely consistent with the tone of the story. He
also blames himself for not having spoken out when the Negroes

entered the stall, though he still does not understand why he was unable to; which again indicates that his original confusion about his sexual role persists into his adulthood. And he suggests an additional dimension of ambiguity by remarking that the Negroes were "maybe partly funning." The Negroes thus come to seem subjective shadows of the boy's psychic terror: his experience spins directly from the dislocated center of his self; and the story may be read as if the boy has never actually been molested by the Negro swipes but has erupted into hysteria as a result of accumulated anxieties about his sexual role.

"The Man Who Became a Woman" gains greatly from having an adult narrator who is deeply involved in his own story, for despite his insistence that he is now thoroughly rid of "all that silly nonsense about being a girl" he reveals how persistently, and poignantly, the adult mind struggles to control the memories of adolescence. Herman Dudley may even be, as he insists, a normal man, but to grant this somewhat desperate claim is to record the precariousness and internal ambiguity of adult normality itself. And this, indeed, is the particular achievement of the story, that through a recollection of adolescence it subtly portrays a complex state of adult emotion.

"Death in the Woods" is the only one of Anderson's stories that may accurately be compared, as so many have been, to Russian fiction. Like Turgeniev and Chekhov, Anderson uses the "pathetic fallacy," which is no fallacy at all, to build up the atmosphere of death, and relies on effects of mood and devices of pacing rather than conflict between characters to pull his story into climax. And like Turgeniev and Chekhov in many of their stories, Anderson uses an elemental experience to convey the sense of the ultimate unity of nature, an harmonic oneness of all its parts and creatures bunched in the hand of death.

The story's narrator tells about an old woman, the wife of a lazy and brutal farmer, who has "got the habit of silence." The woman "had to scheme all her life about getting things fed, getting the pigs fed so they would grow fat and could be butchered in the fall." Beaten by her husband and abused by her son, she is the tongueless servant of every living creature near her; "the stock in the barn cried to her hungrily, the dogs followed her about."

On a cold day the old woman wades through snowdrifts to get to town, where she trades her eggs for meat and sugar. With her come four farm dogs, "tall gaunt fellows," who are joined by three other dogs. Carrying a heavy sack of food on her back, she cuts through the woods to reach home before her drunken husband will return from a horse-trading journey. She stops to rest at the foot of a tree, and falls asleep. The day darkens, the moon comes out. The dogs become aroused and begin circling the tree beneath which she sleeps. "Round and round they ran, each dog's nose at the tail of the next dog. In the clearing, under the snow-laden trees and under the wintry moon they made a strange picture, running thus silently, in a circle their running had beaten in the soft snow. The dogs made no sound. They ran round and round in a circle." When the woman dies, the dogs gather round her, do not touch her body but in tearing the food off her back rip her dress. A day or two later the body is found and the boy who is later to remember the incident notices that "She did not look old, lying there in that light, frozen and still. . . . My body trembled with some strange mystical feeling and so did my brother's."

Though bare as a winter tree, the story is marvelously rich in substance. In a note for an anthology Anderson wrote that "the theme of the story is the persistent animal hunger of man. There are these women who spend their whole lives, rather dumbly, feeding this hunger. . . . [The story's aim] is to retain the sense of mystery in life while showing at the same time, at what cost our ordinary animal hungers are sometimes fed." This description is apt, though necessarily limited. For Anderson could hardly have failed to notice that the story may be read as an oblique rendering of what he believed to be the central facts about his mother's life: a silent drudgery in the service of men, an obliteration of self to feed their "persistent animal hunger," and then death.

But "Death in the Woods" obviously strikes much deeper: it is gaunt and elemental, its characters not particularized, the old woman simply a drudge who does not even enjoy the pathetic consolations of Flaubert's Félicité, the husband as brutal as any peasant in Dostoievsky, and the old woman's end as loveless as the most anonymous death. At first the old woman seems an image of the overwhelmed feminine victim, for even the dogs that attend her death are male, but gradually that image is enlarged to include all human creatures; her story becomes the story of all the unnoticed and uninteresting deaths that litter man's time.

While she lives there is nothing beautiful or redeeming about her, but in death she becomes young and radiant in the eyes of the boy, for she is no longer a farmer's wife. Frozen by the nature that is as benevolent to her in death as it was harsh in life, she comes to represent, both to the boy and the men who carry her body back to the town, something far beyond her individual self or possible attributes; something that may be designated as symbolizing the awe felt before fatality. But the particular power of the story is due to the fact that, out of its humility before all sentience, it makes the death of even this most miserable creature seem significant and tragic. In a sense this is the opposite of what Tolstoy did in *The Death of Ivan Ilytch,* yet the two stories have an ironic similarity in that both dramatize the democracy of human fate. The eerie death ceremony performed by the dogs seems as appropriate as any that men could offer, for the old woman's life was no closer to men than to the dogs that circle her in pure hunger, signaling her return to earth. The ceremony of the dogs resolves the story on one level, pointing to the inevitable process of life feeding on fresh death. But simultaneously there is another, more "human" resolution: through observing the woman's death, the boy has enlarged his knowledge of the human condition to which he too is subject; he has learned that an awareness of death is a condition for an intense immersion in life.

"Death in the Woods" has only one significant flaw: a clumsiness in perspective which forces the narrator to offer a weak explanation of how he could have known the precise circumstances of the old woman's death. But in every other respect the story is unblemished: its language, neither colloquial nor literary, is the purest Anderson ever summoned, and its gravely undulating rhythms successfully take its prose to that precarious point which is almost poetry. The story's most brilliant accomplishment in technique is its pacing, its controlled building up and canny holding back, done in the secure knowledge that the climax will not be imperiled by its initial flatness. Anderson reworked "Death in the Woods" several times; and of all his stories he seems to have felt most strongly toward it, for more than any of his autobiographies it expressed his dominant memory of the dark landscape of childhood.

Where "The Man Who Became a Woman" steadily mounts into terror and "Death in the Woods" into awe, "The Egg" maintains a pace so easy and a  tone so mildly wry that, by comparison, it seems almost benign. Yet of Anderson's three best stories it is surely the most terrible in its view of human life, surely the most grim, despairing, and tragic. In the other stories tone seems directly to brace the movement and define the meaning, to provide, as it were, the rising atmospheric tension they require; but in "The Egg" the bare fable is so appalling that, to prevent a slide into the lugubrious, it needs to be cooled by a prose which is dry and unimpassioned. The result, if less conspicuously dramatic than the other stories, is more complex and ironic, and of all Anderson's short fictions "The Egg" most deserves to be placed among the great stories of the world.

The narrator of "The Egg" begins by recalling his parents: his father had been a contented farm hand until, at the age of 35, he married a schoolteacher. Then "they became ambitious. The American passion for getting up in the world took possession of them." To become wealthy they bought a chicken farm, and here the image of the egg, which is to dominate the story with a crazy and malevolent exuberance, first appears. The narrator dryly remembers how difficult it was to raise egg-laying chickens: "It is all so unbelievably complex. . . . One hopes for so much from a chicken and is so dreadfully disillusioned." After ten years of effort the family moves away, to open a restaurant near a railroad junction. But the father takes with him a box full of glass bottles in which malformed baby chicks—four-legged, two-headed, double-winged—are kept in alcohol. By now obsessed with eggs, the father thinks these grotesques valuable, for "people, he said, liked to look at strange and wonderful things." He displays his treasure on a shelf in his restaurant—and the eggs become a curse on the family.

Prodded by an obsession with success, the father conceives the idea of making the restaurant a social center for the neighboring young people. But one night his dream bursts; an egg in hand, he comes upstairs from the store with "a half insane light in his eyes," and falling on his knees begins to weep. The narrator, deliberately avoiding a direct dramatic line, then quietly tells what happened in the store below.

A young man had come in to wait for a train. The father, his eyes lighting on a basket of eggs, began making conversation, insisting that Christopher Columbus was a cheat for falsely claiming to be able to make an egg stand on its head. He, however, could do it, and after many efforts did, but meanwhile the youth, who thought him mildly insane, had failed to notice his feat. Suppressing his anger, the father tried another trick: he heated an egg in vinegar, began to squeeze it through the neck of a bottle and promised that when "the egg is inside the bottle it will resume its normal shape. . . . People will want to know how you got the egg in the bottle. Don't tell them. Keep them guessing." When he heard the approaching train, the father began to hurry. In a panic to please, he broke the egg, splattering it over himself. The indifferent youth laughed, and then "a roar of anger rose from my father's throat. He danced and shouted a string of inarticulate words. Grabbing another egg . . . he threw it, just missing the head of the young man. . . ."

In this story there are two main forces of movement: the father and the egg. It is possible, however, to read it—profitably, if not exhaustively—as though the egg were mere neutral literary furniture and the father the only actor. In such terms, "The Egg" comes to seem, as Horace Gregory has said, "a burlesque of American salesmanship." Here again is the classic American story: ambition prodding a simple man into a situation he cannot control and thereby bringing about his spiritual destruction. And since Anderson felt no need to write from the condescending stance of "social consciousness" he could engage in a fraternal sort of ridicule: "We did not talk much, but in our daily lives tried earnestly to make smiles take the place of glum looks.

Mother smiled at the boarders and I, catching the infection, smiled at our cat. Father became a little feverish in his anxiety to please."

When once we take into account the sheer power of the egg to frustrate the father, we must be struck by the extent to which he may be seen as standing for Anderson's own father. Irwin Anderson had a robust heartiness the character in the story does not have, but there were moments in his life when he too collapsed in despair at his own ineptness and the world's unwillingness to take him seriously. From that aspect of his father Anderson has built his character—a poignant gesture of filial reconciliation, sharply in contrast to the murderous aggression of *Windy McPherson's Son* and the self-conscious romanticizing of *A Story Teller's Story*.

But when we extend our focus of perception still further, it becomes clear that the story must finally be read, not primarily as a social portrait or a filial gesture, but as a parable of human defeat. Traditionally, the egg arouses the most intimate associations with the processes of life, but in this story it is to be seen less as a symbol of creativity and renewal than as a token of all the energy in the universe—arbitrary, unmotivated, ridiculous, and malevolent—against which man must pit himself. The image of man suggested by "The Egg" is a deeply pessimistic one: he is not merely defeated but is tricked in his defeat, his very hunger for life is the source of his humiliations, his wish to live becomes his impulsion to death. The world in which he lives is unremittently hostile and, in part, the story's point is to show how the boy gradually realizes the full extent of, and his own subjection to, that hostility. The boy's education in defeat is conveyed through a marvelous symbolic contrast in which the story's tragicomic tone is most sharply realized. He remembers that on Sunday afternoons he used to watch his father sleeping and fancy that the bald path over the top of his head was "a broad road, such a road as Caesar might have made on which to lead his legions" and that he was "going along the road into a far beautiful place where there were no chicken farms and where life was a happy eggless affair." But when, at the moment of his father's humiliation, he sees his mother continually stroking the same bald path, the boy learns where the "broad road" may actually lead to.

As the story proceeds, the egg becomes an increasingly threatening force. It is first seen in its simplest aspect, a commodity to be produced. Then it is a grotesque, the deformation the father values because it is the only kind of egg he can control; an attachment that makes a grotesque out of the father himself. His wish to control the egg and to "entertain" customers are both expressions of a need to enter into workable relations with some force or beings external to himself. But that is beyond his capacity, the egg will be neither toyed with nor controlled, and when, in a revengeful act, he tries to bottle it, the egg breaks over him, causing him his greatest humiliation and driving him still further back into loneliness. In the end, the energy of the egg destroys man.

This is a harsh view, and it is tolerable only because there is nothing harsh in its telling. The egg splatters over the father as the stranger he had sought to please laughs at him—but the boy's mother later runs her hand consolingly over the "bald path." These are the two ultimate images in Anderson's parable of defeat, neither valid without the other, the two together making for the most mature vision of human life Anderson ever had. It is the peculiar virtue of "The Egg" that while each paragraph seems comic its total effect is one of great pathos. And while the story yields a variety of symbolic meanings, it is first and finally a story, thoroughly convincing in the one way a story must be —as a representation of life in which, if one wishes, the egg may even be taken as a mere "real" egg.

The number of Anderson's stories that can be considered completely first-rate is few, probably no more than half a dozen, and of these almost all come under the heading of what has here been called his "oral" story form. But those of his stories that are first-rate rank only a shade or two below the best of Chekhov and Turgeniev; their life is assured. It is sometimes argued that they are of limited significance because they are restricted to the subject matter of adolescence; but, as should by now be evident, in Anderson's best stories adolescence becomes a commanding vantage point for imaginative statements about all of human life. In any case, even if the objection were accurate it would be of little significance, for only the genuinely mature artist can portray immature life. Anderson's "oral" stories, it is true, do not create the large social world that is often demanded of fiction, and they hardly create the kind of world, as does *Winesburg*, that is primarily the outer sign of a subjective vision. But this much they do: they impinge irrevocably on the reader's sensibility, enlarging his knowledge of and insight into men—and that is the ultimate test of fiction.

Anderson's remaining stories are, by and large, not so successful as those based on the pattern of oral narrative. When his stories are patently "written," when they do not depend on a central narrator for their movement and meaning, they lack the tonal unity and structural tidiness of the "oral" stories. (The distinction between Anderson's "oral" and "written" stories is not quite the same as that between his stories in the first and third person, for there are several in the third person, such as "Brother Death" and "An Ohio Pagan," in which one clearly feels the presence of a narrator's voice.) A few of the stories that do not follow the oral pattern are, of course, successful, notably "The Untold Lie" and "The Return," an effective account of a man's disappointing visit to his home town. But in most of the "written" ones there is no sufficiently realized dramatic action or engaging character to replace the oral narrator as a centripetal force. The stories consequently tend to thin into musings or symbolic schemes.

Thematically, this second group of stories is usually concerned with the neurotic costs of the unlived life. In such stories as "Unlighted Lamps" and "The Door of the Trap" people are locked in their inability to communicate, and experience evades them while they hunger for it. Mary Cochran, who appears in both stories, bears the curse of her father's original failure to warm his marriage with the emotion that "was straining and straining trying to tear itself loose." The theme of unlived life receives two major variations, first as a fear of expressing emotion ("Unlighted Lamps") and then as a hesitation to accept sex from which love might follow ("The Door of the Trap"). What the source of this appalling isolation is, Anderson does not feel a need to say; sometimes he hints that it is a heritage of Puritanism or of Midwestern town harshness, but it seems clear that in his deepest feelings he regards isolation as an ineradicable human condition.

Both variations of the theme of unlived life appear in "Out of Nowhere Into Nothing," a long story that is probably his most characteristic expression. Rosalind Westcott returns to her native Iowa town for a brief visit, hoping to talk to her mother and to weigh her life in Chicago, but as she observes the kindly sloth in which her parents live and hears again those terrible "night noises" she had hated as a girl, she realizes that her family cannot help her; she is alone. Like many of Anderson's women, Rosalind Westcott is strong and vital, full of desire for an experience that can engage her emotional capacities. While walking along a railroad track in the corn fields, she meets her next-door neighbor, Melville Stoner, a bachelor who assumes the stance of the reflective observer. She is drawn to him, to his queerness and his trembling wish for companionship. For a moment it seems as if she has found with him "the thing beyond words, beyond passion—the fellowship in living," but Melville Stoner withdraws, pleading that he is too old to abandon his passive role.

Midway, Anderson resorts to long murky flashbacks to Rosalind's Chicago years, and the story slumps badly. But as long as he focuses on Rosalind Westcott and Melville Stoner, who are among his more individualized and memorable characters, the story has a gray, resigned poignancy: the image of these two lonely people walking in the yellow heat of the Iowa corn fields remains fixed in one's mind. The story's greatest strength is as a portrait of male inadequacy, of a good man's refusal to enter the dangerous relationships of love and sex. A woman's desire and a man's loneliness meet, there is a brief parabola of intense feeling and then: parting, each unable to satisfy the other. Of Melville Stoner, Anderson asks, "Did loneliness drive him to the door of insanity, and did he also run through the night seeking some lost, some hidden and half-forgotten loveliness?" Here in one sentence are gathered Anderson's most characteristic and cherished words: *door, run, hidden, half-forgotten, loveliness;* here is his world. The view behind "Out of Nowhere Into Nothing" is untenable in itself: to believe life to be a mere occasional explosion in the darkness and to insist so literally on human isolation is a kind of perverse romanticism. But when enough feeling enters into Anderson's fictional rendering of this view, it becomes enlarged and complicated in a way its abstract statement never can be—which is a measure of the artist's triumph.

In most of the stories that deal with the theme of unlived life there is, however, as great an emotional deprivation in their own telling as their characters are supposed to suffer; Anderson allows his dominating notion to weed promiscuously and to choke off the dramatic representation necessary to fiction. When one examines such stories as "Another Man's Wife," "The Man's Story," "Unused," "The Door of the Trap," and "The New Englander," one is struck by how remarkably devoid they are of any account of external experience, how vague in background and hazy in evocation of place and thing. The typical Anderson characters are here all so very familiar: all straining, bursting into nothingness, all lost. Though Anderson's intention is a call to experience, these stories are often evasions of the writer's obligation to focus on particular segments of experience; they create an unprovisioned and unlimned world, a neither-nor area suspended between reality and symbol. Toward his undifferentiated gargoyles Anderson feels and shows the tenderest of loves, but his absorption in a world that is neither descriptively faithful nor symbolically coherent can lead to nothing but a declining sputter of emotion at the end of each story. Having abandoned or rather having never fully accepted realism, he could not find, in these stories, another method for perceiving the objective world. He was trapped in a halfway house: he could neither build realistic structures nor find an adequate means of transcending the need for them.

In this second group of his stories he would often employ elaborate systems of symbolism to sustain his story where neither his action nor his characters could. In "The New Englander," for example, there is an extraordinary skein of symbols but the story itself lacks the conviction of reality; there is nothing viable in relation to which the symbols can act. Anderson is not presenting genuinely conceived characters, he is redecorating the legend of Puritan repression through such symbols as the rock, the trapped rabbit, the imprisoned bird. Here symbols do not enlarge upon reality; they crush it.

Another frequent sign of disintegration in these stories is Anderson's resort to rigid verbal rhythms which he apparently hoped would serve as the controlling and soothing center of his prose. In those pieces where he is most at sea imaginatively, the rhythm is most insistently established, as for example in the story "Unused":

> How cruelly the town had patronized May, setting her apart from the others, calling her smart. They had cared about her because of her smartness. She was smart. Her mind was quick, it reached out.

Here the deliberate reiteration of one simple word makes for an increasingly stiff cadence and an irritatingly false simplicity. When Anderson has his writing under control the rhythm is subterranean and bracing; as soon as the relationship between medium and meaning is disturbed, the rhythmic beat becomes a grating staccato responsible for that air of disingenuous folksiness which disfigures so much of his writing.

In Anderson's stories it is thus possible to see most clearly that major contrast in quality which is present in all of his work. The first group of stories, together with *Winesburg,* is his most valuable achievement, unquestionably an enrichment of the American imagination; the second group is not merely bad in itself but soon comes to seem a portent of the particular kind of badness which is to pervade both Anderson's later novels and much of American fiction in the twentieth century.

# "Death in the Woods" and the Artist's Self in Sherwood Anderson

## by Jon S. Lawry

Sherwood Anderson's autobiographical works attest his continuing absorption with the incidents and the form of his short story "Death in the Woods." [1] In his *Memoirs* he says that he tried to write the story "a dozen times over as many years." [2] It appears in a tentative early version in *Tar*.[3] Many of its episodes are used in a seldom-read fragment entitled "Father Abraham," which supposedly developed the life of Lincoln; indeed, the story's materials occupy a dominant position in that strange, often autobiographical work.[4] Elsewhere in his *Memoirs* (pp. 310–12), he relates the incident of the dogs' death ritual as having happened to himself. We may doubt the literal truth of that account, since Anderson himself repeatedly questions whether the event was fact or dream; in any case, however, the story was filled, for Anderson, with great personal and artistic significance.

I do not propose here to discuss the several versions of the story, even though the final form is a remarkable improvement over other versions. I wish instead to take the final version and ask of it what the story is "about," Anderson's interior explanation being patently insufficient. The meaning of the story will be revealing, I believe, of what Anderson intended in his occasional statements about the "self" and the "imagination" as artistic principles.

"Death in the Woods" contains an explicit interior statement of its own meaning. It comes thereby to share with "The Rime of the Ancient Mariner" the problem of a "moral" or open statement of meaning which is too slight for the preceding fiction, and is even

" 'Death in the Woods' and the Artist's Self in Sherwood Anderson," by Jon S. Lawry. From *PMLA* 74 (1959), 306–11. Reprinted by permission of the Modern Language Association of America.

1 *Death in the Woods and Other Stories* (New York: Liveright, 1933), pp. 3–24. All quotations are from this edition.

2 New York, 1942, p. 286.

3 New York, 1926, pp. 199–222.

4 In *The Sherwood Anderson Reader*, ed. Paul Rosenfeld (Boston: Houghton Mifflin, 1947), pp. 530–602.

discordant with it. We may suppose that, whereas Coleridge knew full well that his "moral" was unnecessary and superficial, Anderson did not suspect that his statement—surrounded as it is with a breathless insistence upon its being a revelation—was too meager for the story. Anderson's statement is, of course, that the life of the old woman of the story was given over to "feeding animal life."

The objective incidents of the story, which in themselves support Anderson's "moral," involve an "old" woman, Mrs. Grimes, who is bent and worn at forty. Abandoned by her unwed mother at birth, the girl had been bound to a German farmer. He later attempted to rape her, and fought over her with Jake Grimes, a sullen young scoundrel. She was then "bound" in marriage to Grimes, bore him a worthless son, and settled into a grinding service to the two men and the animals of the farm, all of whom—"horses, cows, pigs, dogs, men"—had to be fed. On the wintry day of her death, she had gone to town for meat. Feeling weak, she took a short cut through the woods, sank down to rest, and could not bring herself to rise. A pack of dogs circles her as she dies. Upon her death, they wolf the raw meat that she had carried and rip the clothing from her body. A hunter finds the body, thinks it to be that of a young girl, and leads a group of village men to the scene. "No one knew who she was," and each man finds her beautiful. The boyish narrator and his brother receive a partly prurient, partly mystical shock upon seeing her thin girlish body, frozen, like marble, in the snow. The town blacksmith carries her tenderly back into the village.

"She had spent all her life feeding animal life": that statement of the meaning of the story, unnecessary in itself, is wholly insufficient for all that follows the discovery of the body, and for the eerie death ritual that precedes it. The revelation of the woman to the boys, gathered into a context of idealization of woman and rejection of actual sexual experience, and the tender care of the village men for the dead woman they knew but did not know, has no relation to such a "moral." The statement is even more inadequate for the extremely important element in the story omitted in the sketch above: the narrator, who "creates" the meaning of the story. For him it becomes, after his own experience of life and fragmentary recollections of the woman and her death, "music," a revelation created upon memory by contemplation. For him the meaning is, moreover, a conscious, willed creation: "The notes had to be picked up slowly one at a time," if the music was to be heard. It is the narrator, then, who realizes the "meaning," yet for him the ascribed meaning is especially incomplete.

The narrator is a man, now, recalling the events. At first he scarcely remembers them. Every town, he says, has some old woman, not

known, never spoken to, a thing alone, who each week trades a few
eggs or chickens for groceries; so, he recalls—mostly as a datum for
generalization—did the town of his boyhood. He remembers from
those days only her appearance, at first. Next he recovers her name
and the historical details of her birth, bondage, and marriage. There-
after, gradually, her full personal sensations become his own. He feels
with her the bondage to "horses, cows, pigs, dogs, men." Once this
communion is effected, an arc swings from her life to his own: as he
evokes her death, he recalls that he too once faced a circling pack
of dogs on a freezing day. Finally, their lives converge directly as the
narrator remembers that he, as a boy, saw the body of the "old"
woman transformed by death into that of a young girl, wholly beautiful. The boy, it would seem, had even striven to continue the contact
of their lives, for he had later been drawn to the abandoned farm-
house and had seen there two dogs still prowling, still waiting to be
fed. From these recollections (or this created fiction), the man extracts
the statement that the woman had fed animal life, and claims that
her story is a beautiful "whole" which he heretofore had been unable
to comprehend.

But his statement is flat, largely because he—the explicator or
creator—is unaccounted for. Also, the transformation of the woman
is absent, save in a merely pitiable application (only in death was
she other than a drudge for animal hungers).

It therefore becomes clear that the story is really concerned not
with the woman alone, but with the receiving (here, a creating) consciousness—the "I" of the story. His progress is revealing. Like the
townspeople, the German family, and the Grimes men, he had at
first seen only an anonymous thing (in the words later used to describe her corpse, "no one knew who she was"): one "old woman,"
no different from her kind in any other town. Some few historical
details collect around her, but he still recalls her with indifference.
As he nears his own experience through rendering hers, however, he
fully enters into her life as an *old* woman, realizing now that she was
blank only because life had been drained from her. Their lives converge, as we have seen, culminating in the sense of revelation the narrator feels in seeing the unknown woman's body, perfected in death,
which permits him to see the *young* woman and, beyond her, the freed
human being behind the anonymous thing called "Mrs. Grimes." This
wholeness of realization had, however, to await the mature man's
creation, for the boy had seen only two different women, both to
some extent "unknown" and unrelated one to the other, and both
senses of the woman had faded from his memory.

The narrator has progressed from blank observation of historical
fragments, through pity, to whole knowledge. But that knowledge

is not of the old woman, primarily; it is of himself. The story is, in almost every sense, about him as well as by him. Not only had the old woman and her experience been insignificant, merely historical, but so as well had his own experience, heretofore. He had not known that his experience of the death ritual of the dogs had human relationship and meaning; he had not known that his seeing the dead woman in the snow was no mere event, but rather definition for him of the mystery and beauty of woman. The creation of the woman's story, the discovery (through sympathy and communion) of *her* self, leads him into whole recognition of *his* being. He is no longer "I" as a statistic, a recorder of isolated experiences. With her, because of her, he becomes complete; his own experiences now take on significant human relationship, symbolic fullness. In reaching to and beyond the unknown woman resident in the labeled thing, he finds or constructs the "I" which is not only part of what he has met but also the human center wherein experience achieves meaning.

It is important to note that this process of discovery existed, in stunted form, for the men of the town who were present at the death scene. When they had discovered the woman, nameless in the snow, she had been for them all a "beautiful young girl." But we may suspect that for the men, as for the young boy, the recovered name of the woman—"Mrs. Grimes"—had destroyed or erased the ideal beauty they had witnessed. Only the one mature man recovers and absorbs the two aspects of the woman. Anderson has through him led us to a further emphasis upon this consciousness. The narrator is now revealed as an artist in the essential gesture of art: creation, minting from his own and others' objective experiences the personal expression of meaning, the personal ingathering to form. Such an act justifies the ascription of "music" to the story, and the feeling of the creator that he has given coherence and beauty to unrelated fragments.

In "Death in the Woods," then, the discovery of "I" necessarily involves the artistic expression of that discovery. The process whereby human sympathy gives rise to self-discovery is presented as one creative act. There is no realized "I" until entry has been gained into general human meaning, just as experience remains mere history until the significant "I" emerges.

Anderson's interior explanation of "meaning" is revealed to be only a preliminary statement. It perhaps indicates an attempt on his part to give firmness and resolution to the story, conscious as he was of objections that his stories evaporated or collapsed. But the attempt was surely misguided. This story actually is uncharacteristically stable and dynamic, largely because of the narrator's progress from recorder to creator. Instead of clarifying the story, Anderson's explicit comment obscures its real concern, which is not the death of the old woman but the creation her history gives rise to. Only in that creation is she given her due.

The creative narrator of this story is not, as is usually the case with narrators in Anderson's stories, involved with his subject through personal concerns, familial relation, or friendship. The distance between them, however, serves to enhance their sympathetic contact; they have only disinterested humanity in common. Even their shared experiences, being so different in cause, are unrelated save in that most general, yet finally most immediate, of relationships. Such distance permits this narrator—one among Anderson's "oral" narrators who is "deeply involved in the outcome of his own story" [5]—to achieve a similarly paradoxical contact-through-distance with his audience. The story is not "told" to any assumed audience direct. Instead its process of growth and contact is discovered by the audience, through the act itself rather than through the narrator's relation of the act. The audience is invited to enter as individuals into a process almost identical with that of the narrator and to reach with him for contact with another life. The narrator's own discovery, conveyed for the most part in intensely simple and quiet repetitions of statement that indicate a range of feeling from vague bafflement to a nearly mute, consoling sympathy with suffering, is so little an objective story, so much a tender and half-inarticulate gesture of caring, that the audience must in turn become private, groping beings directly involved in the narrator's action (see Howe, pp. 149–53). The unacknowledged audience is asked, by such a style, to share directly not only the narrator's responses but his act of discovering and creating those responses. The very distance and privacy of the narrator's record become its insurance of personal reception from an audience.

It is noteworthy that a first-person creative narrator does not appear in the other versions of the story. Nor does such a narrator-artist appear elsewhere in Anderson (although he himself sometimes acts as such, with results that we will see later), save perhaps in George Willard, who gives of himself to Winesburg but gains much more from it; out of its passionate failures he constructs a whole being in himself and could not, we may suppose, do so without them. But in Willard there is little of the artist. He absorbs meaning; he does not create it.

"Death in the Woods" exhibits striking parallels with Anderson's occasional aesthetic propositions. His reflections upon "self" and "imagination," which occur in nearly all his statements upon art, are—after some reservations—almost a critical prescription for the method of this story.

[5] Irving Howe, *Sherwood Anderson,* American Men of Letters Ser. (New York: William Sloane Associates, 1951), p. 149.

His statements upon "self" are so simple as to seem at first contradictory. As humans, and especially as artists, he holds, men must get rid of self, but at the same time the whole task of art is to gain knowledge of self. "Self" in the first sense clearly means self-concern, self-interest, failure to "connect"; it is "the grand disease . . . we all are trying to lose." [6] To lose that restricting self through sympathy with others is to find the true self: "Man cannot think clearly of self, cannot see himself except through others. The self you seek, the true self you want to face, to accept, perhaps to love, is hidden away. . . . It is everywhere in others" (*Memoirs*, p. 6). The achievement of this whole, generous, fully human self seemed to Anderson to rest with art, which, he felt, was "likely to get you to thinking more and more of others . . . leading you more and more out of yourself"; only in others did "life [go] on" (*Letters*, pp. 433, 287). The self surrendered into and discovered in others was, for Anderson, the signal gift of the artist: "How people ever lose themselves who are not artists I do not know" (*Letters*, p. 167). In telling of his first conviction of success in art, with the story "Hands," he writes significantly, "There was a story of another human, quite outside myself" which, when accomplished, gave him for the first time "belief in self" (*Memoirs*, pp. 279–80). The artist's self is gained only through imaginative sympathy with other human lives, an act which is, for Anderson, the fundamental premise of art.

Yet this communion is by no means a purely social gesture. Anderson repeatedly insists that his concern is only for the individual man, and, moreover, for that man as an imaginative rather than as an historical realization; the expression of sympathy was to result in artistic rather than political or social expression. "Attempting to feel toward others in the mass," he held, "is an attempt to . . . feel in a vacuum" (*Memoirs*, p. 497). Furthermore, he wanted not the biographical unraveling of another person but his "essential," immediate revelation. During his apprenticeship as a Chicago writer, he says, he saw many a person's "whole life story" by a "single glance into the face" (*Memoirs*, p. 208); once such an intuitive realization has occurred, he told a college audience, "I cannot ever even see him or her again" (*Reader*, p. 338). The artist, in short, surrenders himself to the imaginative revelations from others in order to give not aid, but understanding and expression, to their experiences. In turn, he believed his stories could reach out to the "hidden voices in others," or inform the original object of his received meaning: "It may be that is all we are after—that he shall know" (*Letters*, pp. 53, 357).

This belief that the essential human self can be discovered only through the surrender of self-concern, especially and perhaps only

[6] Howard Mumford Jones and Walter B. Rideout, *Letters of Sherwood Anderson* (Boston: Little, Brown, 1953), p. 167.

by the artist, is pursued at length in terms of Anderson's own career in *A Story Teller's Story*,[7] a work unreliable as autobiography but acceptable enough in its record of an "American man striving to become an artist, to become conscious of himself, filled with wonder concerning himself and others," through which process "the life outside oneself is all, everything" (pp. 307, 290). The boy and youth turn to selfish, escapist dreams of personal glory, but the young man is the while being instructed in the loss of self by two sufferers, Judge Turner and Alonzo Berners, who have the capacity to "inject into [confessions] the essence of truth" and to enter "into [a] man's thoughts" in order to give him "sympathetic understanding without sentimentality" (pp. 162, 247). Dedicated to like reception of human needs, the beginning writer attempts "a more direct and subtle expression of our common lives than we have ever yet had" (p. 324). Later, the acknowledged author, practicing a kind of negative capability activated by sympathy, opposes the professional writer who serves only his own success: "a peculiar . . . credulousness must result to the writer" when he divorced himself from "actual life," and "such a writer woke . . . to find himself irrevocably dead" (p. 354). We should note that Anderson believed such contact with others would preserve "essential" reality; he insists repeatedly that in this way the artist avoids any flight into the past or escape into dream.

Part of Anderson's dedication to "actual life" involved his using only American materials, the source of his being and his experience. The American artist, he held, must "stay, in spirit at least, at home" (*Story*, p. 385); in one sense this decision was the last measure of selflessness, for it carried with it the great difficulty of expressing lives barren of tradition and interrelation (Epilogue, *Story*). However, the nature of such lives, once felt, elevated their need for sympathy into an imperative, for no other means of reaching them could succeed. Eventually Anderson's aim of expressing the lonely American's "secret inner life" (*Story*, p. 388) led him to an ambitious corollary: infidelity in representing such lives would be "betraying all of life," whereas fidelity to them through human sympathy could "in the end, pull mankind out of its mess" (*Letters*, p. 388).

These somewhat pretentious attitudes are really little more than extensions of Anderson's belief that the "truth" of a man must be derived from an exact reception of his inner self, and that this truth was not manufactured by the writer but received in inarticulate form direct from experience. The writer had simply to permit his words to express what life mutely offered him. In that reception, however, the artist is dangerously passive, as we will see; for the most part, "loss of self" cannot produce art, but only its condition.

---

[7] New York, 1924; page references following are to this work.

*Imagination* has in Anderson's usage a meaning akin to that of *self*, both involving the private, "essential" areas of human consciousness. The character of *imagination*, however, raised serious problems, for the term drew attention to active creation rather than the somewhat passive reception of "tales" from other "selves." For Anderson, *imagination* or *fancy* stand always as the opposites of fact, and are the sole agents of truth about men: "men do not exist in facts. They exist in dreams" (*Memoirs*, p. 9). Even the historical elements of his own life were transformed into whatever Anderson "felt them" imaginatively to be (*Memoirs*, p. 8). The imaginative world alone is real for the artist, for only by such "lying" (so far as literal fact was concerned) could he reach essential truth; but it also is the only real world for any men, whose lives in every case are "lived out there in the imaginative world" (*Letters*, pp. 100, 436). It is in that world that the central meaning of the man—his desires, hopes, fears, beliefs—exists. For this reason, Anderson sometimes yearned to write a story without "physical action" (*Letters*, p. 441), for he could then be most true, or most relevant, to his characters' imaginations.

However, these terms were for Anderson ambivalent, capable of suggesting not only essential as opposed to "factual" truth about men, but suggestive also of falsehood, escape, and selfish dream, as was charged against the imagination of the young man in *A Story Teller's Story*. A more satisfactory sense of the artistic imagination as Anderson conceived it is conveyed by *intuition*, which he used as a synonym for imagination (*Letters*, p. 225). If we limit the meaning of *intuition* to his sense of the artistic imagination—that of the acutely perceptive understanding of one person by another—we can move near the center of his practice in fiction, and the rare success he achieved in stories such as "Death in the Woods."

In the first place, reliance upon intuition tended almost of necessity to produce a static condition in many of his works. Anderson himself unwittingly pointed to the danger when he described the impulse to such imagination: "little illuminating . . . things happened" in life; "the true history of life is but a history of moments" (*Story*, pp. 437, 309); in Chicago, "minute little happenings in the lives of many people" were "revealed" to him (*Letters*, p. 19). Frequently these revelations were called subtle, queer, or strange. Although illuminations of this unusual sort avoid "plot," which Anderson despised, they are on the other hand limited to a brief flash of understanding for a fixed state of consciousness.

Second, intuition could not completely achieve that sympathetic contact Anderson so wished for. The "reality" or truth of the intuition is referable only to the intuiting mind. Although the intuition may be virtually true in its own terms, it may have no real contact with the truth of the object of intuition at all; in any case, the object of intuition becomes almost irrelevent, once the intuition is formed. Anderson, perhaps again unwittingly, sensed this difficulty upon one occasion. In insisting that an unnamed writer had not got close to reality, he explained that the man "had seemed to me to have very little to give out of himself . . . [he] had confused the life of reality with the life of the imagination . . . imagination will always remain separated from the life of reality" (*Reader*, p. 343). The key word here is "himself"; reality lay not in realistic detail applied to the object, but in the validity of the writer's response.

Third, the writer might eventually be driven back to autobiography or fragmentary impressions autobiographical in nature. Autobiography becomes the ultimate end of intuition: "I have felt" replaces "They have been or known." Fixed perceptions will tend to replace artistic imitation. In this area, too, Anderson at times sensed the danger of his position. In his middle and later career, he spoke at times of putting "clothes" on his characters, and of using in his novels "more mind" instead of depending so utterly "on pure feeling" (*Letters*, p. 333).

Fourth, dependence of intuition could, and probably did, reduce the problem of form and style to the accidental nature of the intuition itself. The product of such helplessness on the part of the writer may have been impatient remarks such as these: "I have . . . tried to work out of pure feeling, having the conviction that . . . the form I wanted would follow," and "Form is, of course, content. It is nothing else, can be nothing else" (*Letters*, pp. 331, 202). Again, Anderson on some occasions perceived that the artist himself must be finally responsible for formal control of his materials. Expression might, he conceded, itself create feeling, apart from the object (*Letters*, p. 324). He could conceive also of the artist's impressing order upon the disorganized "life of reality," and making his tale "true and real to the theme, not to life" (*Reader*, p. 345).

These several glimpses by Anderson into the danger of reliance upon intuition alone are comparatively rare. The uncritical acceptance of "imagination" as the sole agency of art is, on the other hand, almost always on his lips. The logical end of such a principle is found in Anderson's "Father Abraham," which in many ways fulfills his notions of art when the reservations shown above were not allowed to operate. The nature of this fragment is made quite clear by Anderson's description of the work in his letters: "Now I am frankly going to make my own story. . . . I want [Lincoln] on my own terms, as I understand such a man, having come from the same kind of background," and "The thing projected is not a life, but an attempt to make felt the final opening out of that strange, grotesque, sweet man" (*Letters*, pp. 125, 121). The characteristic Anderson intuitive sympathy is here apparent, but also at once apparent is the possessive impelling of the artist's own experience and intuition upon an object. In effect, Lincoln would be what Anderson felt—felt not about Lincoln, but in and of himself. Only by such reliance upon his own feeling could he have been induced to transfer the "Death in the Woods" incidents into an expression of Lincoln, and to have used them to explain Lincoln's sympathy. The same reliance upon intuition rather than imitation no doubt helps to explain Anderson's steady return to autobiography, in *Tar, A Story Teller's Story,* his *Notebook,* and the *Memoirs,* to say nothing of the *Letters,* many of which are fragments of autobiography.

The reservations shown above did, however, operate with fine effect in some of his best works, producing there a control and ordering of both selfless sympathy and momentary intuition. By displacing his direct feeling into a first-person narrator, or into the effect of intuitions revealed at second hand to a boy who grows in consciousness under their effect (the George Willard of Winesburg), or into the awakening personal and artistic process of the narrator of "Death in the Woods," he seems to me to have achieved the goal he established. Sympathy is developed as discovery and growth in a character—as imitation—rather than as static intuition by the author. The points of correspondence between his adjusted artistic beliefs and "Death in the Woods" are striking.

In "Death in the Woods," the narrator surrenders self, only to gain it. By his imaginative *and* creative communion with the woman—by discovering her—he discovers a greater reality within himself. Only in the narrator's creative imagination (going far beyond bare intuition, which really stopped with the realization that she fed animal life) can his experience of the woman both as "Mrs. Grimes" and the girl in the snow become one meaning. Only in the exercise of creative imagination can his experience of himself—as the boy seeing the woman's body, the young man facing a circle of dogs, the older man bearing still an ideal picture of woman—become whole. The story so nearly parallels Anderson's personal and artistic beliefs operating under the fine control of an artistic discipline that it becomes almost a practice of those beliefs. We may even tentatively suggest that Anderson's unsuccessful short stories fail in the degree to which his practice fell short of those beliefs, as qualified above. They may perhaps stand as failures to transform self and actual occurrence into an imaginative reality that is carefully moved beyond the artist's own autobiographical "feeling."

# Sherwood Anderson

## *by Lionel Trilling*

I find it hard, and I think it would be false, to write about Sherwood Anderson without speaking of him personally and even emotionally. I did not know him; I was in his company only twice and on neither occasion did I talk with him. The first time I saw him was when he was at the height of his fame; I had, I recall, just been reading *A Story-Teller's Story* and *Tar*, and these autobiographical works had made me fully aware of the change that had taken place in my feelings since a few years before when almost anything that Anderson wrote had seemed a sort of revelation. The second time was about two years before his death; he had by then not figured in my own thought about literature for many years, and I believe that most people were no longer aware of him as an immediate force in their lives. His last two novels (*Beyond Desire* in 1932 and *Kit Brandon* in 1936) had not been good; they were all too clearly an attempt to catch up with the world, but the world had moved too fast; it was not that Anderson was not aware of the state of things but rather that he had suffered the fate of the writer who at one short past moment has had a success with a simple idea which he allowed to remain simple and to become fixed. On both occasions—the first being a gathering, after one of Anderson's lectures, of eager Wisconsin graduate students and of young instructors who were a little worried that they would be thought stuffy and academic by this Odysseus, the first famous man of letters most of us had ever seen; the second being a crowded New York party—I was much taken by Anderson's human quality, by a certain serious interest he would have in the person he was shaking hands with or talking to for a brief, formal moment, by a certain graciousness or gracefulness which seemed to arise from an innocence of heart.

I mention this very tenuous personal impression because it must really have arisen not at all from my observation of the moment

"Sherwood Anderson." From *The Liberal Imagination: Essays on Literature and Society,* by Lionel Trilling (New York: The Viking Press, 1950). Copyright 1941, 1947, © renewed 1969 by Lionel Trilling, Reprinted by permission of The Viking Press, Inc., and Martin Secker & Warburg Limited.

but rather have been projected from some unconscious residue of admiration I had for Anderson's books even after I had made all my adverse judgments upon them. It existed when I undertook this notice of Anderson on the occasion of his death, or else I should not have undertaken it. And now that I have gone back to his books again and have found that I like them even less than I remembered, I find too that the residue of admiration still remains; it is quite vague, yet it requires to be articulated with the clearer feelings of dissatisfaction; and it needs to be spoken of, as it has been, first.

There is a special poignancy in the failure of Anderson's later career. According to the artistic morality to which he and his friends subscribed—Robert Browning seems to have played a large if anonymous part in shaping it—Anderson should have been forever protected against artistic failure by the facts of his biography. At the age of forty-five, as everyone knows, he found himself the manager of a small paint factory in Elyria, Ohio; one day, in the very middle of a sentence he was dictating, he walked out of the factory and gave himself to literature and truth. From the wonder of that escape he seems never to have recovered, and his continued pleasure in it did him harm, for it seems to have made him feel that the problem of the artist was defined wholly by the struggle between sincerity on the one hand and commercialism and gentility on the other. He did indeed say that the artist needed not only courage but craft, yet it was surely the courage by which he set the most store. And we must sometimes feel that he had dared too much for his art and therefore expected too much merely from his boldness, believing that right opinion must necessarily result from it. Anderson was deeply concerned with the idea of justification; there was an odd, quirky, undisciplined religious strain in him that took this form; and he expected that although Philistia might condemn him, he would have an eventual justification in the way of art and truth. He was justified in some personal way, as I have tried to say, and no doubt his great escape had something to do with this, but it also had the effect of fatally fixing the character of his artistic life.

Anderson's greatest influence was probably upon those who read him in adolescence, the age when we find the books we give up but do not get over. And it now needs a little fortitude to pick up again, as many must have done upon the news of his death, the one book of his we are all sure to have read, for *Winesburg, Ohio* is not just a book, it is a personal souvenir. It is commonly owned in the Modern Library edition, very likely in the most primitive format of that series, even before it was tricked out with its vulgar little ballet-Prometheus; and the brown oilcloth binding, the coarse paper, the bold type crooked on the page, are dreadfully evocative. Even the introduction by Ernest Boyd is rank with the odor of the past, of the day when criticism existed in heroic practical simplicity, when it was all truth against hypocrisy, idealism against philistinism, and the opposite of "romanticism" was not "classicism" but "realism," which—it now seems odd—negated both. As for the Winesburg stories themselves, they are as dangerous to read again, as paining and as puzzling, as if they were old letters we had written or received.

It is not surprising that Anderson should have made his strongest appeal, although by no means his only one, to adolescents. For one thing, he wrote of young people with a special tenderness; one of his best-known stories is called "I Want To Know Why": it is the great adolescent question, and the world Anderson saw is essentially, and even when it is inhabited by adults, the world of the sensitive young person. It is a world that does not "understand," a world of solitude, of running away from home, of present dullness and far-off joy and eventual fulfillment; it is a world seen as suffused by one's own personality and yet—and therefore—felt as indifferent to one's own personality. And Anderson used what seems to a young person the very language to penetrate to the heart of the world's mystery, what with its rural or primeval willingness to say things thrice over, its reiterated "Well . . ." which suggests the groping of boyhood, its "Eh?" which implies the inward-turning wisdom of old age.

Most of us will feel now that this world of Anderson's is a pretty inadequate representation of reality and probably always was. But we cannot be sure that it was not a necessary event in our history, like adolescence itself; and no one has the adolescence he would have liked to have had. But an adolescence must not continue beyond its natural term, and as we read through Anderson's canon what exasperates us is his stubborn, satisfied continuance in his earliest attitudes. There is something undeniably impressive about the period of Anderson's work in which he was formulating his characteristic notions. We can take, especially if we have a modifying consciousness of its historical moment, *Windy MacPherson's Son,* despite its last part which is so curiously like a commercial magazine story of the time; *Marching Men* has power even though its political mysticism is repellent; *Winesburg, Ohio* has its touch of greatness; *Poor White* is heavy-handed but not without its force; and some of the stories in *The Triumph of the Egg* have the kind of grim quaintness which is, I think, Anderson's most successful mood, the mood that he occasionally achieves now and then in his later short pieces, such as "Death in the Woods." But after 1921, in *Dark Laughter* and *Many Marriages,* the books that made the greatest critical stir, there emerges in Anderson's work the compulsive, obsessive, repetitive quality which finally impresses itself on us as his characteristic quality.

Anderson is connected with the tradition of the men who maintain a standing quarrel with respectable society and have a perpetual bone to pick with the rational intellect. It is a very old tradition, for the Essenes, the early Franciscans, as well as the early Hasidim, may be said to belong to it. In modern times it has been continued by Blake and Whitman and D. H. Lawrence. Those who belong to the tradition usually do something more about the wrong way the world goes than merely to denounce it—they *act out* their denunciations and assume a role and a way of life. Typically they take up their packs and leave the doomed respectable city, just as Anderson did. But Anderson lacked what his spiritual colleagues have always notably had. We may call it *mind,* but *energy* and *spiritedness,* in their relation to mind, will serve just as well. Anderson never understood that the moment of enlightenment and conversion—the walking out—cannot be merely celebrated but must be developed, so that what begins as an act of will grows to be an act of intelligence. The men of the anti-rationalist tradition mock the mind's pretensions and denounce its restrictiveness; but they are themselves the agents of the most powerful thought. They do not of course really reject mind at all, but only mind as it is conceived by respectable society. "I learned the Torah from all the limbs of my teacher," said one of the Hasidim. They think with their sensations, their emotions, and, some of them, with their sex. While denouncing intellect, they shine forth in a mental blaze of energy which manifests itself in syntax, epigram, and true discovery.

Anderson is not like them in this regard. He did not become a "wise" man. He did not have the gift of being able to throw out a sentence or a metaphor which suddenly illuminates some dark corner of life—his role implied that he should be full of "sayings" and specific insights, yet he never was. But in the preface to *Winesburg, Ohio* he utters one of the few really "wise" things in his work, and, by a kind of irony, it explains something of his own inadequacy. The preface consists of a little story about an old man who is writing what he calls "The Book of the Grotesque." This is the old man's ruling idea:

> That in the beginning when the world was young there were a great many thoughts but no such thing as a truth. Man made the truths himself and each truth was a composite of a great many vague thoughts. All about in the world were truths and they were all beautiful.
>
> The old man listed hundreds of the truths in his book. I will not try to tell you all of them. There was the truth of virginity and the

truth of passion, the truth of wealth and of poverty, of thrift and of
profligacy, of carelessness and abandon. Hundreds and hundreds were
the truths and they were all beautiful.

And then the people came along. Each as he appeared snatched up
one of the truths and some who were quite strong snatched up a
dozen of them.

It was the truths that made the people grotesques. The old man
had quite an elaborate theory concerning the matter. It was his notion
that the moment one of the people took one of the truths to himself,
called it his truth, and tried to live his life by it, he became a
grotesque and the truth he embraced became a falsehood.

Anderson snatched but a single one of the truths and it made
him, in his own gentle and affectionate meaning of the word, a
"grotesque"; eventually the truth itself became a kind of falsehood.
It was the truth—or perhaps we must call it a simple complex of
truths—of love-passion-freedom, and it was made up of these "vague
thoughts": that each individual is a precious secret essence, often
discordant with all other essences; that society, and more particularly
the industrial society, threatens these essences; that the old good
values of life have been destroyed by the industrial dispensation;
that people have been cut off from each other and even from themselves. That these thoughts make a truth is certain; and its importance is equally certain. In what way could it have become a falsehood and its possessor a "grotesque"?

The nature of the falsehood seems to lie in this—that Anderson's
affirmation of life by love, passion, and freedom had, paradoxically
enough, the effect of quite negating life, making it gray, empty, and
devoid of meaning. We are quite used to hearing that this is what
excessive intellection can do; we are not so often warned that emotion, if it is of a certain kind, can be similarly destructive. Yet when
feeling is understood as an answer, a therapeutic, when it becomes
a sort of critical tool and is conceived of as excluding other activities
of life, it can indeed make the world abstract and empty. Love and
passion, when considered as they are by Anderson as a means of
attack upon the order of the respectable world, can contrive a world
which is actually without love and passion and not worth being
"free" in.[1]

[1] In the preface of *The Sherwood Anderson Reader,* Paul Rosenfeld, Anderson's
friend and admirer, has summarized in a remarkable way the vision of life which
Anderson's work suggests: "Almost, it seems, we touch an absolute existence, a
curious semi-animal, semi-divine life. Its chronic state is banality, prostration, dis-
memberment, unconsciousness; tensity with indefinite yearning and infinitely stretch-
ing desire. Its manifestation: the non-community of cranky or otherwise asocial
solitaries, dispersed, impotent and imprisoned. . . . Its wonders—the wonders of
its chaos—are fugitive heroes and heroines, mutilated like the dismembered

In Anderson's world there are many emotions, or rather many instances of a few emotions, but there are very few sights, sounds, and smells, very little of the stuff of actuality. The very things to which he gives moral value because they are living and real and opposed in their organic nature to the insensate abstractness of an industrial culture become, as he writes about them, themselves abstract and without life. His praise of the racehorses he said he loved gives us no sense of a horse; his Mississippi does not flow; his tall corn grows out of the soil of his dominating subjectivity. The beautiful organic things of the world are made to be admirable not for themselves but only for their moral superiority to men and machines. There are many similarities of theme between Anderson and D. H. Lawrence, but Lawrence's far stronger and more sensitive mind kept his faculty of vision fresh and true; Lawrence had eyes for the substantial and even at his most doctrinaire he knew the world of appearance.

And just as there is no real sensory experience in Anderson's writing, there is also no real social experience. His people do not really go to church or vote or work for money, although it is often said of them that they do these things. In his desire for better social relationships Anderson could never quite see the social relationships that do in fact exist, however inadequate they may be. He often spoke, for example, of unhappy, desperate marriages and seemed to suggest that they ought to be quickly dissolved, but he never understood that marriages are often unsatisfactory for the very reasons that make it impossible to dissolve them.

His people have passion without body, and sexuality without gaiety and joy, although it is often through sex that they are supposed to find their salvation. John Jay Chapman said of Emerson that, great as he was, a visitor from Mars would learn less about life on earth from him than from Italian opera, for the opera at least suggested that there were two sexes. When Anderson was at the height of his reputation, it seemed that his report on the existence of two sexes was the great thing about him, the thing that made his work an advance over the literature of New England. But although the visitor from Mars might be instructed by Anderson in the mere fact of bisexuality, he would still be advised to go to the Italian opera if he seeks fuller information. For from the opera, as never from

---

Osiris, the dismembered Dionysius. . . . Painfully the absolute comes to itself in consciousness of universal feeling and helplessness. . . . It realizes itself as feeling, sincerity, understanding, as connection and unity; sometimes at the cost of the death of its creatures. It triumphs in anyone aware of its existence even in its sullen state. The moment of realization is tragically brief. Feeling, understanding, unity pass. The divine life sinks back again, dismembered and unconscious."

Anderson, he will acquire some of the knowledge which is normally in the possession of natives of the planet, such as that sex has certain manifestations which are socially quite complex, that it is involved with religion, politics, and the fate of nations, above all that it is frequently marked by the liveliest sort of energy.

In their speech his people have not only no wit, but no idiom. To say that they are not "real" would be to introduce all sorts of useless quibbles about the art of character creation; they are simply not *there*. This is not a failure of art; rather, it would seem to have been part of Anderson's intention that they should be not there. His narrative prose is contrived to that end; it is not really a colloquial idiom, although it has certain colloquial tricks; it approaches in effect the inadequate use of a foreign language; old slang persists in it and elegant archaisms are consciously used, so that people are constantly having the "fantods," girls are frequently referred to as "maidens," and things are "like unto" other things. These manner-isms, although they remind us of some of Dreiser's, are not the result, as Dreiser's are, of an effort to be literary and impressive. Ander-son's prose has a purpose to which these mannerisms are essential— it has the intention of making us doubt our familiarity with our own world, and not, we must note, in order to make things fresher for us but only in order to make them seem puzzling to us and remote from us. When a man whose name we know is frequently referred to as "the plowmaker," when we hear again and again of "a kind of candy called Milky Way" long after we have learned, if we did not already know, that Milky Way is a candy, when we are told of someone that "He became a radical. He had radical thoughts," it becomes clear that we are being asked by this false naïveté to give up our usual and on the whole useful conceptual grasp of the world we get around in.

Anderson liked to catch people with their single human secret, their essence, but the more he looks for their essence the more his characters vanish into the vast limbo of meaningless life, the less they are human beings. His great American heroes were Mark Twain and Lincoln, but when he writes of these two shrewd, enduring men, he robs them of all their savor and masculinity, of all their bitter resisting mind; they become little more than a pair of sensitive, suffering happy-go-luckies. The more Anderson says about people, the less alive they become—and the less lovable. Is it strange that, with all Anderson's expressed affection for them, we ourselves can never love the people he writes about? But of course we do not love people for their essence or their souls, but for their having a certain body, or wit, or idiom, certain specific relationships with things and other people, and for a depend-able continuity of existence: we love them for being there.

We can even for a moment entertain the thought that Anderson himself did not love his characters, else he would not have so thoroughly robbed them of substance and hustled them so quickly off the stage after their small essential moments of crisis. Anderson's love, however, was real enough; it is only that he loves under the aspect of his "truth"; it is love indeed but love become wholly abstract. Another way of putting it is that Anderson sees with the eyes of a religiosity of a very limited sort. No one, I think, has commented on the amount and quality of the mysticism that entered the thought of the writers of the twenties. We may leave Willa Cather aside, for her notion of Catholic order differentiates her; but in addition to Anderson himself, Dreiser, Waldo Frank, and Eugene O'Neill come to mind as men who had recourse to a strong but undeveloped sense of supernal powers.

It is easy enough to understand this crude mysticism as a protest against philosophical and moral materialism; easy enough, too, to forgive it, even when, as in Anderson, the second births and the large revelations seem often to point only to the bosom of a solemn bohemia, and almost always to a lowering rather than a heightening of energy. We forgive it because some part of the blame for its crudity must be borne by the culture of the time. In Europe a century before, Stendhal could execrate a bourgeois materialism and yet remain untempted by the dim religiosity which in America in the twenties seemed one of the likeliest of the few ways by which one might affirm the value of spirit; but then Stendhal could utter his denunciation of philistinism in the name of Mozart's music, the pictures of Cimabue, Masaccio, Giotto, Leonardo, and Michelangelo, the plays of Corneille, Racine, and Shakespeare. Of what is implied by these things Anderson seems never to have had a real intimation. His awareness of the past was limited, perhaps by his fighting faith in the "modern," and this, in a modern, is always a danger. His heroes in art and morality were few: Joyce, Lawrence, Dreiser, and Gertrude Stein, as fellow moderns; Cellini, Turgeniev; there is a long piece in praise of George Borrow; he spoke of Hawthorne with contempt, for he could not understand Hawthorne except as genteel, and he said of Henry James that he was "the novelist of those who hate," for mind seemed to him always a sort of malice. And he saw but faintly even those colleagues in art whom he did admire. His real heroes were the simple and unassuming, a few anonymous Negroes, a few craftsmen, for he gave to the idea of craftsmanship a value beyond the value which it actually does have—it is this as much as anything else that reminds us of Hemingway's relation to Anderson—and a few racing drivers of whom Pop Geers was chief. It is a charming hero worship, but it does not make an adequate antagonism to the culture which Anderson opposed, and in order to make it compelling and effective Anderson reinforced it with what is in effect the high language of religion, speaking of salvation, of the voice that will not be denied, of dropping the heavy burden of this world.

The salvation that Anderson was talking about was no doubt a real salvation, but it was small, and he used for it the language of the most strenuous religious experience. He spoke in visions and mysteries and raptures, but what he was speaking about after all was only the salvation of a small legitimate existence, of a quiet place in the sun and moments of leisurely peace, of not being nagged and shrew-ridden, nor deprived of one's due share of affection. What he wanted for himself and others was perhaps no more than what he got in his last years: a home, neighbors, a small daily work to do, and the right to say his say carelessly and loosely and without the sense of being strictly judged. But between this small, good life and the language which he used about it there is a discrepancy which may be thought of as a willful failure of taste, an intended lapse of the sense of how things fit. Wyndham Lewis, in his attack in *Paleface* on the early triumphant Anderson, speaks of Anderson's work as an assault on responsibility and thoughtful maturity, on the pleasures and uses of the mind, on decent human pride, on Socratic clarity and precision; and certainly when we think of the "marching men" of Anderson's second novel, their minds lost in their marching and singing, leaving to their leader the definitions of their aims, we have what might indeed be the political consequences of Anderson's attitudes if these were carried out to their ultimate implications. Certainly the precious essence of personality to which Anderson was so much committed could not be preserved by any of the people or any of the deeds his own books delight in.

But what hostile critics forget about Anderson is that the cultural situation from which his writing sprang was actually much as he described it. Anderson's truth may have become a falsehood in his hands by reason of limitations in himself or in the tradition of easy populism he chose as his own, but one has only to take it out of his hands to see again that it is indeed a truth. The small legitimate existence, so necessary for the majority of men to achieve, is in our age so very hard, so nearly impossible, for them to achieve. The language Anderson used was certainly not commensurate with the traditional value which literature gives to the things he wanted, but it is not incommensurate with the modern difficulty of attaining these things. And it is his unending consciousness of this difficulty that constitutes for me the residue of admiration for him that I find I still have.

# Introduction to *Letters of Sherwood Anderson*

## *by Howard Mumford Jones*

G. K. Chesterton once remarked that there is no such thing as a novel by Charles Dickens, but only something cut off from the vast and flowing stream of his personality. In the same way one can assert that there is no such thing as a work of fiction by Sherwood Anderson. The novels are autobiographical, the autobiographical books have in them the elements of fiction, the letters read like the first draft of a novel. There are short stories so compact they might become novels, and there are novels that are at best only dilated short stories. Yet this library, at once unified and variegated, has its common denominator. The books represent facets of Sherwood Anderson, that enigmatic and engaging personality whose friends ranged from Gertrude Stein to the stoneworker near Ripshin farm in Virginia, and whose alternating moods of exaltation and despair are as kaleidoscopic as ever Byron's were.

The letters here printed, most of them for the first time, read like a posthumous novel. But they also read like something buttressed and substantiated by whatever Anderson's books had already told us of the writer. Surely there are not many other instances in which a man's letters thus neatly confirm his works, and his works confirm his letters.

A sample paragraph will illustrate this intimate relationship as well as a dozen could do. Anderson writes:

> I have been to Nebraska, where the big engines are tearing the hills to pieces; over the low hills runs the promise of the corn. You wait, dear Brother; I shall bring God home to the sweaty men in the corn rows. My songs shall creep into their hearts and teach them the sacredness of the long aisles of growing things that lead to the throne of the God of men.

This might come from *Dark Laughter,* or from *Many Marriages,* or from a short story, or it might even be a preliminary note for some-

"Introduction to *Letters of Sherwood Anderson,*" by Howard Mumford Jones. From *Letters of Sherwood Anderson,* ed. by Howard Mumford Jones, in Association with Walter B. Rideout (Boston: Little, Brown and Company, 1953), pp. vii-xviii. Copyright 1953 by Eleanor Anderson. Reprinted by permission of Little, Brown and Company, and Howard Mumford Jones.

thing in *Mid-American Chants*. It appears as a matter of fact in an early letter to Waldo Frank. Of course there are readers who do not like epistolary writing of this sort. It makes them uncomfortable, and they murmur something about posturing before a mental mirror. But others will remark upon the identity of style in the letters with that in the books. Either way, favorably or unfavorably, what you get is Sherwood Anderson.

The qualities of this style are evident. It continues throughout this collection, as if all the letters were written at one time. It is a style that is supple, conversational, vivid, lyrical, having a touch of artifice, having also, perhaps, a touch of the amateur, but it is a style that presents us the author in his habit as he lived. It begins with the first letter and it extends through the last. The first letter is dated 1916 and was written when Anderson was forty; and since there are almost five thousand letters in the great Newberry Library collection, it may reasonably be asked why no earlier letter appears in this collection.

The answer is simple. One day, so to speak, Anderson woke up and said, "I am a writer." As a writer he was born adult or at any rate as mature as he was ever to be. There is no good exhuming letters written by Anderson the businessman, a quite different fellow, and the few letters in the collection about writing and written before 1916 do not say what is said in the letters here printed.

The myth which pictures Sherwood Anderson walking out of his office in the midst of dictating a letter is historically false but symbolically true. When he discovered his purpose in life was not money-making but writing, the discovery was absolute. Of course there was a period of hesitation, of course there was a shy, awkward, hidden apprentice time, of course there were later agonizing episodes of doubt or despair. Some of these darker moods are recorded here and some are recorded in letters not reprinted. Nevertheless, the discovery was final in the sense that among the saints conversion is final. From the time of this discovery our writer was a dedicated spirit, a single, if complex and sometimes divided, personality, which, when it published itself to the world, by the strength of its insistence upon subjective, personal, and unconventional values, aroused the hostility of the genteel and the enthusiasm of youth.

There was in Anderson a combination of simplicity and subtlety that lies in a recognizable Midwestern tradition. You can see it in his attitude toward New York. In an early letter to Waldo Frank you find the awe of the child of Middle America before what he conceives to be the superiority of the East. He returned from a visit to New York, he says, filled with "odd feelings of reverence and humbleness." One thinks of Howells's first visit to the enchanted ground of

New England. Then, in the cycle of letters to Van Wyck Brooks, you can watch the alternation of moods. The friendship with Brooks develops, there is never any doubt about it, but Anderson's attitude is patently ambivalent. He loves Brooks, he urges Brooks to write him more freely, he counsels Brooks about Mark Twain—and Anderson, with some justice, thought he had the "feel" of Clemens as Brooks had not. But he is also a little afraid of Brooks, whom he thought of as a scholar, a college man, an intellectualist, a sophisticate critic with all literature at his command.

Brooks, then, was somebody to be both loved and placated. By 1930 Anderson was writing of the power that Brooks exercised over his (Anderson's) mind, since, precisely as when Brooks had been writing about Mark Twain, Anderson had obediently thought about Twain, so now, when Brooks is writing about Henry James, Anderson reads James. Then, suddenly, another facet of Anderson appears, the subtle side, in a revealing paragraph guaranteed to raise the hackles of every intellectualist critic in the country. Anderson writes:

> You may be interested to know my reactions to some solid weeks of James reading—the feeling of him as a man who never found anyone to love, who did not dare love. I really can't care much for any character after he gets through with it; he, in short, takes my love away from me too.
>
> I've a fancy—can it be true that he is the novelist of the haters? Oh, the thing infinitely refined and carried far into the field of intellectuality, as skillful haters find out how to do.

One's response to this passage may be one of three kinds, perhaps of more. One may, for example, be instantly confirmed in the opinion that Anderson was a minor writer, of limited range, deserving the oblivion contemporary neglect wants to consign him to. Or one can say that East is East and West is West, and in American literature never the twain shall meet. Or, once past the shock of the thing, one can be struck by Anderson's penetration. I suggest there is some truth in each of these responses.

Certainly Anderson's range was limited. (So, for that matter, was Thackeray's.) Out of his voluminous publications it is at least possible that only *Winesburg, Ohio,* and a handful of the short stories will survive, marvelous as some pages in *Tar,* for example, or in *Dark Laughter* may be. Moreover, his Midwestern qualities determine and limit his work and keep him apart from the world of the *Nation* and the *New Republic*—those fellows, he thought, were too analytical—and from the aesthetic movement on the Atlantic Coast. Note, in this connection, a late letter to Paul Rosenfeld, in which Anderson finds it necessary to justify, against his aesthetic friend, an interest in the common man. Finally, but more importantly, the insight is really acute. The very phrasing is Jamesian—"Oh, the thing infinitely refined and carried far into the field of intellectuality, as skillful haters find out how to do" may, to all appearances, exist somewhere in James's prefaces or in the fiction. What is more to the point is the truth in Anderson's remark. There is a real sense in which skillful haters do carry the thing refined far into the field of intellectuality, and there is a real sense in which James is the novelist of the haters, as any prolonged study of Jamesian criticism will by-and-by reveal.

Anderson, though he had the subtlety to make this comment, never carried anything to this pitch of intellectual refinement, not merely because his sensitivity was alien to that of James, but also because, whether James is or is not the novelist of the haters, hatred in this degree was omitted from Anderson's make-up. He was capable of indignation, but that is another thing. "I want," he wrote the Copenhavers in 1934, "to write one joyous book before I die . . . not at all sentimentally joyous, but having in it a deeper joy. . . . Isn't there a deeper lesson God wants us to know, and that we, like perverse children —that's what we are, quite hopelessly children—that we will not know?" In contemporary fiction joy has become unfashionable, and love is seldom discussed except when one is discussing Kierkegaard or Dostoevski. But love and joy are central to Sherwood Anderson.

At this point, of course, the mean sensual man sagely wags his head. Love, he will aver in his ribald way, love is, indeed, the word for a novelist who was married four times, whose works were sometimes banned because of their frank sexuality, and whose writing is supposed in part to have prepared the way for Freudian fiction in the United States. The mean sensual man, however cogent he sounds, is, I think, essentially irrelevant. The point at issue is not eroticism but generosity of spirit. Read the letters to young writers in this book. Read the letters in which Anderson expresses his pleasure in discovering a fine personality or a fine work of art. Or read the letters in which Anderson broods over man's inhumanity to man—those, for example, having to do with the Danville strike. His astonishing statement to Paul Kellogg, in a letter of December 14, 1920, that what the country needs is a new leisure class is at once his protest against the gospel of getting on and his demand that there be a larger American margin for love and joy. (One must remember that in 1920 leisure was not yet a problem, but merely an ideal.)

> I want these men and women to stop me on the road or in the
> city streets and talk with me without feeling that I am keeping them
> from their tasks in some factory or office. . . . I want a body of healthy
> young men and women to agree to quit working, to loaf, to refuse to

be hurried or try to get on in the world—in short, to become intense individualists.

That, he added grimly, is "pretty un-American, and I am afraid the Americanization Committee of my home town will get after me for saying it."

Love and joy, however, are commonly by-products, a truth Anderson recognized only occasionally, as when he wrote Trigant Burrow that

> . . . no man knows himself or can arrive at truth concerning himself except by what seems like indirection. I have a desire to take hold of indirection as a tool and use it in an attempt to arrive at truth.

Usually, however, he tried to attain these ends by direct assault. Hence his feverish wanderings over the earth, his incessant beginning of manuscripts that were never finished, his constant self-examination, his devouring sense of incompleteness. Two or three times he refers to himself as a child. Once he admits (to Van Wyck Brooks) that he is the perpetual adolescent. As such, he says, speaking for his generation, "I do represent much." One thinks of Fitzgerald.

In some sense Sherwood Anderson knew himself better than his critics knew him. He was, indeed, the child, he was, indeed, the perpetual adolescent in the kingdoms of this world. Without debating the question of who the inhabitants of the kingdom of heaven truly are, without entering into the vexed problem of whether the eye of the artist is or is not identical with the eye of the child—I have in mind the parallel between Anderson's prose and the painting of his time—one notes the naïveté of his loneliness and of his moments of joy. The latter were the moments of a child happy in the day. The loneliness is the grievance of a child who fancies he is not wanted. In saying this I do not in the least mean to derogate from the genuineness of either the rapture or the suffering, I am merely trying to particularize his moods.

Take, for example, the letter to Horace Liveright in which he describes *Dark Laughter,* a letter which has all the serious appeal of a child who longs for approval:

> Since you were here, I have been working on it every minute of every day, in fact have kept at it so hard and long that each day when I got through, I was so exhausted I could hardly get up from my desk. . . . You see what I am trying to give you now, Horace, is something of the orchestration of the book. The neuroticism, the hurry and self-consciousness of modern life, and back of it the easy, strange laughter of the blacks. There is your dark, earthy laughter—the Negro, the earth, and the river—that suggests the title.
>
> Bet on this book, Horace, it is going to be there with a bang. I wanted to write you about it again and tell you how I feel about it,

> but I have been so absorbed in the novel itself, tearing away scaffolding, laying new foundations, putting in joists and doorsills, that I could not think of anything but building the novel.

The very metaphor, though Anderson uses it often, suggests playing house. But note especially how, as with children, the intensity of absorption in the play becomes identified with value. The novel must be good because he has tried so hard.

In such moments Anderson's simplicity—a simplicity well-nigh embarrassing—is naked and evident. But there is another, mystical aspect to Anderson which places him with Whitman, Twain, Van Gogh, and Dostoevski—even with the religious mystics. There are many instances of this spiritualized pantheism in the letters, but perhaps the noblest expression is a long letter of comfort addressed to Burton Emmett in 1933. We also, says Anderson, are a part of something, of some incomprehensible thing, and this incomprehensible thing is "the real inner glory of life." I believe, he writes, "that it is this universal thing, scattered about in many people, a fragment of it here, a fragment there, this thing we call love that we have to keep on trying to tap." The whole letter breathes such nobility, it is impossible to leave it. He says, for instance:

> In others life goes on. When I have no more courage, it may be that the person sitting next to me or walking beside me in the street is full of courage. Why shouldn't I ask for it, take it when I get it? There is a curious contradiction here. Sometimes when I go like a beggar asking warmth, comfort and love from another, knowing I do not deserve it, I begin living a little in others, and thus I get away from self.

And again:

> As for the end, I have often thought that when it comes, there will be a kind of real comfort in the fact that the self will go then. There is some kind of universal thing we will pass into that will in any event give us escape from this disease of self.

This is perfect writing. It has the clean line and lofty economy of style of the great French moralists.

The longing to escape from self, the desire to merge with others and with the universe, is central in Anderson's complex outlook. He insists, paradoxically, upon both the need of individuality and the curse of self-consciousness. His desire to transcend mere egoism runs throughout his correspondence. It is clear, from the letters concerning the Hedgerow Theatre or his own interest in playmaking, that the warmth and intimacy of the theater had special attraction for him. Again, we read that an unfinished novel, *Immaturity,* was to have illustrated this overcoming of the self. It was to have been a book that

. . . oozes out over the whole landscape and should be in the end the
kind of book that a man takes to bed with him on bleak winter
evenings. . . . The winds and rains come, and the land is black with
fertility. Men will be born, infinite men of broad girth and cocky
eyes. Escape if you can all the art and intellectual talk.

Inasmuch as Anderson is one of our most expressive commentators
on the nature of art, in this context "art and intellectual talk" connotes
the false separatism of art from existence he disliked in the New York
circles.

What *is* the writer's true self, his dream self or the economic unit
that he is? What is the relation of imaginative work to the world of
bargain and sale? How much shall an artist sacrifice to the market
place? Can an honest man split himself in twain, one half of him
creating after his instincts and the other half becoming a literary carpenter at contractor's labor? This theme also runs throughout the correspondence. One finds Anderson in a panic imploring his agent, or a
publisher, or a magazine editor, or a politician to accept a scheme of
hack work he outlines, for which he can get pay; and in a later letter
one finds him roundly condemning the crassness of this very procedure.
It is interesting to watch him demand support for struggling young
artists—the letter to Otto Kahn is an example—while almost simultaneously he shies away from other well-meant attempts to subsidize
free spirits, fearful that he who pays the piper eventually calls the
tune. If his economic thinking in this regard was both confused and
emotional, who has done any better? The letters in this respect give us
a perfect example of the psychological dislocation of the artist in industrial society, a dislocation the more keenly felt because Anderson
had seen business from the inside and felt a lack of integrity in it.

Another theme haunting the correspondence seems likewise pertinent
here. Anderson dreamed of, but never wrote, a book about Lincoln.
For him Lincoln transcended self, he expressed the social mysticism of
the Middle West; and though Sandburg, not Anderson, was to write
the work which supremely set forth the Midwestern interpretation of
our secular saint, Anderson was perpetually drawn to him. Note also,
in this connection, a passage in a letter to Paul Rosenfeld, which runs:

I take these little, ugly factory towns, these big sprawling cities into
something. I wish it would not sound to[o] silly to say I pour a dream
over it, consciously, intentionally, for a purpose. I want to write
beautifully, create beautifully, not outside but in this thing in which
I am born, in this place where, in the midsts of ugly towns, cities,
Fords, moving pictures, I have always lived, must always live.

This was true self-knowledge. Wander as he might, Anderson remained perpetually the troubled Midwesterner, alternately revolting

against industrialism and finding poetry in machines, rejoicing in American productive energy and pitying the joyless workers, believing both in the mass and in the individual, yet acutely conscious of the limitations in these antithetical concepts. His radicalism was a function of this need for self-transcendence, and it expressed itself confusedly, as in the vague, inconclusive symbolism of *Marching Men*. His radicalism was never essentially economic or political—not once but many times he repudiated the Communists—for it was always mystical, the radicalism of the poet, the child, and the pragmatist. I think it still has much to say to the thirst after democracy in our times.

Radicalism in another sense was deep-sunk in Anderson's own nature, and permits us to have from him a fresh view of the nature of the imaginative process itself. The great prefaces by Henry James, prefaces which only Ellen Glasgow's book, *A Certain Measure,* can approach in illumination, are by common consent the most revealing statement in American letters of the way of the writer with his material. Great as these essays are, they are inevitably the expression of a second stage in the creative process—the stage wherein the writer reflects upon what he has done in the perspective of time and tells us of the relation he now sees among intention, craftsmanship, fulfillment, and reception. They show us, they admirably show us, how best to understand the work of art. A very large part of Anderson's discourse in these letters concerns an earlier and more primitive stage in the creative process. He brings us down to a more primary level of the psychology of writing— to writing as obsession, to writing as rhythm, to writing as a function in large degree of a subconscious, certainly of a nonrational, part of the psyche.

Thus of *Marching Men* he tells us that the concept appealed strongly to "my rather primitive nature," that

> . . . the beat and rhythm of the thing would come and go; a thousand outside things would flow in. I worked madly; then I threw the book away. Again and again I came back to it. In the end I had no idea as to whether it was good or bad. I only knew that the thing was out of me. . . .

Three or four times he compares literary composition to the experience of pregnancy and deliverance, and also to the poles of maleness and femaleness in life. After *Mid-American Chants* had, as he thought, liberated him from the reproach of "sentimental liberalism," he again insisted upon the primacy of rhythm—

> I want to achieve in it rhythm of words with rhythm of thought. . . . In making this book I have felt no call to responsibility to anything but my own inner sense of what is beautiful in the arrangement of words and ideas . . .

and he distinguished an outward technique from an inward technique, a kind of compulsion to truth:

> One day I found out that when I sat down to write, it was the more difficult to lie. The lie lay before one on the paper. It haunted one at night.

"I have," he said, "a great fear of phrase-making, for words are very tricky things," and "I do not want to make them rattle."

When the thing came off, when the divine afflatus was upon him, the effect was like the effect of vision on the mystic. He always remembered that the writing of "Hands" was such a moment of obsession; later he described another such seizure:

> I have begun working again and yesterday, for the 1st time in months, sat at my desk, here in this little country hotel, for hours with no consciousness of time passing, completely lost, the words and sentences with a fine rhy[th]mic flow, ideas coming like flights of birds, for the time, at least, completely happy. No. Happiness is not the word. To be happy there must be consciousness of self as happy, and in this state there is no self.

The trouble with the creative impulse, he said later, is that

> . . . it tends to lift you up too high into a sort of drunkenness and then drop you down too low. There is an artist lurking in every man. The high spots for the creative man come too seldom.

When they did not come, however they were desired, the result was an almost unbearable desolation. A sequence of letters to Paul Rosenfeld, in 1927, graphically records this spiritual dryness; and another sequence, addressed to his son John, perhaps unique in literature, adjures the son as a beginning artist to avoid some of these sorrows:

> You have to pay dearly for being an imaginative person. Learn to give as little time as possible to self-pity. It is ten times as important to be devoted as it is to succeed. You will be a fool if you think ever that you have succeeded in the arts.

The self, that old enemy, was again the perplexing element in the problem. As he wrote John—

> I presume it is the power of losing self. Self is the grand disease. It is what we are all trying to lose. . . . How people ever lose themselves who are not artists I do not know.

In the end, "perhaps a man has to manufacture his own interest in life."

> A man who is really sensitive has moments that lift him up higher than the average man. He wants to stay up there and can't. Then

he begins to feel life is unfair to him. He broods. Self becomes all-important to him.

For the paradox of self was that it was at once the instrument and the obstacle of the artist, who is

> . . . after all, partly a product of his environment. He can do nothing with nature, cannot draw close unless sensitized. If sensitized, everything beats in on him. He does not escape the general tone and mood of the world in any event.

The only solution to the enigma was simplicity; and his complaint against writing as carried on in America was that it was smart. "Eternal lack of force taking itself out in smartness or cleverness and thinking they've done something," he said of some of the more "sophisticated" of his contemporaries. As for theories of art and aesthetics—

> Well, talking about it all is a little like handling a flower. It gets wilted or soiled. One speaks of the matter and then, right away, feels a little stuffy. I can't tell exactly why I think this is true, [yet] the one thing I detest, because it makes me feel detestable, is preaching or being a wise man or seer.

The best thing was to go among living people—human beings, he wrote a librarian, are "my library"—and then, as he said to Dreiser, "when we are simply telling, as we should really always be trying to tell, the simple story of lives, we are doing our best service."

Much could be said of Anderson's feeling for painting, of his incessant wish to unite the two arts in a common vision. But perhaps the best statement of how, in his experience, a work of art comes into being is found in the following passage, again from a letter to John Anderson.

> I used to think that the thing sought by the painter o[r] the sculptor was already in the stone or on the canvas, that something stood between it and the artist. There was what I thought of as the disease of individuality. I don't think this any more. This I have found out: there is in me, as in you, or any working artist, always the danger of a kind of statement. It may be that this only comes because we ourselves, as individuals, get between ourselves and the thing sought. Of course others thrust themselves in there too, but that is not what I am thinking about now. This I have found out from experience, that these floating ideas, always drifting through the mind, if given free play by action, seem to become definite and alive. As the painter might make an infinite number of sketches, often rapidly, but nevertheless making them, as a writer puts down on paper the same kind of passing things, something does often result. Often a sudden realization of beauty. So in human relationships.

For him, therefore, all doctrine of external form was meaningless. He sought, instead, the under surface, the subconscious meaning of a human situation; and form, as he told Dwight Macdonald in a long and unfortunately somewhat illegible letter, is not something imposed, but is brought to life by the mystery of creation itself. So far as Anderson could explicate it, he tried, in the letter to Mary Chryst Anderson here reprinted, to show at once his debt to Gertrude Stein ("she taught me to recognize the second person in myself, the poet-writing person"), and the mechanism of imaginative work, not mechanical and automatic, yet

> . . . all of the more beautiful and clear, the more plangent and radiant writing I have done, has all been done by a kind of secondary personality that at such times takes possession of me.

In the perspective of time it becomes increasingly clear that the generation of the 1920's stood on the watershed that divides the old American literature from the new. The pre-World-War-I tradition, despite notable exceptions, was Apollonian; the generation of Anderson, Dionysiac. The tradition of form, of propriety, of idealism ended, so to speak, with the sinking of the *Lusitania*; the world of subrational psychology, of the mixed genre and the indeterminate work of art— the world, for better or worse, of modern writing—began about the time Sherwood Anderson discovered that he was a writer, but that a writer could go to no school and follow no program. To a surprising degree, therefore, the roots and beginnings of our contemporary notions of literature and of the creative process are to be found in these occasional letters by a man described as "groping," "confused," "immoral," and various other pejorative things by timid or genteel critics. We, for whom Anderson's experimentalism opened paths, are not so likely to condemn experiments or even failures from which we have profited. The letters of Sherwood Anderson stand at the fountainhead of American modernism.

# Sherwood Anderson: American Mythopoeist

## by Benjamin T. Spencer

### I

It is not surprising that during the past generation Sherwood Anderson's literary reputation should have suffered an eclipse, for the renascent American literature which he envisioned and in part exemplified half a century ago was rooted in the soil and in a sense of wonder and mystery alien both to the realism which preceded it and to the sophisticated naturalism that followed it. To be sure, his work has rarely evoked the degree of condescension found in the dictum of Miss Susan Sontag, who, somewhat ironically upbraiding Anderson for taking himself too seriously, recently dismissed *Winesburg, Ohio,* as "bad to the point of being laughable." In view of her addiction to the New Wave of French fiction, with its commitment to sensory surfaces and psychic fragmentation as contrasted with Anderson's concern for inwardness and identity, her verdict is inevitable.[1]

That such a reversal in his literary fortunes would occur Anderson himself surmised over forty years ago. Acknowledging himself to be not a great writer but rather a "crude woodsman" who had been "received into the affection of princes," he prophesied that "the intellectuals are in for their inning" and that he would be "pushed aside." And indeed, though more judiciously than Miss Sontag, estimable critics have concurred in assigning Anderson a lesser rank than did his early contemporaries. Soon after the author's death Lionel Trilling, while confessing a "residue of admiration" for his integrity and his authenticity as the voice of a groping generation, nevertheless adjudged him too innocent of both the European literary heritage and the role of ideas in psychic maturity. More recently Tony Tanner, in an analysis of the naïveté of American writers, found in Anderson a distressing

"Sherwood Anderson: American Mythopoeist," by Benjamin T. Spencer. From *American Literature,* 41 (March 1969), 1–18. © 1969 by Duke University Press, Durham, North Carolina. Reprinted by permission of the publisher and the author.

1 S. Sontag, "Notes on 'Camp,'" in *Against Interpretation* (New York: Farrar, Straus, 1966), p. 284.

example of such writers' penchant for "uncritical empathy" and for dealing in discrete moments of feeling without that "exegetical intelligence" which has shaped all durable literature.[2]

Between these two extremes of detraction grounded on the one hand in an aversion to "meaning" and on the other in an intellectualization of art through formal control and complexity, Anderson has consistently had, as a recent volume assessing his achievement shows, his body of apologists. Faulkner, Van Wyck Brooks, Irving Howe, Malcolm Cowley have been among those who have found a distinctiveness and a distinction in the best of his work, especially when it is related to the literary atmosphere of the first quarter of the century. Indeed, Anderson himself throughout his career could never separate his writing from its national context, and this cisatlantic cultural context impelled him toward the mythic, toward the archetypal and the elemental, rather than toward the urban and sociological. Repeatedly he spoke of his love for America, sometimes as "this damn mixed-up country of ours," sometimes as a land "so violent and huge and gorgeous and rich and willing to be loved." Moreover, he thought of himself as representatively and comprehensively "the American Man," as he wrote Brooks, explaining that by virtue of his varied occupational background he could take into himself "salesmen, businessmen, foxy fellows, laborers, all among whom I have lived." But not only did he feel himself to be "a composite essence of it all"; he also could experience, he declared with Whitman-like assurance, an "actual physical feeling of being completely *en rapport* with every man, woman, and child along a street" and, in turn on some days "people by thousands drift[ed] in and out" of him. Like Whitman, too, he contained multitudes and contradictions; he was, as he said, a compound of the "cold, moral man of the North" and "the warm pagan blood of the South . . . striving to become an artist" and "to put down roots into the American soil and not quite doing it." [3]

In reiterating through the second and third decades of the century his view that the crucial deficiency among American writers was that "Our imaginations are not yet fired by love of our native soil," Anderson had in mind of course more than the affirmation of a simple American pastoralism. The "soil," indeed, included the darker lives of the

2 S. Anderson, *Saturday Review of Literature*, IV, 364–65 (December 3, 1927); *Letters*, ed. H. M. Jones and W. B. Rideout (Boston: Little, Brown, 1953), pp. 36, 38, 108; L. Trilling, *Kenyon Review*, III, 293 ff. (Summer 1941); IV, 171 (Spring 1942); T. Tanner, *The Reign of Wonder* (Cambridge, Eng.: Cambridge U. Press, 1965), pp. 206, 209 ff.

3 See *The Achievement of Sherwood Anderson*, ed. Ray Lewis White (Chapel Hill: U. of North Carolina Press, 1966), *passim*; S. Anderson, *Letters*, pp. 95, 104, 275; *A Story Teller's Story* (New York: B. W. Huebsch, Inc., 1924), pp. 307, 308.

people who lived on it or near it; or, as he wrote to Dreiser in the mid-1930's, the redemption of such lives must lie so far as the writer is concerned not in any philosophical or ideological projection from his pen but in telling "the simple story of lives" and by the telling, counteracting the loneliness and "terrible dullness" that afflicted the American people. He had in mind, no doubt, such a story as the first which he had drafted for *Winesburg,* as he later related its genesis in "A Part of Earth"—a story called "Hands," in which he conveys the pathetic misunderstanding of the character whom he described as the "town mystery" of Winesburg, Wing Biddlebaum, whose hands reached out to others like "the wings of an imprisoned bird." Later the same motif is repeated in the hero of *Poor White,* whose loneliness and vague ambition impel him to a restless wandering and finally to an awkward and alienated marriage, and in the heroine of *Kit Brandon,* whose intense loneliness Anderson asserts to be characteristic of American life. Indeed Anderson's return to his native "soil" led him to the discovery of what he called "the loneliest people on earth," and his sensitive treatment of these people has led the novelist Herbert Gold to call him one of the purest poets of isolation and loneliness. To Irving Howe he seemed to have expressed the "myth" of American loneliness. Even with this theme, therefore, the mythopoeic Anderson apparently had initially found his imaginative stance. He was not, of course, in the strict etymological sense of the word a "mythopoeist," a maker of myths; but his imagination achieved its finest expression in narratives such as "Death in the Woods" or in parts of *Dark Laughter* where the preternatural or archetypal not only gave it unity and direction but also evoked a connotative style approaching the idiom of poetry. The term is therefore broadly used here as the most adequately comprehensive one to indicate the orientation and mode of Anderson's fiction as contrasted with those of such contemporary naturalists or realists as Dreiser and Lewis.[4]

## II

This persistent concern with loneliness both in Anderson's own life and in that of his characters, Lionel Trilling has asserted, is in part traceable to his excessive reliance on intuition and observation and to

[4] S. Anderson, *A Story Teller's Story,* p. 79; *Letters,* pp. 344–45, 455; "A Part of Earth," in *The Sherwood Anderson Reader,* ed. Paul Rosenfeld (Boston: Houghton Mifflin, 1947), pp. 321–28; *Memoirs* (New York: Harcourt, Brace, 1942), pp. 6, 184–85; *Kit Brandon* (New York: Scribner, 1936), p. 255; H. Gold, *Hudson Review,* X, 548 ff. (Winter 1957–58); I. Howe, *Sherwood Anderson* (New York: William Sloane Associates, 1951), p. 129.

his unfortunate assumption that his community lay in the "stable and the craftsman's shop" rather than in the "members of the European tradition of thought." That Anderson was only superficially and erratically involved with the literary and philosophical past of Europe is undoubtedly true. As late as 1939 he could declare that he did not know what a "usable past" is, and that his concern was rather to live intensely in the present. In effect Anderson was emphasizing the inductive and the autochthonous as primary in the literary imagination, as Emerson, Thoreau, and Whitman had done before him; or, in anticipation of William Carlos Williams, he was committing himself to the principle that only the local thing is universal. By concentrating on the elemental tensions of provincial life he was assuming, as Mark Twain had done with the Mississippi, that the archetypes of human character and situation would most surely emerge, and that by returning to "nature" or the "soil" American literature would find at once its uniqueness and its authenticity. Hence his dismissal also of recent European art as a model for American artists. How irrelevant is Whistler's pictorial mode, he wrote in the 1920's, to a valid expression of the "rolling sensuous hills . . . voluptuously beautiful" in California; and how silly are those painters who follow Gauguin when the varied life and color of New Orleans is available to them. The "half-sick neurotics, calling themselves artists" as they stumbled about the California hills, apparently resembled the "terrible . . . shuffling lot" of Americans he later observed in Paris. Yet from writers whom he venerated as the great fictional craftsmen of Europe—Turgenev, Balzac, Cervantes—he induced what seemed to him to be the fundamental principle for a durable American literature: indigenous integrity. These authors were "deeply buried . . . in the soil out of which they had come," he asserted in *A Story Teller's Story*; they had known their own people intimately and had spoken "out of them" with "infinite delicacy and understanding." With this indigenous commitment, Anderson believed, he and other American writers could belong to "an America alive . . . no longer a despised cultural foster child of Europe." [5]

Though Anderson found only a limited relevance for the cisatlantic writer in the literary modes and cultural traditions of Europe, he was by no means indifferent to the American past. His involvement lay deeper than the love which he professed to Gertrude Stein for "this damn mixed-up country of ours"; it approached, indeed, a mythic assent to what he viewed as a liberating cultural destiny often reiterated

[5] L. Trilling, *Kenyon Review*, IV, 171 (Spring 1942); I. Howe, *Sherwood Anderson*, pp. 245–46; W. C. Williams, *Selected Essays* (New York: Random House, 1954), pp. 118–19, 132; S. Anderson, *Letters*, pp. 126, 165; *Dark Laughter* (New York: Liveright, 1952), pp. 45, 47; *A Story Teller's Story*, pp. 390, 395.

from the early days of the Republic—a belief in what his younger contemporaries Pound and Fitzgerald praised as the old largeness and generosity which they felt had marked the ante-bellum national character. The substance and inclination of Anderson's nationality may be inferred from the names of the five Americans whom he concluded, in an evening's discussion with his wife, to be the greatest his country had produced: Jefferson, Lincoln, Emerson, Whitman, and Henry Adams. For Lincoln and Whitman, as well as for Twain and Dreiser, he confessed a special affinity because they, with origins like his own, had had to take time to put roots down in a thin cultural soil and, ingenuous and confused, to confront a "complex and intricate world." The somewhat unexpected inclusion of Henry Adams may be accounted for by the common anxiety that both authors felt not only about the shattering effects of the machine on the older American values but also about the redemptive agency of some new mythic force which would bring unity out of multiplicity in American life. A more sustained influence, however, Anderson felt in Whitman, whose attempt to supplant a narrow and repressive Puritanism with large democratic vistas of brotherhood and loving perceptions he believed had been betrayed by later generations of American authors. Like Whitman he tried to project the democratic beyond concept into myth—into man's link with primordial forces of earth and into an eventual return to what the older poet in "Passage to India" had called "reason's early paradise." [6]

Though early in his literary career Anderson was puzzled that Twain had not generally been placed with Whitman "among the two or three really great American artists," he was especially drawn to the Missouri author as a salient example of the American writer's plight and failure. In Twain he perceived a literary pioneer whom the "cultural fellows," as he termed them, had tried in vain to get hold of. Yet ironically, despite Twain's brave achievement and his bold disregard of literary precedent, Anderson sadly observed, he had never been able to attain full literary stature because the America which nurtured him was a "land of children, broken off from the culture of the world." As a part of this, Twain seemed to Anderson to have been caught up in the country's dominant shrillness and cheapness, with his literary talent thereby perverted and dwarfed. But an additional factor in Twain's failure seemed to Anderson to be his voluntary removal during the latter half

[6] S. Anderson, *Letters*, pp. [3], 37, 40–41; cf. B. T. Spencer, "Pound: The American Strain," *PMLA*, LXXXI, 460, 465–66 (December 1966); "Fitzgerald and the American Ambivalence," *South Atlantic Quarterly*, LXVI, 374, 377–80 (Summer 1967); R. L. White, ed., *The Achievement of Sherwood Anderson*, p. 149; S. Anderson, *Windy McPherson's Son* (Chicago: U. of Chicago Press, 1965), pp. 33–40; *Memoirs*, p. 440.

of his literary life to the East, where he became subservient to what the latter termed the "feminine force" of the "tired, thin New England atmosphere." It is not surprising, therefore, that in *Dark Laughter* Anderson, through his hero Bruce Dudley, should charge Twain with deserting the imaginatively rich Mississippi River milieu and reverting to childhood or trivial themes which could be summed up as "T'witchetty, T'weedlety, T'wadelty, T'wum!" By ignoring the "big continental poetry" of rivers before it was choked off by the invasions of commerce, Twain in Anderson's eyes was in part responsible for the fact that the great River had become a "lost river," now "lonely and empty," and perhaps symbolic of the "lost youth of Middle America." Indeed *Dark Laughter* may be viewed as Anderson's mythopoeic projection of the repressed Dionysiac forces which the early Twain at times adumbrated and then gradually abandoned for genteel values and concerns. At the heart of the book is Anderson's elegy for a literary ancestor who should have expressed the mythic force of the heartland but who lost his touch with elemental things.[7]

For Anderson, therefore, America evoked both intense devotion and recurrent despair—perhaps an inevitable dualism in one whose deepest cultural convictions were grounded in an ante-bellum version of the American dream as articulated by his five greatest Americans. Jeffersonian as he essentially was, he inclined to trace the confusion and vulgarity of his age to the displacement of the agrarian base of American society. This older America he could envision in *Windy McPherson's Son* as a kind of pastoral paradise, a land of milk and honey wherein the shocks of abundant corn were "orderly armies" which the American pioneer had conscripted from the barren frontier, as it were, "to defend his home against the grim attacking armies of want." It was this agrarian faith, he wrote in *Mid-American Chants,* that had lured the immigrant races westward and had developed a deep affinity with the earth spirit, with the fields as "sacred places" in whose fertility the impulses to human aggression had vanished. And as small organic centers in this agrarian richness, he felt, there had developed the Midwestern villages, which, in turn, had nurtured a vital individualism whereby both men and women lived with courage and hope and with a pride in craftsmanship and independence such as that joyously possessed by Sponge Martin in *Dark Laughter*. Hence Anderson's characterization of Bidwell, Ohio, the setting of much of *Poor White*: it was a pleasant and prosperous town whose people were like a "great family," and, like those in other Midwestern towns in the 1880's, were undergoing a "time of waiting" as they tried to understand themselves

7 S. Anderson, *Letters,* pp. [3], 31, 33, 34, 41, 43; *Dark Laugher,* chaps. ii, xi, *passim.*

and turned inward to ponder the utopianism of Bellamy and the atheism of Ingersoll.[8]

The snake which had crept into this agrarian Eden and its village culture was, in Anderson's reiterated view, a new reliance on the external benefits supposedly conferred by technological progress rather than on the inner resources conferred by Nature and the Soul on the Emersonian and Thoreauvian and Whitmanian self. On this contest of the humane self and the nonhuman machine most of Anderson's major works revolve—especially *Windy McPherson's Son, Winesburg, Poor White, Dark Laughter,* and *Beyond Desire.* During his youth, Anderson told a college audience in 1939, the increasing obsession with getting ahead had resulted in a pervasive confusion through the identification of happiness with possessions. Inevitably the towns had become tainted with a competitiveness and greed which left them, as he phrased it in *Windy McPherson's Son,* "great, crawling slimy thing[s] lying in wait amid the cornfields." Young Sam McPherson's success in Chicago, like Anderson's, brought its disenchantment with such "blind grappling for gain"; having "realised the American dream" in its perverted form at the end of the century, Sam felt impelled toward the larger quest of seeking truth—toward the risks of that "sweet Christian philosophy of failure [which] has been unknown among us." Because of a ruthless greed whetted by the new industrialism, Anderson suggests in the novel, "Deep in our American souls the wolves still howl." The consequent dehumanization of the old communities could be seen in both city and village. Reflecting on the brutal crowds in New York, Sam is no doubt expressing Anderson's attitude when he concludes that "American men and women have not learned to be clean and noble and natural, like their forests and their wide, clean plains." And in villages like Winesburg, as Anderson declared in his *Memoirs,* the blind faith in machines had not brought beauty but had left a residue of fragmented grotesques—villagers who, as he explains in introducing the stories of *Winesburg,* in the disintegration of the agrarian community had been driven to seize upon some narrow or partial truth and, in a desperate attempt to sustain their lives, to make it an obsessive and destructive absolute. In a disconsolate mood of acceptance Anderson conceded in his *Memoirs* that "it may just be that America had promised men too much, that it had always promised men too much." In effect he was conceding the subversion of a major myth—one fused by his own experience from the old dream of the garden, Jeffersonian agrarianism, Transcendentalism, the repudiation of Puritanism, and

---

8 S. Anderson, *Memoirs,* pp. 87, 289, 396; *Windy McPherson's Son,* pp. 57–58; *Mid-American Chants* (New York: B. W. Huebsch, Inc., 1923), pp. 69–71; *Poor White,* in *The Portable Sherwood Anderson,* ed. Horace Gregory (New York: Viking, 1949), pp. 153–55, 156, 162, 271–72.

the pastoral abundance of the West. His vision of a land where the earth and brotherhood would allow the satisfaction of the basic human desires had yielded to the reality of masses of "perverse children," lost and lonely.[9]

## III

Anderson's mythic focus, however, lay below the national or politico-economic level. America and the West were at last but symbolic media or indices for him, as they had been for the Transcendentalists—transient entities to be valued only to the degree that they proved instrumental in releasing the deific forces or primal satisfactions of man's being. This assumption Anderson made clear in his early days as a writer by insisting in the *Little Review* that the so-called "new note" in American literature was in reality "as old as the world," involving as it did the "reinjection of truth and honesty into the craft" of writing and also the "right to speak out of the body and the soul of youth, rather than through the bodies and souls of master craftsmen who are gone. [¶] In all the world there is no such thing as an old sunrise, an old wind upon the cheeks. . . ." Similarly, as he later recalled in his *Memoirs,* he and other members of the Chicago group during the First World War were, above all, trying "to free life . . . from certain bonds" and "to bring something back," including the "flesh" which the genteel realism of the preceding generation had excluded. In short, they wished to divert American literature from what they conceived to be its secondary focus on the socio-political and redirect it to the primary and recurring experiences—to what Anderson in his later years was willing to call "the great tradition" which, he said, goes on and on and is kept straight only with difficulty. "All the morality of the artist," he concluded, "is involved in it." [10]

Convinced as he was that the greatest obstacle to the return to the "oldness" and the "great tradition" lay in the fidelity to fact espoused by the realistic school, Anderson insisted that American writers look primarily within themselves, for "there is this common thing we all have . . . so essentially alike, deep down the same dreams, aspirations, hungers." In effect Anderson was urging a mythopoetic approach to the same native scenes that Howells and Twain had often depicted. Like Conrad, he believed that "the artist descends within himself" and "ap-

[9] *The Sherwood Anderson Reader,* ed. P. Rosenfeld, pp. 337 ff., 342; S. Anderson, *Windy McPherson's Son,* pp. 66, 98–106, 131, 242, 244, 294, 324, 325; *Memoirs,* pp. 80, 396, 401, 495, 501; *The Achievement of . . . Anderson,* ed. R. L. White, p. 34. For the larger context of the garden myth, see Leo Marx, *The Machine in the Garden* (New York: Oxford U. Press, 1964).

[10] *Little Review,* I, 23 (March 1914); *Memoirs,* pp. 240–45; *Letters,* p. 442.

peals to that part of our being which is not dependent on wisdom" by speaking to "our capacity for delight and wonder, to the sense of mystery surrounding our lives; to our sense of pity, and beauty, and pain. . . ." In the Midwestern lives about him Anderson found the "dreams, aspirations, hungers" which could evoke the "sense of mystery . . . of pity, and beauty, and pain," and the transatlantic understanding and approval which his stories had elicited confirmed his belief that the American writer could best strike the universal note through such an emphasis. That the "subjective impulse" and the imagined world should take precedence for the author over fact he continued to affirm throughout his life, proclaiming consistently the satisfactions that he had found as a "slave to the people of . . . [his] imaginary world." [11]

As the clearest repository of archetypal emotions and situations Anderson, like Hawthorne and Twain before him, used the small town or village for his settings. In the commonplace Midwest world, he wrote in 1918 in "A New Testament," there is a "sense of infinite things." As an illustration of this "sense" he proffered his story "In a Strange Town," in which the persona observes an ordinary couple—a woman and a man accompanying her to place her husband's coffined body on the train. The people are of no importance, he explained in a comment on the story, but they are involved with Death, which *is* "important, majestic." The very strangeness of the town, he also explained, served to afford a kind of aesthetic distance in which the irrelevant and superficial disappeared and the elemental constants of mortality emerged. To be sure, Anderson at times and for the most part in nonfictional works, did view the town, both Midwestern and Southern, in a sociological perspective. But even here he frequently sounded mythic overtones, as he did in his perceptive remark in *Home Town* (1940) that the small community had always been the "backbone of the living thing we call America" because it lies halfway between the cities (which breed ideas) and the soil (which breeds strength).[12]

On this soil as an autochthonous matrix Anderson consistently relied for the vital norms of his stories as well as of the villages themselves, enclosed as they generally were with their cornfields. It was the soil which in his belief gave the "power" to life and literature (to use

[11] S. Anderson, *Little Review*, I, 16–17 (April 1914); *Memoirs*, pp. 445, 495; *Notebook* (New York: Boni & Liveright, 1926), pp. 139–46; *Letters*, p. 457; "Man and His Imagination," in *The Intent of the Artist*, ed. A. Centeno (Princeton, N.J.: Princeton U. Press, 1941), *passim;* for Conrad, see Preface to *The Nigger of the "Narcissus."*

[12] S. Anderson, *Little Review*, VI, 4 (October 1918); *Short Stories*, ed. M. Geismar (New York: Hill and Wang, 1962), pp. 155–57; "Home Town," in *The Sherwood Anderson Reader*, pp. 743–47.

Emerson's dual terminology from "Experience") as the towns and cities gave the "form." The towns and villages, therefore, of *Winesburg* or *Dark Laughter* and *Poor White*, rich as they may be in human archetypes, are never autonomous, but always have their traffic with the surrounding fields and woods. Acknowledging the "bucolic" in his nature, Anderson spoke of himself as a "Western novelist" and of his region as the "corn-growing, industrial Middle West." It is "my land," he wrote in 1918 to Van Wyck Brooks. "Good or bad, it's all I'll ever have." But only incidentally was he concerned with its industrial aspects; for what he wished to do, he said, was to "write beautifully, create beautifully . . . in this thing in which I am born—indeed, to "pour a dream over it." His perspective was thus visionary; his imagination was committed to distant vistas, not merely democratic but essentially mythic. Stirred during the years of the Chicago renaissance by something new and fresh in the air, as he said in the *Little Review*, he was convinced that "the great basin of the Mississippi . . . is one day to be the seat of the culture of the universe." The current industrialism of the region he interpreted in a quasi-mythic figure as a cold and damp winter beneath whose lifeless surface something was "trying to break through." Envisioning that vernal rebirth in the West when "newer, braver gods" would reign and a new and joyous race would develop, he composed his *Mid-American Chants*—essentially a volume of free-verse hymns extolling an American paradise where nature and man were one. In the very term "chants" Anderson suggested both the style and purpose of his poems. Eschewing both the elegiac disenchantment with the region to be found in Masters's *Spoon River Anthology* and the virile bravado of Sandburg's contemporaneous *Cornhuskers,* these visionary poems in the diction and movement and tone are Anderson's most explicit venture into the mythopoeic strain.[13]

In the *Chants* Anderson essentially invoked the earth spirit, as he wrote in "Mid-American Prayer," with its Indian memories and rites to supplant the Puritanism dominant in the region and to remind the Midwestern people of the "lurking sounds, sights, smells of old things." The theme of the repressive sterility of New England was, indeed, an oft-reiterated one in Anderson's most prolific years, for he had come to feel that the major mission of the Midwestern writer, as he explained in his *Memoirs,* was on behalf of a new race to put "the flesh back in our literature" and thereby to counteract the "feminine force" of the older section. The New England notion of America was not blood deep, he asserted in a Lawrentian vein in *A Story Teller's Story*; and

<hr />

13 S. Anderson, *Letters*, pp. 7, 10, 13, 21, 43, 79, 80; *Memoirs*, pp. 241–42; *Mid-American Chants* (New York, 1923), pp. 18, 51, 71; *Little Review*, VI, 6 (October 1918); I. Howe, *Sherwood Anderson*, pp. 57–58, 73–74.

since blood will tell, the increasingly thinner blood of the Northeastern man must yield to that type more richly blended from the "dreaming nations" which had settled the Midwest. In place of an "old-maid civilization" derived from a cold, stony New England, Anderson saw emerging from the "rich warm land" and polyglot racial strains a kind of Dionysiac brotherhood in which the humane spirit of Lincoln would be the heroic and brooding presence. Thus, as he wrote in *Dark Laughter,* the "whole middle American empire" would be restored as a land of rivers and prairies and forests "to live in, make love in, dance in." [14]

Despite Anderson's invocation of rivers and forests and the "old savages" therein "striving toward gods," the dominant symbol in *Mid-American Chants* was the pastoral cornfield—a symbol indigenous to the country as a whole, though especially so to the Upper Mississippi Valley. Confessing himself to be a "kind of cornfed mystic," Anderson was always moved by the sight of a cornfield, and later in his life at Marion, Virginia, he remarked that such fields were distinctively American. Not surprisingly, the cabin where he chose to do his first writing in Virginia was, as he wrote Stieglitz, a "deserted one in a big cornfield on top of a mountain. Cowbells in the distance, the soft whisper of the corn." Nearly a decade earlier, in *Windy McPherson's Son* he had protested the popular conception of corn as being merely the feed for horses and steers; instead the shocks of corn stood for him as majestic symbols of a land in which man had been freed from hunger. Yet two years later, in *Mid-American Chants* the cornfields moved from a mere symbol of well-being into the sacramental: they became a "sacred vessel" filled with a sweet oil which had reawakened man to a sense of the beautiful, old things. Moreover, the long aisles of corn in their orderly planting not only signified man's conquest of the forest; they seemed even to run to the throne of the gods. "Deep in the cornfields the gods come to life," he wrote in "War," / "Gods that have waited, gods that we knew not." In the cornfields, indeed, Anderson found a new impulse to prayer through what he felt to be their mythic reincarnation of the earth spirit; in them he found an elemental vitality to counteract the sterile religious tradition of New England. Back of the "grim city," Chicago, he saw "new beauties in the standing corn" and, in "Song to New Song," dreamt of "singers yet to come" when the city had fallen dead upon its coal heap. Or again, in "Song for Lonely Roads," he reasserted his faith that "The gods wait in the corn, / The soul of song is in the land." During these years, indeed, as he wrote in one of his letters, he felt that "a man cannot be a pessimist who lives near a brook or a cornfield"; and in another he confessed to the "no-

---

14 S. Anderson, *Mid-American Chants,* pp. 69–71; *Memoirs,* pp. 246, 247; *A Story Teller's Story,* pp. 80, 101; *Dark Laughter,* pp. 68–69; *Letters,* pp. 40–41, 43.

tion" that none of his writing "should be published that could not be read aloud in the presence of a cornfield." [15]

## IV

By the 1930's, and especially with the stringencies of the economic depression, Anderson's corn gods had proved illusory. In his earlier romantic commitment to the divinely organic he had construed the machine as a seductive threat to a Mid-American reunion with the earth. In those days he could still believe in the triumph of the egg—to use the title of one of his volumes which contains the story "The Egg," a humorous treatment of the effort of the persona's father to subdue a simple egg by standing it on end or forcing it into a bottle. His humiliating defeat, one may suppose, may be taken to reflect Anderson's earlier view of the futility of human attempts to contain or subdue the primal, organic forces of nature. From a similarly organic perspective the inventor-hero of *Poor White* (1920), appearing at evening and pantomiming with his flailing arms and mechanical strides the motions of his cabbage-planting machine, becomes for the farmers a frightening specter whose grotesque movements are a graphic index to consequences which Anderson felt must follow the replacement of the organic by the mechanical. As imposed behavior and technological demands had succeeded freedom and personal pride in craftsmanship, he commented in *Poor White*, men and women had become like mice; and in *Dark Laughter* he spoke of the "tired and nervous" cities, with their "murmur of voices coming out of a pit." Over a decade later in his Southern novel *Kit Brandon* only a few of the mountain girls seemed to him to have retained a self-respect and proud individualism akin to that of "the day of America's greater richness." Of this older richness another symbol was the horse, which as a boy in the livery stable he had found to be the most beautiful thing about him and superior to many of the men with whom he had to deal. In the industrial era, he wrote in *A Story Teller's Story*, since machines had supplanted horses, his own nightmare as a writer was that of being caught as a prisoner under the "great iron bell"—that is, we may interpret, under the great humanly wrought inanimate doom. Perhaps his vivid story "The Man Who Became a Woman," in which a young boy whose devotion to the horse Pick-it-boy has cleansed his lustful thoughts and dreams and who, mistaken for a girl at night in the stable loft by the drunken horse-swipes, flees naked to the neighboring slaughterhouse yard and undergoes a kind of traumatic burial in the skeleton of a horse—perhaps

---

15 S. Anderson, *Memoirs*, p. 360; *Windy McPherson's Son*, pp. 57–58, 246; *Mid-American Chants*, pp. 11–12, 13, 22, 29, 30, 35, 38–40, 47, 60, 62–63; 67, 68, 69–71; *Letters*, pp. 21, 33, 145.

this story reflects something of the psychic effect on Anderson of the destruction of his mythopoeic America. At any rate, even by the time of the publication of *Horses and Men* (1923), in which he celebrated both the vibrant fascination of the horse and the innocence of youth, he confessed to Stieglitz that he had learned at last that horses and men are different and that in the confrontation of human dilemmas the equine would no longer "suffice." [16]

Though by the mid-1920's Anderson felt obliged to abandon many of the mythic assumptions of his Midwestern years, he could not renounce entirely the demands of his mythopoeic imagination. During the last fifteen years of his life, therefore, he sought new centers and media for a viable myth which would bring unity and beauty to his life. This he found in the mill towns of the new industrial South and in the girls who worked therein. Formerly the South had been for Anderson New Orleans and the southern Mississippi, where the dark, ironic laughter of the Negroes had seemed to express for him an elemental spontaneity and a vital sense of life—a "touch with things" such as stones, trees, houses, fields, and tools, as Bruce Dudley enviously concedes in *Dark Laughter*—which made the members of a subject race humanly superior to the sterile life about them. In the later Southern novels the Negroes have all but disappeared, and though the mill girls, who as a vital center supplant them, are too much at the mercy of their factory world to embody any mythic assurance, they do point to a redemptive feminine principle which Anderson, like Henry Adams, found in his later years the surest counteragent to the disintegrating power of the machine. It was the American woman, he concluded in the 1930's, who alone could reintroduce the "mystery" which a technological age had dispelled and without which "we are lost men." Since American women at their best had not yet been "enervated spiritually" by the machine or accepted from it a "vicarious feeling of power," perhaps women, he argued in his book entitled by that phrase, might rescue the American man "crushed and puzzled" as he was in a mechanical maze. [17]

Yet, just as Anderson's phrase "perhaps women" suggests an acknowledged tentativeness in his later mythic formulations, so his treatment of the machine in his late works often discloses a new ambiguity. As his recourse to woman for salvation reflects Adams's adoration of the Virgin, so his discovery of the poetry as well as the power of the machine follows the example of another of his five "greatest Americans," Whitman, who abandoned the pastoral milieu of "the splendid

16 S. Anderson, *Poor White*, in *The Portable Sherwood Anderson*, pp. 188, 215; *Dark Laughter*, p. 75; *Kit Brandon*, pp. 84, 85; *Memoirs*, p. 79; *Letters*, p. 106; *A Story Teller's Story*, pp. 187–90.

17 S. Anderson, *Letters*, pp. 58, 68; *Dark Laughter*, chaps. vii, xi; *Perhaps Women* (New York: Horace Liveright, Inc., 1931), pp. 41–43, 112, 113, 142.

silent sun" to discover the poetry of ferries and locomotives and crowded streets. Yet Anderson, with his earlier sustained distrust of the machine, could not free himself from an ambivalence in his later years; he felt both awe and impotence, he confessed, in the presence of the vast order and power and beauty of machinery, and his tribute to Lindbergh as an emergent culture hero, the new type of machine man, as well as his sympathetic portrayal of the speed-obsessed Kit Brandon, the heroine of a late novel, betrays an uneasiness not present, say, in his characterizations of Sponge Martin and the Negroes in *Dark Laughter*. Yet watching the superb technology of the whirling machines, his hero Red Oliver, in *Beyond Desire*, no doubt reflected much of Anderson's later attitude by confessing that he felt "exultant" and that here was "American genius" at work—America at "its finest." Two years earlier, in 1930, Anderson had declared that he would no longer be "one of the . . . protestors against the machine age" but henceforth would "go to machinery" as if it were mountains or forest or rivers. Hence his poem to the beneficence of the automobile and his attempts to catch the excitement of the cotton mills in his "Machine Song" or "Loom Dance." Yet he also felt impelled to express the more sinister admixture of fear and awe experienced in the presence of the textile machines, whose hypnotic speed and incessant shuttle rhythms could induce in Molly Seabright, a mill girl in *Beyond Desire*, an indifference and confusion which led to a loss of identification with the human world about her. Modern American industry, he concluded ambivalently in *Perhaps Women* (1932), was indeed a "dance," a "flow of refined power," to which men lifted up their eyes in worshipful adoration. Surely in such statements the failure of Anderson to approach the machine as if it were mountains and rivers is manifest. The earlier mythopoeic imagination has become bifurcated into myth and poetry; the validity of the myth is not felt, and the poetry is an act of will rather than of imagination. In this bifurcation and desiccation one may no doubt find much of the explanation for Anderson's decline in his later years.[18]

## V

To his inclination and commitment to a mythopoeic approach to American experience both Anderson's literary achievements and his shortcomings may ultimately be traced. From the time of the First World War until his death at the beginning of the Second, he consistently aligned his writing with a focal purpose summarily stated in *A*

---

[18] S. Anderson, *Perhaps Women*, pp. 9 ff. 14–17, 21–29, 30 ff., 36, 107–8, 125–26; *Beyond Desire* (New York: Liveright 1961), pp. 49–51, 288–89; *Letters*, pp. 202–3, 206, 207, 208.

*Story Teller's Story:* "It is my aim to be true to the essence of things."
In probing for the "essence" he ran the romantic risk of neglecting the
existential substance of American experience, and hence one may feel,
as Lionel Trilling has asserted, a deficiency of the sensory and concrete
in his work. If one adds to this mythic concern for patterns and forces
behind the phenomenal world Anderson's addiction to the psychic and
intuitive as the arbiters of reality, one approaches what to Anderson
seemed the "poetic" factor in the mythopoeic imagination. Hence
neither the region nor the nation was a substantial entity for him;
neither ideologies nor sociological formulas were significant norms for
his fictional perspective. The "new note" in American literature, as he
said, was really a return to the old sensations and desires; and hence
his women have few social concerns or ambitions, nor are they regional
types: Aline Grey and Clara Butterworth and Kit Brandon play their
roles as versions of the White Goddess reasserting primal humanity, as
did Adams's Virgin.[19]
Anderson's style, like his larger fictional perspective, is an organic
product of his mythopoeic approach. Rooted in the naive, in wonder,
in the mystic and the intuitive, his expression shapes itself subjectively
from emotions or associations, as Tanner has shown, at the expense of
tight syntax, controlled structure, and purified or precise diction. And
yet Anderson's vagaries are, for the most part, those which he inherited
(and somewhat intensified) through a major native tradition initiated
by the Transcendentalists and involving in its course Whitman, Twain,
Stein, and Salinger. If from Anderson's pen this style becomes one in
which each sentence affords only a fragmentary glimpse, as Tanner
contends, perhaps the limitation is in part explained by Anderson's
conclusion that in an immense land where all men are strangers to one
another, the writer can "only snatch at fragments" and be true to his
"own inner impulses." That a cisatlantic orientation may be necessary
to the full comprehension of Anderson's style, with its indigenous tone
and idiom, is suggested by Gertrude Stein's contention that "Anderson had a genius for using the sentence to convey a direct emotion,
this was in the great american [*sic*] tradition, and that really except
Sherwood there was no one in America who could write a clear and
passionate sentence." Early in his career Anderson in "An Apology for
Crudity" asserted that if American writing were to have force and authenticity, it would have to forgo objectivity for the "subjective impulse," and that an honest crudity would have to precede the "gift of
beauty and subtlety in prose." However consciously stylized and contrived his own apparent artlessness may be, his "subjective impulse"

---

[19] S. Anderson, *A Story Teller's Story*, p. 100; *Little Review,* I, 23 (March 1914);
L. Trilling, *Kenyon Review,* III, 298–99 (Summer 1941).

extended outward like Whitman's in an effort to catch "the essence of things," and his reputation will be most secure among those who can accept the mythopoeic assumptions which nurtured and shaped his imagination.[20]

20 T. Tanner, *The Reign of Wonder*, pp. 206 ff., 220–21; S. Anderson, *The Modern Writer* (San Francisco: The Lantern Press, 1925), pp. 2–3, 37; "An Apology for Crudity," *Dial*, LXIII, 437–38 (November 8, 1917); G. Stein in *Sherwood Anderson / A Bibliography*, ed. E. P. Sheehy and K. A. Lohf (Los Gatos, Calif.: The Talisman Press, 1960), p. [x].

# Sherwood Anderson: An Appreciation

## by William Faulkner

One day during the months while we walked and talked in New
Orleans—or Anderson talked and I listened—I found him sitting on a
bench in Jackson Square, laughing with himself. I got the impression
that he had been there like that for some time, just sitting alone on
the bench laughing with himself. This was not our usual meeting place
We had none. He lived above the Square, and without any especial
prearrangement, after I had had something to eat at noon and knew
that he had finished his lunch too, I would walk in that direction and
if I did not meet him already strolling or sitting in the Square, I myself would simply sit down on the curb where I could see his doorway
and wait until he came out of it in his bright, half-racetrack, half-Bo-
hemian clothes.

This time he was already sitting on the bench, laughing. He told me
what it was at once: a dream: he had dreamed the night before that he
was walking for miles along country roads, leading a horse which he
was trying to swap for a night's sleep—not for a simple bed for the
night, but for the sleep itself; and with me to listen now, went on from
there, elaborating it, building it into a work of art with the same tedi-
ous (it had the appearance of fumbling but actually it wasn't: it was
seeking, hunting) almost excruciating patience and humility with which
he did all his writing, me listening and believing no word of it: that is,
that it had been any dream dreamed in sleep. Because I knew better.
I knew that he had invented it, made it; he had made most of it or at
least some of it while I was there watching and listening to him. He
didn't know why he had been compelled, or anyway needed, to claim it
had been a dream, why there had to be that connection with dream and
sleep, but I did. It was because he had written his whole biography into
an anecdote or perhaps a parable: the horse (it had been a racehorse at
first, but now it was a working horse, plow carriage and saddle, sound
and strong and valuable, but without recorded pedigree) representing

"Sherwood Anderson: An Appreciation," by William Faulkner. From *The Atlantic
Monthly*, 191 (June 1953), 27–29. Copyright 1953 by Estelle Faulkner and Jill Faulkner
Summers. Reprinted from *Essays, Speeches and Public Letters*, ed. by James B.
Meriwether, by permission of Random House, Inc., and Chatto and Windus Limited.

the vast rich strong docile sweep of the Mississippi Valley, his own America, which he in his bright blue racetrack shirt and vermilion-mottled Bohemian Windsor tie, was offering with humor and patience and humility, but mostly with patience and humility, to swap for his own dream of purity and integrity and hard and unremitting work and accomplishment, of which *Winesburg, Ohio* and *The Triumph of the Egg* had been symptoms and symbols.

He would never have said this, put it into words, himself. He may never have been able to see it even, and he certainly would have denied it, probably pretty violently, if I had tried to point it out to him. But this would not have been for the reason that it might not have been true, nor for the reason that, true or not, he would not have believed it. In fact, it would have made little difference whether it was true or not or whether he believed it or not. He would have repudiated it for the reason which was the great tragedy of his character. He expected people to make fun of, ridicule him. He expected people nowhere near his equal in stature or accomplishment or wit or anything else, to be capable of making him appear ridiculous.

That was why he worked so laboriously and tediously and inde-fatigably at everything he wrote. It was as if he said to himself: "This anyway will, shall, must be invulnerable." It was as though he wrote not even out of the consuming unsleeping appeaseless thirst for glory for which any normal artist would destroy his aged mother, but for what to him was more important and urgent: not even for mere truth, but for purity, the exactitude of purity. His was not the power and rush of Melville, who was his grandfather, nor the lusty humor for living of Twain, who was his father; he had nothing of the heavy-handed disregard for nuances of his older brother, Dreiser. His was that fumbling for exactitude, the exact word and phrase within the limited scope of a vocabulary controlled and even repressed by what was in him almost a fetish of simplicity, to milk them both dry, to seek always to penetrate to thought's uttermost end. He worked so hard at this that it finally became just style: an end instead of a means: so that he presently came to believe that, provided he kept the style pure and intact and unchanged and inviolate, what the style contained would have to be first rate: it couldn't help but be first rate, and therefore himself too.

At this time in his life, he had to believe this. His mother had been a bound girl, his father a day laborer; this background had taught him that the amount of security and material success which he had attained was, must be, the answer and end to life. Yet he gave this up, re-pudiated and discarded it at a later age, when older in years than most men and women who make that decision, to dedicate himself to art, writing. Yet, when he made the decision, he found himself to be only a one- or two-book man. He had to believe that, if only he kept that style pure, then what the style contained would be pure too, the best. That was why he had to defend the style. That was the reason for his hurt and anger at Hemingway about Hemingway's *The Torrents of Spring,* and at me in a lesser degree since my fault was not full book-length but instead was merely a privately-printed and subscribed volume which few people outside our small New Orleans group would ever see or hear about, because of the book of Spratling's caricatures which we titled *Sherwood Anderson and Other Famous Creoles* and to which I wrote an introduction in Anderson's primer-like style. Neither of us—Hemingway or I—could have touched, ridiculed, his work itself. But we had made his style look ridiculous; and by that time, after *Dark Laughter,* when he had reached the point where he should have stopped writing, he had to defend that style at all costs because he too must have known by then in his heart that there was nothing else left.

## 2

The exactitude of purity, or the purity of exactitude: whichever you like. He was a sentimentalist in his attitude toward people, and quite often incorrect about them. He believed in people, but it was as though only in theory. He expected the worst from them, even while each time he was prepared again to be disappointed or even hurt, as if it had never happened before, as though the only people he could really trust, let himself go with, were the ones of his own invention, the figments and symbols of his own fumbling dream. And he was some-times a sentimentalist in his writing (so was Shakespeare sometimes) but he was never impure in it. He never scanted it, cheapened it, took the easy way; never failed to approach writing except with humility and an almost religious, almost abject faith and patience and willingness to surrender, relinquish himself to and into it. He hated glibness; if it were quick, he believed it was false too. He told me once: "You've got too much talent. You can do it too easy, in too many different ways. If you're not careful, you'll never write anything." During those after-noons when we would walk about the old quarter, I listening while he talked to me or to people—anyone, anywhere—whom we would meet on the streets or the docks, or the evenings while we sat somewhere over a bottle, he, with a little help from me, invented other fantastic char-acters like the sleepless man with the horse. One of them was supposed to be a descendant of Andrew Jackson, left in that Louisiana swamp after the Battle of Chalmette, no longer half-horse half-alligator but by now half-man half-sheep and presently half-shark, who—it, the whole fable—at last got so unwieldy and (so we thought) so funny, that we decided to get it onto paper by writing letters to one another such as two temporarily separated members of an exploring-zoological expedition might. I brought him my first reply to his first letter. He read it. He said:—

"Does it satisfy you?"

I said, "Sir?"

"Are you satisfied with it?"

"Why not?" I said. "I'll put whatever I left out into the next one." Then I realized that he was more than displeased: he was short, stern, almost angry. He said:—

"Either throw it away, and we'll quit, or take it back and do it over." I took the letter. I worked three days over it before I carried it back to him. He read it again, quite slowly, as he always did, and said, "Are you satisfied now?"

"No sir," I said. "But it's the best I know how to do."

"Then we'll pass it," he said, putting the letter into his pocket, his voice once more warm, rich, burly with laughter, ready to believe, ready to be hurt again.

I learned more than that from him, whether or not I always practised the rest of it any more than I have that. I learned that, to be a writer, one has first got to be what he is, what he was born; that to be an American and a writer, one does not necessarily have to pay lip-service to any conventional American image such as his and Dreiser's own aching Indiana or Ohio or Iowa corn or Sandburg's stockyards or Mark Twain's frog. You had only to remember what you were. "You have to have somewhere to start from: then you begin to learn," he told me. "It dont matter where it was, just so you remember it and aint ashamed of it. Because one place to start from is just as important as any other. You're a country boy; all you know is that little patch up there in Mississippi where you started from. But that's all right too. It's America too; pull it out, as little and unknown as it is, and the whole thing will collapse, like when you prize a brick out of a wall."

"Not a cemented, plastered wall," I said.

"Yes, but America aint cemented and plastered yet. They're still building it. That's why a man with ink in his veins not only still can but sometimes has still got to keep on moving around in it, keeping moving around and listening and looking and learning. That's why ignorant unschooled fellows like you and me not only have a chance to write, they must write. All America asks is to look at it and listen to it and understand it if you can. Only the understanding aint important either: the important thing is to believe in it even if you dont understand it, and then try to tell it, put it down. It wont ever be quite right, but there is always next time; there's always more ink and paper, and something else to try to understand and tell. And that one probably wont be exactly right either, but there is a next time to that one, too. Because tomorrow America is going to be something different, something more and new to watch and listen to and try to understand; and, even if you cant understand, believe."

To believe, to believe in the value of purity, and to believe more. To believe not in just the value, but the necessity for fidelity and integrity; lucky is that man whom the vocation of art elected and chose to be faithful to it, because the reward for art does not wait on the postman. He carried this to extremes. That of course is impossible on the face of it. I mean that, in the later years when he finally probably admitted to himself that only the style was left, he worked so hard and so laboriously and so self-sacrificingly at this, that at times he stood a little bigger, a little taller than it was. He was warm, generous, merry and fond of laughing, without pettiness and jealous only of the integrity which he believed to be absolutely necessary in anyone who approached his craft; he was ready to be generous to anyone, once he was convinced that that one approached his craft with his own humility and respect for it. During those New Orleans days and weeks, I gradually became aware that here was a man who would be in seclusion all forenoon—working. Then in the afternoon he would appear and we would walk about the city, talking. Then in the evening we would meet again, with a bottle now, and now he would really talk; the world in minuscule would be there in whatever shadowy courtyard where glass and bottle clinked and the palms hissed like dry sand in whatever moving air. Then tomorrow forenoon and he would be secluded again —working; whereupon I said to myself, "If this is what it takes to be a novelist, then that's the life for me."

So I began a novel, *Soldiers' Pay.* I had known Mrs. Anderson before I knew him. I had not seen them in some time when I met her on the street. She commented on my absence. I said I was writing a novel. She asked if I wanted Sherwood to see it. I answered, I dont remember exactly what, but to the effect that it would be all right with me if he wanted to. She told me to bring it to her when I finished it, which I did, in about two months. A few days later, she sent for me. She said, "Sherwood says he'll make a swap with you. He says that if he doesn't have to read it, he'll tell Liveright (Horace Liveright: his own publisher then) to take it."

"Done," I said, and that was all. Liveright published the book and I saw Anderson only once more, because the unhappy caricature affair had happened in the meantime and he declined to see me, for several years, until one afternoon at a cocktail party in New York; and again there was that moment when he appeared taller, bigger than anything he ever wrote. Then I remembered *Winesburg, Ohio* and *The Triumph of the Egg* and some of the pieces in *Horses and Men,* and I knew that I had seen, was looking at, a giant in an earth populated to a great —too great—extent by pygmies, even if he did make but the two or perhaps three gestures commensurate with gianthood.

# Chronology of Important Dates

1876     Anderson born, September 13, in Camden, Ohio. Third of seven children of Irwin M. Anderson, a harnessmaker, and Emma Smith Anderson.

1884     Family moved to Clyde, Ohio, the setting for *Winesburg, Ohio*. Anderson attended public schools.

1896 or 1897     Went to Chicago, worked as unskilled laborer in a warehouse.

1898     Enlisted in U.S. Army during Spanish-American War; stationed in Cuba after end of hostilities.

1899     Entered Wittenberg Academy, Springfield, Ohio, for final year of formal education.

1900     Became copywriter in a Chicago advertising firm; soon began contributing articles and sketches to trade paper, *Agricultural Advertising*.

1904     Married Cornelia Lane of Toledo, Ohio.

1906     Became president of United Factories Company, a Cleveland mail-order firm.

1907     Moved to Elyria, Ohio, and set up a company to distribute, later also to manufacture, paint. Begin to write stories and novels soon afterward.

1912     In late November had nervous breakdown, crucial event in his decision to be a writer rather than a businessman.

1913     Resumed job as advertising copywriter in Chicago while trying to establish himself as a writer of fiction.

1916     Divorced Cornelia Lane Anderson and married Tennessee Mitchell. Published his first novel, *Windy McPherson's Son*.

1917     *Marching Men*, novel.

1918     *Mid-American Chants*, poems.

1919     *Winesburg, Ohio*, stories, published by B. W. Huebsch.

1920      *Poor White,* novel.

1921      *The Triumph of the Egg,* stories. Became acquainted with Ernest
          Hemingway. Paul Rosenfeld, critic, took the Andersons to
          France, where they met Gertrude Stein and James Joyce. Anderson
          received first *Dial* Award for his contribution to American writing.

1923      *Many Marriages,* novel, and *Horses and Men,* stories.

1924      Divorced Tennessee Mitchell Anderson, married Elizabeth Prall.
          Moved to New Orleans. *A Story Teller's Story,* fanciful memoir.

1925      On lecture tour, then became acquainted with William Faulkner
          in New Orleans. *Dark Laughter,* novel, his one financial success.

1926      Built "Ripshin," country home in Troutdale, near Marion, Vir-
          ginia. *Sherwood Anderson's Notebook,* essays and sketches; *Tar:
          A Midwest Childhood,* semiautobiography. Began second trip to
          Europe.

1927      Returned from Europe. Purchased the two weekly newspapers
          in Marion and edited them for about two years. *A New Testa-
          ment,* prose-poems.

1929      *Hello Towns!,* pieces from the Marion newspapers.

1931      *Perhaps Women,* essays and sketches.

1932      Divorced from Elizabeth Prall Anderson. *Beyond Desire,* novel.

1933      Married Eleanor Copenhaver. *Death in the Woods,* stories.

1934      *No Swank,* articles.

1935      *Puzzled America,* articles describing Depression life in the United
          States.

1936      *Kit Brandon,* novel.

1937      *Plays, Winesburg and Others,* plays.

1940      *Home Town,* commentary with photographs.

1941      Started for visit to South America, but on March 8 died of
          peritonitis at Colón, Panama Canal Zone.

1942      *Sherwood Anderson's Memoirs,* autobiography, published post-
          humously.

# Notes on the Editor and Contributors

WALTER B. RIDEOUT, editor of this volume in the Twentieth Century Views series, is Harry Hayden Clark Professor of English at The University of Wisconsin, Madison. Associate editor of *Letters of Sherwood Anderson,* he is writing a critical biography of Anderson.

REX BURBANK is Professor of English at California State University, San Jose. His *Sherwood Anderson* and *Thornton Wilder* both appeared in Twayne's United States Authors Series.

MALCOLM COWLEY, critic and historian of twentieth-century American literature, is the author of, among other volumes, *Exile's Return, The Literary Situation,* and *A Second Flowering.*

WILLIAM FAULKNER (1897–1962) was the American novelist.

WALDO FRANK (1889–1967), novelist and critic of North and South American culture, was an editor of *The Seven Arts* magazine, which published several of the *Winesburg* tales in 1916–17.

EDWIN FUSSELL, Professor of American Literature at the University of California, San Diego, is the author of *Edwin Arlington Robinson* and *Frontier: American Literature and the American West,* and has translated Cesare Pavese's *American Literature: Essays and Opinions.*

BLANCHE HOUSMAN GELFANT, author of *The American City Novel* and a number of articles on contemporary literature, is Professor of English at Dartmouth College.

ERNEST HEMINGWAY (1899–1961) was the American novelist and short-story writer.

IRVING HOWE is Distinguished Professor of English at Hunter College, City University of New York, and editor of the magazine *Dissent.* Besides studies of Anderson and Faulkner, he has published a number of volumes on literature, on politics, and on the relationship between the two.

HOWARD MUMFORD JONES, A. Lawrence Lowell Professor of the Humanities Emeritus of Harvard University, has published many books, articles, and essays on American and British literature, and is one of the founders of the teaching of American literature in American universities.

JON S. LAWRY is Professor of English at Laurentian University, Sudbury, Ontario. He is the author of *The Shadow of Heaven: Matter and Stance in Milton's Poetry* and *Sidney's Two Arcadias.*

ROBERT MORSS LOVETT (1870–1956) taught from 1893 to 1936 in the Department of English at the University of Chicago, was government secretary to the Virgin Islands (1939–43), and was active in the defense of American civil liberties.

WILLIAM L. PHILLIPS, author of one of the basic articles in Anderson scholarship, is Associate Professor of English and Associate Dean of the College of Arts and Sciences at the University of Washington.

BENJAMIN T. SPENCER is Professor of English Emeritus of Ohio Wesleyan University. A specialist in Elizabethan and Jacobean drama, he has also published *The Quest for Nationality: An American Literary Campaign.*

GERTRUDE STEIN (1874–1946), though born in the United States, lived most of her adult life in France. For nearly half a century she was a creator of experimental writing.

LIONEL TRILLING is University Professor at Columbia University. His books of literary and cultural criticism include *The Liberal Imagination, The Opposing Self,* and *Beyond Culture.*

T(HOMAS) K(ING) WHIPPLE (1890–1939) taught for many years in the Department of English at the University of California, Berkeley. In addition to his volume *Spokesmen: Modern Writers and American Life,* another collection of essays was published, posthumously, as *Study Out the Land.*

# Selected Bibliography

## Books

Anderson, David D. *Sherwood Anderson: An Introduction and Interpretation.* New York: Holt, Rinehart and Winston, 1967.

Appel, Paul P. (ed.). *Homage to Sherwood Anderson: 1876–1941.* Mamaroneck, N.Y.: Paul P. Appel, Publisher, 1970. Reprints "Homage to Sherwood Anderson" Issue of *Story,* 19 (September–October 1941).

Burbank, Rex. *Sherwood Anderson.* New York: Twayne Publishers, 1964.

Ferres, John H. (ed.). *Sherwood Anderson, WINESBURG, OHIO: Text and Criticism.* New York: The Viking Press, 1966.

Howe, Irving. *Sherwood Anderson.* New York: William Sloane Associates, 1951. Reprinted Stanford, Calif.: Stanford University Press, 1966.

Schevill, James. *Sherwood Anderson: His Life and Work.* Denver, Colo.: The University of Denver Press, 1951.

Sutton, William A. *The Road to Winesburg: A Mosaic of the Imaginative Life of Sherwood Anderson.* Metuchen, N.J.: The Scarecrow Press, 1972.

Weber, Brom. *Sherwood Anderson.* Minneapolis, Minn.: University of Minnesota Press, 1964. (Pamphlet.)

White, Ray Lewis (ed.). *The Achievement of Sherwood Anderson: Essays in Criticism.* Chapel Hill, N.C.: The University of North Carolina Press, 1966.

## Articles, Essays, Sections of Books

Abcarian, Richard. "Innocence and Experience in *Winesburg, Ohio,*" *University Review,* 35 (Winter 1968), 95–105.

Anderson, Karl James. "My Brother, Sherwood Anderson," *Saturday Review of Literature,* 31 (September 4, 1948), 6–7, 26–27.

Babb, Howard S. "A Reading of Sherwood Anderson's 'The Man Who Became a Woman'," *PMLA,* 80 (September 1965), 432–35.

Beach, Joseph Warren. *The Outlook for American Prose* (Chicago: The University of Chicago Press, 1926), pp. 247–80.

Bishop, John Peale. "The Distrust of Ideas (D. H. Lawrence and Sherwood Anderson)," in *The Collected Essays of John Peale Bishop* (New York: Charles Scribner's Sons, 1948), pp. 233–40.

Bowden, Edwin T. *The Dungeon of the Heart: Human Isolation and the American Novel* (New York: The Macmillan Company, 1961), pp. 114–24.

Boynton, Percy H. "Sherwood Anderson," *North American Review,* 224 (March–April–May 1927), 140–50.

Bridgman, Richard. *The Colloquial Style in America* (New York: Oxford University Press, 1966), pp. 152–64.

Budd, Louis J. "The Grotesques of Anderson and Wolfe," *Modern Fiction Studies,* 5 (Winter 1959–60), 304–10.

Ciancio, Ralph. " 'The Sweetness of the Twisted Apples': Unity of Vision in *Winesburg, Ohio,*" *PMLA,* 87 (October 1972), 994–1006.

Crane, Hart. "Sherwood Anderson," *The Double Dealer,* 2 (July 1921), 42–45.

Dahlberg, Edward. *Alms for Oblivion: Essays by Edward Dahlberg* (Minneapolis, Minn.: University of Minnesota Press, 1964), pp. 3–19.

Duffey, Bernard. *The Chicago Renaissance in American Letters: A Critical History* (East Lansing, Mich.: The Michigan State College Press, 1954), pp. 194–209.

Farrell, James T. "A Memoir on Sherwood Anderson," *Perspective* 7 (Summer 1954), 83–88.

Flanagan, John T. "Hemingway's Debt to Sherwood Anderson," *Journal of English and Germanic Philology,* 54 (October 1955), 507–20.

Geismar, Maxwell. *The Last of the Provincials: The American Novel, 1915–1925* (Boston: Houghton Mifflin Company, 1947), pp. 223–84.

Gregory, Horace (ed.). *The Portable Sherwood Anderson* (New York: The Viking Press, Revised Edition, 1972), pp. 3–31.

Hansen, Harry. *Midwest Portraits: A Book of Memories and Friendships* (New York: Harcourt, Brace and Company, 1923), pp. 109–79.

Hoffman, Frederick J. *Freudianism and the Literary Mind* (Baton Rouge, La.: Louisiana State University Press, 1957), pp. 229–50.

Lorch, Thomas M. "The Choreographic Structure of *Winesburg, Ohio,*" *CLA Journal,* 12 (September 1968), 56–65.

Love, Glen A. "*Winesburg, Ohio* and the Rhetoric of Silence," *American Literature,* 40 (March 1968), 38–57.

McAleer, John J. "Christ Symbolism in *Winesburg, Ohio,*" *Discourse,* 4 (Summer 1961), 168–81.

Mellard, James M. "Narrative Forms in *Winesburg, Ohio,*" *PMLA,* 83 (October 1968), 1304–12.

Phillips, William L. "Sherwood Anderson's Two Prize Pupils," *University of Chicago Magazine,* 47 (January 1955), 9–12.

Rideout, Walter B. "Why Sherwood Anderson Employed Buck Fever," *The Georgia Review,* 13 (Spring 1959), 76–85.

Rosenfeld, Paul. *Port of New York: Essays on Fourteen American Moderns* (New York: Harcourt, Brace and Company, 1924), pp. 175–98.

San Juan, Epifanio, Jr. "Vision and Reality: A Reconsideration of Sherwood Anderson's *Winesburg, Ohio,*" *American Literature,* 35 (May 1963), 137–55.

Sherwood Anderson Memorial Number. *The Newberry Library Bulletin,* Second Series, No. 2 (December 1948).

Sherwood Anderson Number. *Shenandoah,* 13 (Spring 1962).

Special Sherwood Anderson Number. *The Newberry Library Bulletin,* 6 (July 1971).

Stewart, Maaja A. "Scepticism and Belief in Chekhov and Anderson," *Studies in Short Fiction,* 9 (Winter 1972), 29–40.

Tanner, Tony. *The Reign of Wonder: Naivety and Reality in American Literature* (Cambridge, Eng.: Cambridge University Press, 1965), pp. 205–27.

Thurston, Jarvis. "Anderson and 'Winesburg': Mysticism and Craft," *Accent,* 16 (Spring 1956), 107–28.

Walcutt, Charles Child. *American Literary Naturalism, A Divided Stream* (Minneapolis, Minn.: University of Minnesota Press, 1956), pp. 222–39.

West, Michael D. "Sherwood Anderson's Triumph: 'The Egg'," *American Quarterly,* 20 (Winter 1968), 675–93.

White, Ray Lewis (ed.). *Return to Winesburg: Selections from Four Years of Writing for a Country Newspaper* (Chapel Hill, N.C.: The University of North Carolina Press, 1967), pp. 3–23.